First World War
and Army of Occupation
War Diary
France, Belgium and Germany

47 DIVISION
141 Infantry Brigade
London Regiment
18th (County of London) Battalion (London Irish Rifles)
9 March 1915 - 31 March 1919

WO95/2737/3

The Naval & Military Press Ltd
www.nmarchive.com
Published in association with The National Archives

Published by

The Naval & Military Press Ltd

Unit 10 Ridgewood Industrial Park,

Uckfield, East Sussex,

TN22 5QE England

Tel: +44 (0) 1825 749494

www.naval-military-press.com

www.nmarchive.com

This diary has been reprinted in facsimile from the original. Any imperfections are inevitably reproduced and the quality may fall short of modern type and cartographic standards.

© **Crown Copyright**
Images reproduced by permission of The National Archives, London, England, 2015.

Contents

Document type	Place/Title	Date From	Date To
Heading	WO95/2737/2		
Heading	47th Division 141st Infy Bde 18th Bn London Regt Mar 1915-Feb 1919		
Heading	141st Inf Bde 47th Division War Diary 18th London Regt March 1915 (9.3.15-31.3.15)		
Heading	On His Majesty's Service.		
War Diary	St Albans	09/03/1915	09/03/1915
War Diary	Le Havre	10/03/1915	12/03/1915
War Diary	Winnezeele	12/03/1915	18/03/1915
War Diary	St Venant & Burbure	19/03/1915	19/03/1915
War Diary	Burbure	19/03/1915	31/03/1915
Heading	141st Inf. Bde. 47th Division War Diary 18th London Regt April 1915		
Heading	On His Majesty's Service.		
War Diary	Burbure	01/04/1915	06/04/1915
War Diary	Bethune	07/04/1915	19/04/1915
War Diary	Bethune & Gorre	19/04/1915	19/04/1915
War Diary	Gorre	20/04/1915	23/04/1915
War Diary	Festubert	24/04/1915	25/04/1915
War Diary	Gorre	26/04/1915	27/04/1915
War Diary	Festubert	28/04/1915	30/04/1915
Heading	141st Inf. Bde. 47th Division War Diary 18th London Regt May 1915		
Miscellaneous	On His Majesty's Service.		
War Diary	Gorre & Festubert	01/05/1915	01/05/1915
War Diary	Festubert	01/05/1915	04/05/1915
War Diary	Gorre	05/05/1915	05/05/1915
War Diary	La Beuvriere	06/05/1915	08/05/1915
War Diary	Les Glaughes	09/05/1915	09/05/1915
War Diary	Les Facons	10/05/1915	10/05/1915
War Diary	Le Touret	11/05/1915	12/05/1915
War Diary	Bethune	13/05/1915	13/05/1915
War Diary	Givenchy	14/05/1915	18/05/1915
War Diary	Le Preol	19/05/1915	19/05/1915
War Diary	Givenchy & Le Preol	19/05/1915	19/05/1915
War Diary	Le Preol	20/05/1915	22/05/1915
War Diary	Givenchy	23/05/1915	31/05/1915
Heading	141st Inf. Bde. 47th Division War Diary 18th London Regt June 1915		
Miscellaneous	On His Majesty's Service.		
War Diary		01/06/1915	04/06/1915
War Diary	Annaquin	04/06/1915	08/06/1915
War Diary	(Fosse No 4)	08/06/1915	10/06/1915
War Diary	Masingarbe	11/06/1915	12/06/1915
War Diary	Ndeux Les Mines	13/06/1915	24/06/1915
War Diary	Les Brebis	25/06/1915	28/06/1915
War Diary	W3	29/06/1915	30/06/1915
Miscellaneous	Report On Advanced Second Line From M.I.D To Bully-Grenay-Rutoire Rd		

Heading	141st Inf. Bde. 47th Division War Diary 18th London Regt July 1915		
Miscellaneous	On His Majesty's Service.		
War Diary	Maroc	01/07/1915	06/07/1915
War Diary	Mazingarbe	07/07/1915	14/07/1915
War Diary	Fosse No7	15/07/1915	25/07/1915
War Diary	Philosophe	26/07/1915	29/07/1915
War Diary	Mazingarbe	30/07/1915	31/07/1915
Heading	141st Inf. Bde. 47th Division War Diary 18th London Regt August 1915		
Miscellaneous	On His Majesty's Service.		
War Diary	Mazangarbe	01/08/1915	03/08/1915
War Diary	Allouagne	04/08/1915	18/08/1915
War Diary	Noeux Les Mines	19/08/1915	29/08/1915
War Diary	Houchin	30/08/1915	31/08/1915
Heading	141st Bde. 47th Division War Diary 1/18th London Regiment September 1915		
War Diary	Houchin	01/09/1915	07/09/1915
War Diary	(Les Brebis)	08/09/1915	11/09/1915
War Diary	Noeux Les Mines	12/09/1915	20/09/1915
War Diary	Houchin	21/09/1915	21/09/1915
War Diary	Houchin Les Brebis	22/09/1915	23/09/1915
War Diary	Les Brebis	24/09/1915	24/09/1915
War Diary	Loos	25/09/1915	27/09/1915
War Diary	Les Brebis	28/09/1915	29/09/1915
War Diary	Hesidigneul	30/09/1915	30/09/1915
Miscellaneous	18th Battalion London Regiment London Irish Rifles Preliminary Instructions		
Heading	141st Inf. Bde. 47th Division War Diary 18th London Regt October 1915		
Miscellaneous	On His Majesty's Service.		
War Diary	Hesdigneul	01/10/1915	04/10/1915
War Diary	Haillicourt	05/10/1915	12/10/1915
War Diary	Mazengarbe	12/10/1915	14/10/1915
War Diary	Trenches Of North Loos	15/10/1915	23/10/1915
War Diary	In Trenches	24/10/1915	31/10/1915
Miscellaneous	Appendix 1.		
Map	Map		
Heading	141st Inf. Bde. 47th Division War Diary 18th London Regt November 1915		
Heading	On His Majesty's Service.		
War Diary	Mazangarbe	01/11/1915	14/11/1915
War Diary	Rimbert	15/11/1915	30/11/1915
Heading	141st Inf. Bde. 47th Division War Diary 18th London Regt December 1915		
Heading	On His Majesty's Service.		
War Diary	Raimbert	01/12/1915	01/12/1915
War Diary	Raimbert-Rebecque	02/12/1915	03/12/1915
War Diary	Raimbert	04/12/1915	13/12/1915
War Diary	Noeux Les-Mines & La Bourse	13/12/1915	15/12/1915
War Diary	Hairpin Section	15/12/1915	18/12/1915
War Diary	Verquin	19/12/1915	23/12/1915
War Diary	Hoenzolern Section	24/12/1915	25/12/1915
War Diary	Sailly	26/12/1915	29/12/1915
War Diary	Vermelles	30/12/1915	31/12/1915
War Diary	La Bourse	01/01/1916	01/01/1916

War Diary	Verquin	02/01/1916	02/01/1916
War Diary	Les Brebis	03/01/1916	03/01/1916
War Diary	Loos	04/01/1916	12/01/1916
War Diary	Les Brebis	13/01/1916	15/01/1916
War Diary	Maroc Centre Sub Sect	16/01/1916	31/01/1916
War Diary	Loos	01/02/1916	05/02/1916
War Diary	Les Brebis	06/02/1916	08/02/1916
War Diary	Maroc	09/02/1916	16/02/1916
War Diary	Raimbert	16/02/1916	29/02/1916
Miscellaneous	RFA		
War Diary	Raimbert	01/03/1916	04/03/1916
War Diary	Erny St Julien	05/03/1916	09/03/1916
War Diary	Sachin	10/03/1916	10/03/1916
War Diary	Bruay	10/03/1916	12/03/1916
War Diary	Villers	13/03/1916	13/03/1916
War Diary	Carency Section	14/03/1916	15/03/1916
War Diary	Carency & Villers	16/03/1916	19/03/1916
War Diary	Verdrel	20/03/1916	25/03/1916
War Diary	Bouvigny	26/03/1916	27/03/1916
War Diary	Lorette Sector	28/03/1916	31/03/1916
War Diary	Lorrette Reserve Trenches	01/04/1916	01/04/1916
War Diary	Villers Au Bois	02/04/1916	06/04/1916
War Diary	Verdrel	07/04/1916	19/04/1916
War Diary	Gouy	19/04/1916	20/04/1916
War Diary	A Sub Section	21/04/1916	29/04/1916
War Diary	Maisnil	30/04/1916	30/04/1916
War Diary	Maisnil Bouche	01/05/1916	07/05/1916
War Diary	Q B Centre Sector	08/05/1916	17/05/1916
War Diary	Maisnil Bouchi	18/05/1916	31/05/1916
War Diary	Marest	01/06/1916	10/06/1916
War Diary	Marest Coupigny	11/06/1916	16/06/1916
War Diary	Angres Sector & Bouvigny	17/06/1916	17/06/1916
War Diary	Bouvigny	18/06/1916	20/06/1916
War Diary	Bully	21/06/1916	23/06/1916
War Diary	Angres Sector	24/06/1916	28/06/1916
War Diary	Sains & Bully	29/06/1916	30/06/1916
Heading	141st Brigade 47th Division 1/18th Battalion The London Regiment July 1916		
Miscellaneous	A Form Messages And Signals		
War Diary	Fosse.10	01/07/1916	02/07/1916
War Diary	Bouvigny	03/07/1916	06/07/1916
War Diary	Souchez (1)	07/07/1916	14/07/1916
War Diary	Ablain & Lorette Hts	15/07/1916	19/07/1916
War Diary	Bouvigny	20/07/1916	27/07/1916
War Diary	Divion	28/07/1916	31/07/1916
Heading	141st Brigade 47th Division 1/18th Battalion London Regiment August 1916		
War Diary	Fortel	01/08/1916	02/08/1916
War Diary	Neuilly-Le-Dyen	03/08/1916	04/08/1916
War Diary	Gapennes	05/08/1916	20/08/1916
War Diary	Ergnies & Goronflos	20/08/1916	20/08/1916
War Diary	Goronflos	20/08/1916	20/08/1916
War Diary	Flesselles	21/08/1916	21/08/1916
War Diary	Molliens	22/08/1916	22/08/1916
War Diary	Bresle	23/08/1916	14/09/1916
War Diary	High Wood	15/09/1916	15/09/1916

War Diary	High	15/09/1916	16/09/1916
War Diary	Mametz	17/09/1916	17/09/1916
War Diary	High Wood	17/09/1916	19/09/1916
War Diary	Albert	20/09/1916	20/09/1916
War Diary	Bresle	21/09/1916	26/09/1916
War Diary	Becourt	27/09/1916	28/09/1916
War Diary	Bazantin	29/09/1916	30/09/1916
Heading	War Diary 18th London Regt October 1916 Vol 19		
War Diary	High Wood to Courcelette	01/10/1916	01/10/1916
War Diary	Eaucourt L'Abbaye	01/10/1916	01/10/1916
War Diary	O.B.I	02/10/1916	02/10/1916
War Diary	Eaucourt L'Abbaye	03/10/1916	04/10/1916
War Diary	Bechcourt	05/10/1916	06/10/1916
War Diary	Franvillers	07/10/1916	15/10/1916
War Diary	Bussus	16/10/1916	17/10/1916
War Diary	Wagenbruge Steenvoorde	17/10/1916	19/10/1916
War Diary	Scottish Camp	20/10/1916	28/10/1916
War Diary	Bde Reserve	29/10/1916	31/10/1916
Heading	War Diary 1/18 Bn London Regt November 1916		
War Diary		01/11/1916	14/11/1916
War Diary	Ypres Left Sub Sector	15/11/1916	18/11/1916
War Diary	Scottish Lines	19/11/1916	30/11/1916
Heading	War Diary 1/18th London Regiment December 1916 Vol 21		
War Diary		01/12/1916	31/12/1916
Heading	War Diary 1/18th London Regiment From 1st January 1917 To 31st January 1917 Vol 22		
War Diary	Bluff Sector	01/01/1917	18/01/1917
War Diary	Scottish Lines	19/01/1917	26/01/1917
War Diary	Halifax Camp	27/01/1917	30/01/1917
War Diary	Hill 60	31/01/1917	31/01/1917
Operation(al) Order(s)	1/17th London Regiment Operation Order No. 17	06/01/1917	06/01/1917
Heading	War Diary 1/18th Bn London Regt February 1917 Vol 23		
War Diary		01/02/1917	28/02/1917
Heading	War Diary 1/18th London Rgt March 1917 Vol 24		
War Diary		01/03/1917	31/03/1917
Operation(al) Order(s)	Operation Order No. 3 by Major C. Beresford Commanding Q Battn	17/03/1917	17/03/1917
Heading	War Diary Of 1/18th London Regiment For April 1917 Vol 25		
War Diary		01/04/1917	30/04/1917
Operation(al) Order(s)	Operation Orders No.155 by Lt. Col. D.B. Parry Commanding 1/18th Battn. London Regt., 1st London Irish Rifles	01/04/1917	01/04/1917
Miscellaneous	Schedule A Detail Of Medical Arrangements		
Miscellaneous	Schedule B Communications		
Miscellaneous	Schedule C Dispositions Price To The Assembly		
Miscellaneous	Code		
Miscellaneous	A Form Messages And Signals		
Miscellaneous		07/04/1917	07/04/1917
Miscellaneous	C Form Messages And Signals	07/04/1917	07/04/1917
Miscellaneous	B Form Messages And Signals	07/04/1917	07/04/1917
Miscellaneous	B Form Messages And Signals		
Miscellaneous	C Form Messages And Signals	07/04/1917	07/04/1917
Miscellaneous	B Form Messages And Signals	07/04/1917	07/04/1917

Type	Description	Start	End
Miscellaneous	6 Bn 15Bn	06/04/1917	06/04/1917
Miscellaneous	B Form Messages And Signals	07/04/1917	07/04/1917
Miscellaneous	C Form Messages And Signals	07/04/1917	07/04/1917
Miscellaneous	B Form Messages And Signals		
Miscellaneous	C Form Messages And Signals	07/04/1917	07/04/1917
Miscellaneous	B Form Messages And Signals	07/04/1917	07/04/1917
Miscellaneous	C Form Messages And Signals	07/04/1917	07/04/1917
Miscellaneous	O.C. 6N	06/04/1917	06/04/1917
Miscellaneous	A Form Messages And Signals		
Operation(al) Order(s)	140th Infantry Brigade Order No. 152	04/04/1917	04/04/1917
Heading	War Diary Of 1/18th Bn London Regt For May 1917		
War Diary	Reninghelst	01/05/1917	10/05/1917
War Diary	Spoil Bank	11/05/1917	19/05/1917
War Diary	Swanchateau	20/05/1917	28/05/1917
War Diary	Spoil Bank	29/05/1917	31/05/1917
Miscellaneous	Report Of Work Done By 1/18th Battn London Regt In Spoil Bank Sub-Sector 12th-20th May 1917	21/05/1917	21/05/1917
Heading	War Diary For 1/18th Bn Lon. Regt For June 1917		
War Diary	Spoil Bank	01/06/1917	04/06/1917
War Diary	Dominion Lines	05/06/1917	05/06/1917
War Diary	Dickebusch	06/06/1917	06/06/1917
War Diary	Ecluse Trench	07/06/1917	07/06/1917
War Diary	Old French Tr.	07/06/1917	09/06/1917
War Diary	Blue Line	09/06/1917	14/06/1917
War Diary	Bluff Tunnels	14/06/1917	14/06/1917
War Diary	Heksken	15/06/1917	15/06/1917
War Diary	Caestre	16/06/1917	16/06/1917
War Diary	Racquinghem	17/06/1917	22/06/1917
War Diary	St Martin-Au-Laert	23/06/1917	26/06/1917
War Diary	Sercus	27/06/1917	29/06/1917
War Diary	Godewaersvelde	30/06/1917	30/06/1917
Heading	War Diary Of 1/18th Lon Regt For Month Of July 1917		
War Diary	Mont des Cats Goedewaersvelde	01/07/1917	02/07/1917
War Diary	Ridgewood	03/07/1917	09/07/1917
War Diary	Right Sub Sector M Of Canal	10/07/1917	15/07/1917
War Diary	M.6.D	16/07/1917	31/07/1917
War Diary	Ridgewood	31/07/1917	31/07/1917
Heading	War Diary Of 18th London Regt For Month Of August 1917 Vol 29		
War Diary	Ridge Wood	01/08/1917	08/08/1917
War Diary	M.6.d.5.8	09/08/1917	09/08/1917
War Diary	Esquerdes	10/08/1917	16/08/1917
War Diary	Halifax	17/08/1917	17/08/1917
War Diary	In Line	18/08/1917	21/08/1917
War Diary	In Support	22/08/1917	31/08/1917
Miscellaneous	Operation Orders by Lieut. Col. WW Hughes M.C.	04/08/1917	04/08/1917
Miscellaneous	Amendment No.1 To Operation Order No. 17	03/08/1917	03/08/1917
Operation(al) Order(s)	Operation Order No. 2 by Major C. Beresford Commanding Q Battn	08/08/1917	08/08/1917
Operation(al) Order(s)	Operation Order No. 4 by Major C. Beresford Commanding Q Battn	17/08/1917	17/08/1917
Miscellaneous	A Form Messages And Signals		
Operation(al) Order(s)	Operation Orders No.67 by Lieut. Colonel, W.W. Hughes, M.C. Commanding "Q" Battalion.	20/08/1917	20/08/1917
Heading	1/18th London Regt War Diary For September 1917 Vol 30		

War Diary	Swan Chateau	01/09/1917	01/09/1917
War Diary	G.14.a.1.5	02/09/1917	02/09/1917
War Diary	Micmac Camp H.31.b.3.5	03/09/1917	04/09/1917
War Diary	Dominion Lines	05/09/1917	10/09/1917
War Diary	Line	11/09/1917	16/09/1917
War Diary	Montreal	17/09/1917	17/09/1917
War Diary	Godewearsvelde	18/09/1917	21/09/1917
War Diary	Vandelicourt	22/09/1917	25/09/1917
War Diary	Aubrey Camp	26/09/1917	30/09/1917
Heading	War Diary Of 1/18th Bn London Regt For Month Of October 1917 Vol 31		
War Diary	Aubrey Camp	01/10/1917	02/10/1917
War Diary	Naval Trench	03/10/1917	10/10/1917
War Diary	Roundhay Camp	11/10/1917	17/10/1917
War Diary	Aubrey Camp	18/10/1917	25/10/1917
War Diary	Support	26/10/1917	29/10/1917
War Diary	In Line	30/10/1917	08/11/1917
War Diary	Support	09/11/1917	11/11/1917
War Diary	Maroeuil	12/11/1917	20/11/1917
War Diary	Y Huts	21/11/1917	22/11/1917
War Diary	Fosseux	23/11/1917	23/11/1917
War Diary	Achiet Le Petit	24/11/1917	24/11/1917
War Diary	Rocquigny	25/11/1917	26/11/1917
War Diary	Hindenburg Support	27/11/1917	28/11/1917
War Diary	Bourlon Wood	29/11/1917	30/11/1917
Heading	War Diary 1/18th Bn London Regt December 1917 Vol 33		
War Diary	Bourlon Wood	01/12/1917	01/12/1917
War Diary	Hindenburg Support	02/12/1917	04/12/1917
War Diary	Royaulcourt	05/12/1917	10/12/1917
War Diary	Hindenburg Support	11/12/1917	14/12/1917
War Diary	Bertincourt	15/12/1917	15/12/1917
War Diary	Bouzincourt Area	16/12/1917	31/12/1917
War Diary	Bouzincourt	01/01/1918	04/01/1918
War Diary	Bertincourt	05/01/1918	05/01/1918
War Diary	In Line	06/01/1918	10/01/1918
War Diary	In Reserve	11/01/1918	14/01/1918
War Diary	In Line	15/01/1918	17/01/1918
War Diary	Bertincourt	18/01/1918	23/01/1918
War Diary	In Line	24/01/1918	27/01/1918
War Diary	In Reserve	28/01/1918	31/01/1918
Miscellaneous	Operation Orders Friend	28/01/1918	28/01/1918
War Diary	In Reserve	01/02/1918	01/02/1918
War Diary	In Line	02/02/1918	08/02/1918
War Diary	Bertincourt	09/02/1918	13/02/1918
War Diary	Screw Trench	14/02/1918	22/02/1918
War Diary	Vallulart Camp	23/02/1918	28/02/1918
Operation(al) Order(s)	Operation Order No. 8 by Lt Col W.W. Hughes D.S.O. M.C. Commanding 1/7th London Rgt	13/02/1918	13/02/1918
Heading	47th Division 141st Infantry Brigade War Diary 1/18th Battalion London Regiment March 1918		
War Diary	Vallulart Camp	01/03/1918	20/03/1918
War Diary	Line	21/03/1918	31/03/1918
Heading	141st Brigade 47th Division War Diary 1/18th Battalion The London Regiment April 1918		
War Diary	Senlis	01/04/1918	03/04/1918

War Diary	Bouzincourt	04/04/1918	06/04/1918
War Diary	Senlis	07/04/1918	07/04/1918
War Diary	Acheux	08/04/1918	10/04/1918
War Diary	Mirvaux	11/04/1918	11/04/1918
War Diary	Domart	12/04/1918	12/04/1918
War Diary	Domvast	13/04/1918	29/04/1918
War Diary	Cardonnette	30/04/1918	30/04/1918
Heading	War Diary 18th Bn. London Regt (1st London Irish Rifles) For May-1918		
War Diary	Cardonnette	01/05/1918	01/05/1918
War Diary	Warloy	02/05/1918	09/05/1918
War Diary	In Line	10/05/1918	15/05/1918
War Diary	Corps Reserve	16/05/1918	16/05/1918
War Diary	C.20.6	17/05/1918	22/05/1918
War Diary	In Support	23/05/1918	29/05/1918
War Diary	In Line	30/05/1918	31/05/1918
Miscellaneous	To All Companies After Order	08/05/1918	08/05/1918
Miscellaneous	All Companies		
Miscellaneous	Defence Scheme 18th Bn London Regt		
Miscellaneous	18 Lon Regt	09/05/1918	09/05/1918
Miscellaneous	Defence Scheme 18th Bn London Regt	09/05/1918	09/05/1918
Operation(al) Order(s)	1/18 Battn The London Regiment Operation Order No. 246	28/05/1918	28/05/1918
Operation(al) Order(s)	1/19th Battn The London Regiment Operation Order No. 182	28/05/1918	28/05/1918
Miscellaneous	A Form Messages And Signals		
Miscellaneous			
Miscellaneous	A Form Messages And Signals		
Operation(al) Order(s)	Operation Order L.I.R.242 by Lt. Col. G.B. Thompson D.S.O. Comdg 18th Bn London Regt.		
Miscellaneous	C Form Messages And Signals		
Miscellaneous	Reference B.M.S. 459	02/06/1918	02/06/1918
Miscellaneous	47th Div G.90/1/9	29/05/1918	29/05/1918
Miscellaneous	A Form Messages And Signals		
Heading	War Diary 1/18th Bn London Regt June 1918		
War Diary	In Line	01/06/1918	09/06/1918
War Diary	Divisional Reserve	10/06/1918	30/06/1918
Operation(al) Order(s)	1/18th Bn The London Regt Operation Order No. 247	09/06/1918	09/06/1918
War Diary	Ref Amiens 1/20000 Picquigny	01/07/1918	31/07/1918
Heading	141st Bde 47th Div. 18th Battalion London Regiment August 1918		
Heading	War Diary Of 18th London Regt (1st Lon Irish Rifles) For August 1918		
Miscellaneous	A Form Messages And Signals		
War Diary	Line	01/08/1918	01/08/1918
War Diary	Contay	02/08/1918	03/08/1918
War Diary	In Support	04/08/1918	05/08/1918
War Diary	In Line	06/08/1918	10/08/1918
War Diary	Warloy	11/08/1918	11/08/1918
War Diary	Bois De Mai	12/08/1918	20/08/1918
War Diary	In Support	21/08/1918	25/08/1918
War Diary	Corps Reserve	25/08/1918	28/08/1918
War Diary	Faviere Wood	29/08/1918	31/08/1918
War Diary	Needle Wood	31/08/1918	31/08/1918
Map	Map		
Miscellaneous	Insert Map Ref Or Mark On Map		

War Diary		01/09/1918	11/09/1918
War Diary	Raimbert	12/09/1918	27/09/1918
War Diary	Pierremont	28/09/1918	30/09/1918
Heading	War Diary Of 1/18th London Regt (1st London Irish Rifles) For October 1918		
Miscellaneous	A Form Messages And Signals		
War Diary	Pierremont	01/10/1918	01/10/1918
War Diary	Estaires Area	02/10/1918	31/10/1918
Heading	War Diary Of 1/18th Battn London Regt For November 1918		
Miscellaneous			
War Diary		01/11/1918	30/11/1918
Heading	War Diary Of 1/18 Bn London Regt For December 1918		
Miscellaneous	A Form Messages And Signals		
War Diary		01/12/1918	31/12/1918
Heading	War Diary Of 18 London Regt for Jan 1919		
Miscellaneous	A Form Messages And Signals		
War Diary	Pernes	01/01/1919	28/02/1919
Heading	War Diary Of 18th London Regt For March 1919		
Miscellaneous	Message Form		
War Diary	Pernes	01/03/1919	31/03/1919
Heading	War Diary 1/18 Bn Lon Regt November 1917		
Heading	4th Brigade 1st Bn Herts Regt Vol I-11-31.12.14		
Heading	1/17 London 1917		

WO 95 2737/2

47TH DIVISION
141ST INFY BDE

18TH BN LONDON REGT.
MAR 1915-FEB 1919

Missing 1918 MAR

141st Inf. Bde.
47th Division.

WAR DIARY

18th LONDON REGT.

MARCH

1915
(9.3.15 - 31.3.15)

On His Majesty's Service.

Army Form C. 2118.

WAR DIARY
INTELLIGENCE SUMMARY.
(Erase heading not required.)

Instructions regarding War Diaries and Intelligence Summaries are contained in F. S. Regs., Part II. and the Staff Manual respectively. Title pages will be prepared in manuscript.

Place	Date	Hour	Summary of Events and Information	Remarks and references to Appendices
ST ALBANS	1915 9 May		By train went to SOUTHAMPTON – 1st Train B & D Coys with half Transport – 2nd Train A & C Coys with half Transport. Battalion left S'outhampton in 4 ships – Queen Alexandra (338 men) – (Vandyke) (2 officers & R&F) – Trafford Hall (Transport & officers & 200 R&F) – Viper (2 officers & 250 R&F) Sleight 29 officers 1048 R&F. Uneventful voyage. Rations were retained.	AMH Copy
LE HAVRE	10 "		Batt disembarked at LE HAVRE at various hours & rendezvous took place on quay at 9.30am except post on TRAFFORD HALL which proceeded to camp in a separate party. Battalion around No 2 Camp HAVRE (distance 5 miles) at 12 noon. Inspected by Camp Commandant & issues of various enfants to troops. Rations were to last till midnight on 11th inst. Men's cart issued with hot tea & Transport up to strength.	AMH Copy
"	11 "	7.45am	Battalion paraded in Camp & marched to LE HAVRE stn. Arrived 8.30am 1 officer (W. Rich) & 48 R&F kept as 1st Reinforcement & sent to No 18 Camp HARFLEUR by night	(1st) Copy
		11.55am	Left HAVRE, men 36 to each truck.	
	12 "		Battalion detrained at CAUDESCURE & marched to billets en route WINNEZEELE	
WINNEZEELE (11am)			Trying march & men fatigue due to new kits. Lack of sleep & train wandering & poured road. D Coy divested at RYVELDT & billeted. Coy also stayed at LE TEMPLE & billets. Mr. Magenta & A & B coys to billets at WINNEZEELE. Billets at LE TEMPLE & RYVELDT men in barns. Water too good wells dist water scarce. Billets at WINNEZEELE scattered – men	

1577 Wt.W10791/1773 500,000 1/15 D. D. & L.   A.D.S.S./Forms/C. 2118.

WAR DIARY or INTELLIGENCE SUMMARY

Army Form C. 2118.

Place	Date	Hour	Summary of Events and Information	Remarks and references to Appendices
	March			
	12 (cont)		Cliff in Barn. Billets carried out by O.P.R.O.N. & DE GUNZBERG.	RWH/Capt
WINNEZEELE	13		Rest Day — Men's feet not nearly so bad as expected — 46 paraded with sore feet but notts serious.	RWH/Capt
	14		Companies carried out Musketry instruction & Bayonet fighting — Company Lewis gun teams from divisional school parade.	RWH/Capt
	14+		Of YPRES — 5 cases of demobilia.	RWH/Capt
	15		Musketry Instruction & Night Training in neighbourhood of billets.	RWH/Capt
	16		ditto — Firing heard during afternoon from direction of YPRES.	RWH/Capt
	17.		Route March. Orders received that the Battalion to hold itself in readiness to move. Known Transport left by road route at 7 pm with orders to billet at HAZEBROUCK CASSEL-STEENVOORDE RD for night	RWH/Capt
	18.		Battalion left Billets at 8.30 am & proceeded by road route to a point where it trained at 9.45 under busses & proceeded at 10 am to a pt on the HAZEBROUCK — AIRE road 1 mile NE of STEENBECQUE where it detrained & proceeded by road march to ST VENANT arriving there at 3pm. Men in to billet on the ST VENANT — AIRE road. Very scattered & a great deal of	RWH/Capt

WAR DIARY
INTELLIGENCE SUMMARY
(Erase heading not required.)

Army Form C. 2118.

Place	Date	Hour	Summary of Events and Information	Remarks and references to Appendices
Maul-	18 (ct)		time was wasted in settl[in]g billets due to no maps having been procured by pans) Water - good. Billets (all large farms) very comfortable & inhabitants extremely hospitable. Transport joined up at 2.30 pm - horses very done after expenditure of all night march.	Off/Capt
ST VENANT & BURBURE	19.	8.30 am	Proceeded by road route to BURBURE via LILLERS - ALLOUAGNE. Arriving 2.15 pm - Went into Billets here. Water good. Billets fairly comfortable & concentrated. Battali. HQ situate at ESTAMINET BRANLY BLONDEL very suitable, containing an Officers mess & orderly Room - Horses all under cover.	Off/Capt
BURBURE	20.		Inspection of Battalion by Commanding Officer - 30 cases of sore feet reported by Medical Officer. Training area poor - nearly under cultivation.	Off/Capt
BURBURE	21		Church Parade - Hostile aeroplane observed over LILLERS - two bombs dropped. Battali. Arrangements re rolls & & dealing with approved goods.	Off/Capt

Army Form C. 2118.

WAR DIARY
or
INTELLIGENCE SUMMARY.
(Erase heading not required.)

Instructions regarding War Diaries and Intelligence Summaries are contained in F. S. Regs., Part II. and the Staff Manual respectively. Title pages will be prepared in manuscript.

Place	Date	Hour	Summary of Events and Information	Remarks and references to Appendices
BURBURE	MARCH			
	22	9am	Musketry Instruction & Bayonet Fighting. Inspection of Battalion by Field Marshal	28th Copy
		2.30pm	Sir John French	
	23		Musketry Instruction & Bayonet Fighting & Digging	28th Copy
	24.		Field Training under Company arrangements	28th Copy
	25		" " " "	28th Copy
	26.		Field Training. Recruits musketry at LABAUVRIÈRE — only one target per Battalion. 28th Copy. 40 Recruits fires 10 rounds each. Platoons marched to No 4 mine RAIMBERT at intervals for that.	
	27.		Musketry Instruction & Bayonet Fighting — Recruits musketry continues at LABAUVRIÈRE 28th Copy. All Recruits who do so. Only fires their Recruit course exept Pts. 10 rounds.	
	28		Church Parade. Musketry Instruction after parade lvs.	28th Copy
			at C.O. Concours & two other officers with 3 N.C.O.s went up to NEUVE CHAPELLE & were attached to 1st Batt: South Wales Borderers for instruction in Trench work	
	29.		Early Musketry Instruction & Bayonet fights & Running Parade. Short service by Le Bishop 28th Copy	
			of Laban. Quarter party left for trenches for instruction — (3 officers & N.C.O.s) First party returns	
	30		Digging instruction. Officers Course at Reserve position. Quarter party (5 officers & N.C.O.s 28th Copy	

Army Form C. 2118.

WAR DIARY
or
INTELLIGENCE SUMMARY.
(Erase heading not required.)

Instructions regarding War Diaries and Intelligence Summaries are contained in F.S. Regs., Part II. and the Staff Manual respectively. Title pages will be prepared in manuscript.

Place	Date	Hour	Summary of Events and Information	Remarks and references to Appendices
BORRURE	March (cont) 30		Proceeded to Treule. Second party returned.	Attd Cyst.
"	31		Digging continued — another party for Treule — (3 N.C.O's) — 3rd party returned.	Attd Cyl.
				A.P.Hamilton Capt i/c Kensen Ryl London Irish Ryl.

1577 Wt. W10791/1773 500,000 1/15 D. D. & L.   A.D.S.S./Forms/C. 2118.

141st Inf. Bde.
47th Division.

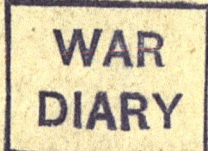

18th LONDON REGT.

APRIL

1915

"On His Majesty's Service."

Army Form C. 2118.

WAR DIARY
or INTELLIGENCE SUMMARY.
(Erase heading not required.)

Instructions regarding War Diaries and Intelligence Summaries are contained in F.S. Regs., Part II. and the Staff Manual respectively. Title pages will be prepared in manuscript.

B. Inf. Bn. — VOL II

Place	Date	Hour	Summary of Events and Information	Remarks and references to Appendices
BURBURE	1915 APRIL 1		Course of Sniping commenced – Sniper fires 10 rounds per man (4 Officers & N.C.Os) on LANAUVRIÈRE range.	A.H. Capt
	2		Battalion carries out digging instruction with South Wales Borderers – previous party returns. 4 men admitted to Hospital.	
			Digging instruction. 6 Officers & 4 N.C.Os left for instruction with Gloucestershire Regt – previous party returns – Divine Service at 3.30 p.m.	A.H. Capt
	3		4 Officers & 4 N.C.Os left for instruction with Gloucestershire Regt.	A.H. Capt
	4		Church Parade – Previous party returns.	A.H. Capt
	5		Company Pioneer Company found for instruction under Lieut MANN. Orders received that no further parties are to proceed for instruction. Orders received that H Battalion will move to BÉTHUNE on the 7th inst & to assemble at THE ORPHANAGE & to attack for instructor to 6th Infy Bde.	
	6		Company Training & A.S.W. Defence during morning & easy afternoon.	A.H. Capt
	7	10.30 am & 2.45 pm	Battalion proceeds 10.30 am & 2.45 pm left for BÉTHUNE at 11.0 am after a stop in front of 5 D.C.E.S.R. L.W. INF. A.P.E. Advance had to wait – the ALGONENE & CHOQUEL Dugouts sent out by GEN. L. OFR CM 26 14th Corps – SUND. BÉTHUNE 2.45 pm & had our quarters in the ORPHANAGE. Quarters not forthcoming & one Company accommodate as best from – the Public Baths being surveyed, the old brewery 4th class & the modern Convent Officers & Adj. proceeds to HQ 6th Inf. Bde & what H Battalion is	A.H.

WAR DIARY
INTELLIGENCE SUMMARY

Army Form C. 2118.

Place	Date	Hour	Summary of Events and Information	Remarks and references to Appendices
BETHUNE	APRIL 7 (cont)		Attacks & reserve billets refers for the incident regimes & covered outdoors the next 8 days. Briefs — One Coy at BETHUNE, One Coy provides Gd. for BETHUNE to Tunnels f as working party — One Coy attck at ANNEQUIN and supplies and parties as required — One coy less 2 platoons in firing line & reserve platoon. — Supposed at HARLEY ST. Battalion HQrs attached to No 1 A section & ordinarily H/Q of H. BETHUNE — LA BASSEE road across the village of CUINCHY. These Coy duties change round every 48 hours & the platoons in the front line reserve change over every 24 hours — thus every platoon in eight days will complete 24 hours in the front line.	
"	8		A Coy paraded at 7.15am & moved via BEUVRY — ANNEQUIN to HARLEY ST. & provided work the Tunnels (less 2 platoons at HARLEY ST. Battln attached to 1/K.R.R. B Coy paraded at 7.30am & resumed the same work & carried out digging operations of EAST ANGLIAN COY. RE. This Company suffered the casualties (2 Riflemen slightly wounded) by shell fire about 305 N of S.M.R.E. HQ on the LA BASSEE road. This Coy returned to billets at ANNEQUIN after work was finished. C Coy paraded at 7.45am & moved via same route reported to O.C. 1st Field Coy. RE for work D " marched at BETHUNE. Men all extremely cheerful & in excellent spirits & behaved very well in dangerous during the shelling etc.	R.H.

WAR DIARY

INTELLIGENCE SUMMARY.

(Erase heading not required.)

Army Form C. 2118.

Instructions regarding War Diaries and Intelligence Summaries are contained in F. S. Regs., Part II. and the Staff Manual respectively. Title pages will be prepared in manuscript.

Place	Date	Hour	Summary of Events and Information	Remarks and references to Appendices
BETHUNE	APL 8 (cont)		road. O.C A Coy reports a quiet night in the trenches. No detail in arrangement about the pioneers of fuel, water & rations to the detached companies.	app
"	9		Companies carried on same procedure except that the platoon of A Coy & his Coy were relieved by the platoon in support. All communications by telephone carried out thro' HQ 1st Div Division where HQ are at BETHUNE — No Casualties	app
"	10		A Coy returns to BETHUNE at 11.30 pm having been relieved by B. Coy. C Coy relieves B Coy at ANNEQUIN & D Coy proceeded to work under the R.E. FRENCH blew up German trench about 200 S of LA BASSÉE road & the boys on heavy shell & rifle fire. No casualties suffered by 1st Battalion. A Coy had its breakfasts served regimentally on their return to BETHUNE	app
"	11		Same procedure except that the platoon of B Coy & his Coy were relieved by the platoon in support. No Casualties. Order received from G.H Bde at Hinges that the Battalion was to have breakfasts between 5.30 am & to remain in readiness for a sudden move until 7.30 am.	app
"	12		C Coy. relieved from B Coy reported from B Coy. B Coy returns to billets at BETHUNE from CHOQUEAUX. Two men wounded —	

WAR DIARY / INTELLIGENCE SUMMARY

Army Form C. 2118.

Place	Date	Hour	Summary of Events and Information	Remarks and references to Appendices
BETHUNE	April 13		Sister News & took over Section A2 from 2/K Batt: Liverpool Regt at 2 pm. One Company in firing line — one in support at CUINCHY SUPPORT pt. Took over the line — A Coy in firing line. B Coy in support. Trenches shallow with tyl. Trav[er]ses with the hich shake in rear. Attack spoke forward to CHR by ... clearing Day &	A4
	4		following night. All quiet except for a few shots from B & C Garrison sent on fire towards their own ally 80 yds from the enemys line. Casualties: six men wounded. Heavy shelling by 9 inch abt 200 x W of CUINCHY Church abt 2 pm. Due to our own artill[er]y firing on German artill[er]y. On actually opened fire yesterday. Relieved by N. Staff Regt at 3.30 pm. D Coy went last — in with 1/6 S(STAFFORD) FIRING left & B Coys out at RUESE — C Coys in Nlverves from it's motion on the 13th to A/B
			Battalion in brigade again in 1st DRAHAYAGE BETHUNE by 6.30 pm today.	A4
	15		Company Drill & general clean up.	
	16		Company Training	
	17		Company Training	
	18		Rest day	
	19		Battalion paraded 11 am & proceeded by road route to GORRE with orders to take over trenches	

Army Form C. 2118.

WAR DIARY
INTELLIGENCE SUMMARY.
(Erase heading not required.)

Instructions regarding War Diaries and Intelligence Summaries are contained in F. S. Regs., Part II. and the Staff Manual respectively. Title pages will be prepared in manuscript.

Place	Date	Hour	Summary of Events and Information	Remarks and references to Appendices
BETHUNE GORRE (old)	19	—	Reld for WORCESTER. REGT and to hold over C2 Subsection from H.L.I. on Sept 23rd Good billets with excellent water supply — Battalion under orders of FIFTH BDE.	APH
GORRE	20		B.H.Q. LOISNE. Two works parties of 100 men each found — 1 man wounded	APH
			Company Drill during morning. Two Working parties of 100 men each paraded — 1st Relief 11K.30 8 p.m. 2nd Relief 11.30 p.m. for work under R.E. Found 1st Relief § A Coy — 2nd Relief by D Coy.	
	21		Company Training + Same works parties found at same hours by B and C Coys.	APH
	22		Company Training [crossed out] by A + D Coys.	APH
	23		Battalion Took over Sec{tor} C2 from H.L.I at 10.15 p.m. First Coy buses 5.30 p.m. at the Potale aerodrome — A Coy & (B) front line — B Coy Reserve — C Coy — C.T's front line, D Coy — Support in FESTUBERT village — No casualty suffered during relief. Relief all quiet — Battalion served ½ rations for 2 Days — very good plan — Regs + Supports + Reserve completed relief due to front line Companies.	APH
	24		All quiet — [illegible]	APH

WAR DIARY
or
INTELLIGENCE SUMMARY.

(Erase heading not required.)

Army Form C. 2118.

Place	Date	Hour	Summary of Events and Information	Remarks and references to Appendices
FESTUBERT	24 (cont)	—	At 11 p.m. message received that Germans (a) blown up a mine on our left in GIVENCHY sector. (b) that South OBS opposite our attack & required our fire support. C2A starts to arrive about 2 p.m. Prov. and Bn in urgency parapet & buildup fire step. One Sergt wounded — bullet wound jaw. Bombers still fire all day — Batt: relieved by TWENTY LON REGT 10.30 p.m.	App 2b
"	25			App 3
GORRE	26		Rest Day.	App 3
"	27		Company Drill during morning — Batt: given roll over C2 from TWENTY LON REGT 10.15 p.m.	App 4
TRENCHES	28.		Dismally wet for Saints Day but little reply by the Germans — little reply firing — contrast in cost of change of parapet & any with 27/28 turn of gap between C2A and C1B.	App 4
"	29		No. of importance occurred — Batt: relieved by TWENTY. LON. REGT at 10.30 p.m. Two men slightly wounded (both bullet wounds)	App 4

Army Form C. 2118.

WAR DIARY
INTELLIGENCE SUMMARY.
(Erase heading not required.)

Instructions regarding War Diaries and Intelligence Summaries are contained in F. S. Regs., Part II. and the Staff Manual respectively. Title pages will be prepared in manuscript.

Place	Date	Hour	Summary of Events and Information	Remarks and references to Appendices
	April 30		Rest Day - Reinforcements from ESSARS & ROUSEGNON in event of Battalion being ordered to reinforce front line as Divisional Reserve. Found their working parties of 100 men each for R.E. - No men killed - bullet wound in shoulder.	Appx

1577   Wt. W10791/1773   500,000   1/15   D. D. & L.   A.D.S.S./Forms/C. 2118.

141st Inf. Bde.
47th Division.

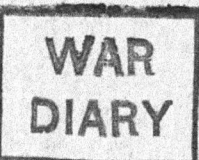

18th LONDON REGT.

M A Y

1 9 1 5

On His Majesty's Service.

Army Form C. 2118.

WAR DIARY
or
INTELLIGENCE SUMMARY.
(Erase heading not required.)

Summary of Events and Information 1/8th LONDON REGT.

Place	Date	Hour	Summary of Events and Information	Remarks and references to Appendices
GORRE & FESTUBERT (C2)	MAY 1ST		Steady shell during morning. Took over Section C2 & from 20 BATT first Coy taking over 8.30 pm - relief complete 10-15 pm. Men Watered for 48 hours. O.C. 1 man killed in Section C2 & about 11-30 pm - shot through head whilst on look out	
FESTUBERT	MAY 2nd		All quiet - 1 man wounded 1 man killed	
"	MAY 3		All quiet.	
"	MAY 4		All quiet - 2 men killed	
GORRE	MAY 5		Batt relieved in C2 by Batt London Regt - 4th Lon Inf. Bde. Batt Proceeded to billets in GORRE.	
LA BEUVRIERE	MAY 6		Batt left for LA BEUVRIERE 2 pm by Companies - very hot day - a tiring march.	
"	MAY 7		Rest day	
"	MAY 8		Left LABEUVRIERE 12 noon after on Sudden orders & proceeded to Rendezvous at LES GLAVIGNES in Brigade area	

Army Form C. 2118.

WAR DIARY
or
INTELLIGENCE SUMMARY
(Erase heading not required.)

Instructions regarding War Diaries and Intelligence Summaries are contained in F. S. Regs., Part II. and the Staff Manual respectively. Title pages will be prepared in manuscript.

1/5 LONDON REGT

Place	Date	Hour	Summary of Events and Information	Remarks and references to Appendices
LES GLAUGETTES	May 9		The 18th Batt arrived at Y Brigade Headquarters LES GLAUGMES West of LE TOURET at 3.40 AM and stood by as part of the First Corps Reserve. Notification had been received the night previously that the British would open a heavy bombardment at 5 AM supplemented by the final Artillery during the previous 30 minutes. At 2 PM the bombardment by the British was resumed for 40 minutes as a prelude to an assault by the First Division & Indians in the neighbourhood of Neuve Chapelle and the BOIS DE BIEZ. Simultaneously the French troops are assaulting South East of LA BASSÉE in the neighbourhood of LOOS and CARENCY. Information was received that GERMAN Machine Guns are apparently firing through bottom of breastworks at 9-45 PM. The Brigade made a move Eastwards to a point on the Rue du Bois about 500 yards West of LE TOURET to stand by as the Second Divisional Reserve.	A24
LES FACONS	May 10		At 3-30 PM the 5th LONDON Brigade (now known as the 141st Brigade of the 47th Division) moved to billets at LES FACONS West of LE TOURET. At 5 PM the billeting area was re-adjusted & the 18th Battalion went into billets in the Rue du Bois about 450 yards west of LE TOURET. Battalion Headquarters at the Estaminet LE PLUS. At 11-30 PM the Battalion	A24

1577 Wt.W10791/1773 500,000 1/15 D.D.&L. A.D.S.S./Forms/C. 2118.

Army Form C. 2118.

WAR DIARY
or
INTELLIGENCE SUMMARY.
(Erase heading not required.)

18th LONDON REGT

Place	Date	Hour	Summary of Events and Information	Remarks and references to Appendices
LE TOURET	11.15		received orders to clear out of billets before 7 AM the next day & to go into bivouac at a point on the NORTH side of the Rue du Bois about 450 yds W of LE TOURET. Bn bivouac all day. Bt 9.10 pm marched to RUE DU BOIS via RICHEBOURG ST VAAST & on to RUE DU BOIS	APP APP
"	12.15		Bivouac proceeded via ESSARS - to BETHONE - Bn bill. with billets around CEMETERY.	APP
BETHUNE	13.15		Batt. reaches BETHONE - Orders received 6.30 pm to proceed by road note at once to GIVENCHY (via S side of CANAL to relieve SCOTS GDS in sector B2.	APP
GIVENCHY	14.15		Sectr B2 taken as follows - C Coy Rgt'l front line - A Coy & 2 sects D Coy left front line - B Coy in Reserve Dugouts - D Coy (less 2 sects) as fillers - 1 platoon KEEP - 1 plat & 1 sect GUNNERS SIDING - two sects HQ Dugouts - 3 sects MAIRIE REDOUBT - 4 MG's in frt line & 2 extra ones for 20H Lr Regt) - Trenches left in excellent condition.	APP
"	15.15		C Coy relieved S.D. A by B. Confidential order received re25 an attack by INSIAN Coy. 7th & 2nd DIVS - 47 DIV in front of GIVENCHY to follow.	APP
"	16.15		Received S & 47 DIV'S order 3.15 am re attack prepared formerly NEF FESTUBERT. One staff & ordnance clothed - lieuts reply correlated & used well of KEEP & NEYLH/HDD app. 2/LIEUT HOUSTON wounded & 2 Oths rank at KEEP	

Army Form C. 2118.

WAR DIARY
or
INTELLIGENCE SUMMARY.
(Erase heading not required.)

18th LONDON REGT.

Place	Date	Hour	Summary of Events and Information	Remarks and references to Appendices
GIVENCHY	17th		Enemy's account of assault - left of the division on our left enlisted - left of 19th to meet on either movement to cause out toward VIOLAINES at 4.10 pm	
			Orders were issued [H Batt] to prepare to await the enemy further delay - put of JB2	
			subsets - Felt disposed were arranged - A Coy assault Coy in reserve - 1st line	
			trench - Coy - support (C Coy) still holds REFT MAIRIE REDOUBT - remainder of Coy to	
			support the advance - assault was to help plan ruled 19 LONDON on our left & its reserves	
			enemy trench - At 7.30pm orders issued for BDE the assault was NOT to take place.	
			About 9pm the enemy exploded a mine on our left front followed up with heavy rifle	
			fire - The mine exploded about 30 yds in front of the centre of the Line at about RD 607	
			assault heavy artillery fire for several minutes. Replied with 1st line	
			direct hits. The assault of HYATT which have been recall explore & the fast had counter-	
			on our own of the enemy. Rifle was cut. [Explosives message on the left of the Battery &c.	App A
			Dr. HYATT for 3 days was sent for C.O.O. 47th DIV.	App A
	18		Offensive occurred on our left on lines had R.S. ent of in our London companies.	App A
LE PREOL	19		Enemy was displays by the western of the enemy Infant.... of JB2	App A
			Batt. relieved by B2 Aug 20 LON REGT - relief complete about 1 am Batt. to billets at	

WAR DIARY of INTELLIGENCE SUMMARY

Army Form C. 2118.

1/8 LONDON REGT.

Place	Date	Hour	Summary of Events and Information	Remarks and references to Appendices
GIVENCHY/ LE PREOL	19		LE PREOL	APH
LE PREOL	20		In billets at LE PREOL. Coy C.O.s reconnts line front B3. Work part 60 men found for B3 at 8 pm. Austln. work part going straight 12 m.n.	APH
"	21.		Inspects of Coys rifles carried by coys oftrs in charge of bilyd turnds due respd – Trenches – Two work parties sent up 7 pm & 8.45 pm to B3. Battn relieved 3 am	APH
"	22		Still in billets LE PREOL. Battn warned to be held in readiness at 7 am & men at work when – Later the orders were amended that the Battn was to be in readiness to move at half an hour's notice to reinforce the Lus. Conference of Coy officers at Battn Offic 10 am to discuss an attack should this made (23rd). Lt Col Concanon CMG 14 Batt: left for STAFF DANCE as Instrl Offer. Capt Atkins Comdng of Batt during on Major Healey.	APH
GIVENCHY	23		18th Battalion LONDON REG to relieve 20 Battalion LON REG. in section B2 in trenches at GIVENCHY, LEZ LA BASSEE. A and C Companies and 2 sections of B Coy in front line. B Coy less 2 sections in keeps and dumps for C (MARIE REDOUBT and GUNNER SIDING) and the HQ dugouts, D Coy in reserve (HARLEY ST) Relief completed at 4 pm. In the absence on sick leave of Lieut Col Concanon DSO, the command of the 18 Battalion is assumed by the Second in	

Army Form C. 2118.

WAR DIARY
or
INTELLIGENCE SUMMARY.
(Erase heading not required.)

1/8 LONDON REGT.

Place	Date	Hour	Summary of Events and Information	Remarks and references to Appendices
GIVENCHY	May 23 (contd.)		Major H M HEALY T.D. 2nd Battalion M O D'Sporonex slightly wounded in the shoulder by a fragment of high explosive shell. Church parade at LE PREOUL for RC's at 10-30 AM. Chaplain Father FLYNN from BEUVRY.	att
"	24		Inspection of trenches Sections B2 (GIVENCHY LES LA BASSEE) by Brigadier General G C NUGENT at 4 PM. The Battalion (1/22 LONDON) on our left belongs to the 142nd Brigade but is temporarily (whilst in the defensive) under Brigadier Gen. NUGENT GC commanding the 141st Brigade. Information received in the forenoon to the effect that the Canadian division had captured work K5. Heavy artillery fire by the enemy throughout the day.	Apps
"	25		The 47th Divn (London) and the Canadians Divn made a vigorous assault on the Enemy's trench & breastwork line East of GIVENCHY LES LA BASSEE. The 141st Inf Bgde was ordered to continue & hold their line as follows: 1/19th Battalion on the right (Astride on the Canal) Section B'. 1/18 Battalion Section B2. 1/19 Batt in reserve in GUNNER SIDING. 1/20 Battalion in reserve at LE PREOUL. The 142nd Inf Bde on our left to assault the enemy trenches at 6-30 P.M. the assaulting Battalions being the 23rd & 24th London. The Canadian Divn to assault at 9 P.M. the 21st & 22nd LONDON in reserve in SIDBURY. The assault by the 23rd & 24th Battalion on our left	

Army Form C. 2118.

WAR DIARY
or
INTELLIGENCE SUMMARY
(Erase heading not required.)

Place: 18th LONDON REGT.

Date	Hour	Summary of Events and Information	Remarks and references to Appendices
May 25 (continued)		quickly succeeded. The 18th Battalion meanwhile keeping up a hot covering fire. [2nd Lieut.] Magnum acted very well as observing officer, on the left of our line. Second Lieut. Steele although suffering from a bullet wound in the forehead stuck to his duty on the advanced trenches for several hours before reporting to the first aid station. A very heavy artillery fire was poured in by the Enemy throughout the evening & night. The first aid Dressing Station & HQ Mess of the 18 Batt was practically destroyed by shell fire. One of the servants (RYAN) & the orderly from Clerk (Cpl WIMSETT) being wounded. Messages received up to midnight from the 141st Inf Brigade Office informed that the 142nd Inf Bde & the Canadian Div. had made substantial progress in occupying Enemy trenches. Messages received from Major Gen. BARTER expressing his appreciation of conduct of troops under his command.	
26		Violent attacks & counter occurred on our left and the early hours. The 24th Batt appears to have gained a position in which they are badly enfiladed by the Enemy. The 18 Batt ordered to give all possible support by covering fire. The enemy's artillery fire has been very heavy. Many breaches have been made in our communication trenches and the KEEP has been badly holed. Casualties on our left (24 & 23 LONDON	

Army Form C. 2118.

WAR DIARY
~~INTELLIGENCE SUMMARY~~
(Erase heading not required.)

Instructions regarding War Diaries and Intelligence Summaries are contained in F. S. Regs., Part II. and the Staff Manual respectively. Title pages will be prepared in manuscript.

18" LONDON REGT.

Place	Date	Hour	Summary of Events and Information	Remarks and references to Appendices
GIVENCHY	May 26		Batt appears to be very heavy. Our own casualties not very serious. [Major Healy slightly wounded on head by shell fire. Three Officers killed and eleven wounded. 8 snipers of the R.E. were killed in the Keep.] The advance of the day's operations appears to have some trenches gained on our left at a very heavy cost. A good nights work was necessary repairs to the KEEP and to the communication trenches were immediate & carried out.	
	27		The following special order of the day by the 44th LON DIV reads as follows :- In the field 27th May 1915 The G.O.C. wishes to express to the Brigadier General & all ranks of the 142nd INF BGDE as well as the other Units of the DIVISION which took part in and R.E. Its great appreciation of their behaviour during the operations of the 25th and 26th instant. They may be assured that the news of their achievement will be received with great satisfaction. Major General BARTER had also much gratification in recording the following message from Lt Gen Sir CHARLES MONRO KCB My best	APX

Army Form C. 2118.

WAR DIARY
or
INTELLIGENCE SUMMARY.
(Erase heading not required.)

1/8th LONDON REGT

Instructions regarding War Diaries and Intelligence Summaries are contained in F. S. Regs., Part II. and the Staff Manual respectively. Title pages will be prepared in manuscript.

Place	Date	Hour	Summary of Events and Information	Remarks and references to Appendices
GIVENCHY	May 27th (continued)		Congratulations to my old comrades of the 2nd (LONDON) Division on their success. Signed C. BARTER, Major Gen. Commanding 47th (LONDON) Division. The section of the enemy trenches captured on our left by the 23rd & 24th LONDON battalions as commanded by higher General (known as the Orchard) still in occupation by the enemy & as heard shelled & bombed. On the night of 27/28 May the 24th Batt was relieved by the LONDON Rest. C Coy (18 Batt) relieved B Coy in the firing line.	
	28		The 20 Batt asked the 18 Batt for assistance in repelling the enemy's bombing attack. The 18 Batt sent a bombing detachment at once good work was done. Sent working parties to 19 Batt. & 20 Batt. An inspection of the tactical situation by the 18th to help the 20 Batt. was made by Gen Nugent during the morning. The following special order of the day by the 141st Infantry Brigade reads as follows In the field 27/5/15	RH

1577 Wt. W10791/1773 500,000 1/15 D. D. & L. A.D.S.S./Forms/C. 2118.

Army Form C. 2118.

WAR DIARY
or
INTELLIGENCE SUMMARY.
(Erase heading not required.)

18th LONDON REGT.

Place	Date	Hour	Summary of Events and Information	Remarks and references to Appendices
GIVENCHY	May 28 (continued)		"The Brigadier has much pleasure in announcing to the Brigade that Major Gen BARTER commanding the 47th (LONDON) Division personally congratulated him on the work of the Brigade during the recent operations. The G.O.C. was especially desirous that all ranks of the Brigade should be made aware of his great appreciation of all he did, & the way they should be requested to be to add this he is the proud of having the honor of commanding them. Signed GEORGE C NUGENT. Brigadier General Commanding 141st Inf. Bde.	aph
	29		The trenches occupied by the 20th Batt on our left has given cause for considerable anxiety. It is commanded by the enemy positions on higher ground & has been persistently bombed & shelled. The bombing party of the 18th has been sent into the 20 BATT (C Company) in the firing line of Section B.2 as support while trench trench mortars to harass the enemy. We relieve the trenches on the 20 Batt. in the afternoon. The 20 BATT. was relieved by the 19 BATT. Before the enemy resumed his bombing tactics. The 18 BATT. communicates with the 19 BATTALION (LONDON) R.F.A. urged them to open a heavy fire on to the	

WAR DIARY or INTELLIGENCE SUMMARY

Army Form C. 2118.

18th LONDON REGT.

Place	Date	Hour	Summary of Events and Information	Remarks and references to Appendices
	May 29th (continued)		enemy positions & to relieve his trench mortars. [Enemy Lieut O.S.] slightly wounded while acting as observing officer on the front trench. The position on our left was reported to the Brigade Office we "little result given." He has lately late in the evening there arrived the Divisional Trench Mortar (Vickers?) Battery for action next morning. A Coy relieved C Coy on the trenches on the left of our line. B Coy relieved D Coy on the right of our line.	AHH AHH
	May 30th		The enemy was very active throughout the night 29/30. May constantly apprehensive of attack. He continuously shelled our front(?) in section 132 and was throwing bombs into our own trench. The position (B3) on the left of our line is still occupied by the 19 Battalion who have continued to supply bothers to advance of our bombing party. [Lance-Corpl HURBUCK] 19 Batt has expressed in a letter to the OC 18 Battalion his thanks for the assistance rendered. Rfm SHIPLEY, 18 Batt was killed while acting as a bomber. The trench occupied by the 19 Batt. Later my company CMS DILLON A Coy. 18 Batt was killed on the trench awhile morning some engineers regarding SHIPLEY. The enemy has kept up a heavy shell	AHH

1577 Wt.W10791/1773 500,000 1/15 D.D.&L. A.D.S.S./Forms/C.2118.

Army Form C. 2118.

WAR DIARY
or
INTELLIGENCE SUMMARY.
(Erase heading not required.)

18 LONDON REGT

Place	Date	Hour	Summary of Events and Information	Remarks and references to Appendices
GIVENCHY	May 30		Previous position all day. The KEEP suffered some direct hits [with the result that two platoons of the garrison were wounded, one enemy is to fall.] Frequent communication by telephone was opened to Regiment. He [Battalion T.M. Mortar Brigade was in support. They rendered valuable service by shelling the enemy position opposite the left of section 13 & [?] Lieut MACKINNON commanded ly Shrapnel on the Road. Late in the evening Lieut Col ATTFIELD Divisional Staff officer called and the object of reconnoitring the the line as a preliminary to the Canadians Division taking over the position of 1/8 Brigade. Subsequently two [?] Very flares. Were observed during dayllight out the day. He [?] position of 1/8 Brigade had apparently been located perfect could be reached [?] made out. He Regimental Light Major of the 19 Batt. reports that the [?] is so much bullet on apparently make it impossible to approve the communication trenches during dayllight and his wounded hook up two also the [?] [?] [?] [?] several by told [?] from more from where he was.	
GIVENCHY	May 31		h.v.c. No change in the located situation. Several officers of the Canadian [?]	

1577 Wt.W10791/1773 500,000 1/15 D. D. & L. A.D.S.S./Forms/C. 2118.

WAR DIARY ~~INTELLIGENCE SUMMARY~~

Army Form C. 2118.

(Erase heading not required.)

Place	Date	Hour	Summary of Events and Information	Remarks and references to Appendices
1st LONDON REGT. (Gibraltar) GIVENCHY	May 31		Division called at H.Q. 1/8 Batt. (London) Regt at 9 AM to reconnoitre the position of Section B2. (GIVENCHY LEZ LA BASSEE) from the Shrine (exclusive) to the DUCKS BILL (inclusive) as when they are going to take over on the 1st June 1915, the position of the line B2 west of the SHRINE (inclusive) will be taken over today by the 4th Division. All arrangements from this morning Brigadier Genl NUGENT was killed by a stray rifle shot while inspecting work in progress at SIDBURY MOUND. General (a.) BETHUNE cemetery at 5.30 PM. Zero officers & Stokers to attend funeral Battalion in the 1/H, 1st INF. BGDE. The funeral was attended by Generals Monro, Barter, Cuthbert, & Willoughby. Late in the evening the late Coy QM Sergt DILLON were buried in the ground attached to the science De Clerk on the PONT FIXE 128.	atts

141st Inf. Bde.
47th Division.

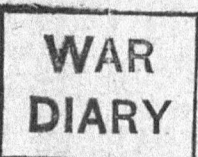

18th LONDON REGT.

JUNE

1915

On His Majesty's Service.

Army Form C. 2118.

18ᵗʰ LON REGT

WAR DIARY
or
INTELLIGENCE SUMMARY.
(Erase heading not required.)

Instructions regarding War Diaries and Intelligence Summaries are contained in F. S. Regs., Part II. and the Staff Manual respectively. Title pages will be prepared in manuscript.

Place	Date	Hour	Summary of Events and Information	Remarks and references to Appendices
	June 1st		The Canadian Division took open from the 18 Lon Regt the portion of the line (Section B2 from the Shrine (exclusive) up to the point clearing Section B² from Section B¹. The remainder of the line section B2 was taken over on the previous night by the Gordon Highlanders (9ᵗʰ Division) the relief by the Canadian division was completed at about 6 PM. The 18 London therefore proceeded by march route to Billets in the Rue d'Ouest at Bethune. Divisional command of the left by Rose has been taken by Lieut Col GODDING commanding the 14 LONDON.	
	2		Officers Commanding Battalions of the 141st Inf Bde attended at 9AM at NOYELLES LES VERMELLES to reconnoitre the line at Vermelles to be taken over today by the 141st Batt from the 1st Guards Brigade (Gloucesters and Cameron Highlanders) Conference at 4 PM at the Bde office to meet Brigadier General THWAITES now appointed to succeed the late Brig Gnl NUGENT. The 18 BATT proceeded in the evening by march route to billets at ANNEQUIN.	
	3		In rest billets at ANNEQUIN	
	4		ditto Working parties detailed for 7-0 PM to night & 6 AM to morrow for Brigade Orders. Billets at ANNEQUIN were shelled by the enemy between 8 & 9 PM	

1577 Wt. W10791/1773 500,000 1/15 D. D. & L. A.D.S.S./Forms/C. 2118.

WAR DIARY
or
INTELLIGENCE SUMMARY.
(Erase heading not required.)

Army Form C. 2118.

18. Lon Reg'

Place	Date	Hour	Summary of Events and Information	Remarks and references to Appendices
ANNAQUIN (continued)	June 1	5	This day. Inspection of 18 BATT. TRANSPORT at SAILLY LABOURSE by Brig Gen. THWAITES. In neat billets at ANNAQUIN. An inspection by the 18 BATT in the afternoon by Brig Gen W THWAITES. Working parties for the trenches as detailed by the Brigade Office. Instruction received later in the day from the Brigade office that the 18 BATT is to proceed tomorrow to LES BREBIS to act temporarily as a Reserve for the 142nd Inf Brigade.	
	6		Inspection in the morning by Brig General THWAITES accompanied by officer commanding 18 & 19 BATT of the trenches to the east of Fosse no 7 at present occupied by the INNISKILLING FUSILIERS. The 18 BATT proceeded by march Route at 10·45 PM to LES BREBIS to act as reserve in the 142nd INF Bde.	
	7		Arrived at LES BREBIS at 1 AM & took over Billets vacated by Kings LIVERPOOL REG'T. Arrival reported to the 142nd INF Bde & also to the 141st INF Bde. Officers commanding Coy s of the 18 BATT proceeded at 10·30 AM to meet guides of the INNISKILLING FUSILIERS at FOSSE no 3 to reconnoitre the trenches to be taken over from them. The 18 BATT left LES BREBIS at 3·30 PM to proceed by march route to Fosse no 3 & took over from the INNISKILLINGS. The transport of the 141st INF Bde moved to HOUCHIN.	
	8		Inspection of trenches by Brig Gen W THWAITES. Companies of the 18 Batt detailed as follows	

Army Form C. 2118.

18 (ON) REG T.

WAR DIARY
or
INTELLIGENCE SUMMARY.

(Erase heading not required.)

Instructions regarding War Diaries and Intelligence Summaries are contained in F. S. Regs., Part II. and the Staff Manual respectively. Title pages will be prepared in manuscript.

Place	Date	Hour	Summary of Events and Information	Remarks and references to Appendices
(FOSSE 7 1/2)	June 8 (Continued)		Having B C and D Coy (each less one platoon)	
	9		Quiet day in trenches. During night enemy put several shells into parapet but damage repaired before day break. Two men wounded.	
	10		Quiet day. Major Healy went on leave and command of Batt assumed by Major Beres ford	
MAZINGARBE	11		Relieved by 20th Batt. went into Reserve billets at MAZINGARBE. Two men wounded	
	12		In reserve (Divisional) marched to Noeux les mines arriving about 10 PM	
NOEUX LES MINES	13		Carried out Company inspections. Issued Batt with clothing etc.,	
	14		Training continued. Bombing & bayonet for practice	
	15		4th Battalion inspected by Brig Gen Thwaites. at Houchin Major Healy returned from leave.	
	16		Training continued. Marched 8-30 PM to position of readiness at Maysing arbe Bivouacked.	
	17		Marched to LES BREBIS took over billets of 22nd Batt. under orders of 142 Bde Relieved 21st Batt. in Subsection W1 AND in front line C in support Bn Reserve	

1577 Wt. W10791/1773 500,000 1/15 D. D. & L. A.D.S.S./Forms/C. 2118.

WAR DIARY or INTELLIGENCE SUMMARY

Army Form C. 2118.

18 Lon REG

Place	Date	Hour	Summary of Events and Information	Remarks and references to Appendices
	July 19		Major Haig went to hospital Command of Battalion assumed by Major Burnfoot	
	20		Quiet day. Enemy bombarded our right & front line	
	21		Nil. Enemy shelled BRENAY afternoon, wounded 2 nd class children 2 & killed 2 One man wounded	
	22		BN HQ Lieut. Henry killed GIVENCHY in afternoon wounded three children close to Bn HQ. Enemy wounded in village	
	23		Quiet day. No shelling of our Section. Heavy Artillery fire on our right in French area. Brig Gen Thwaites inspected Brigade orders received to destroy all pigeons and to collect the crews German wounded in front trenches	
	24		Relieved by 20 Batt went into Brigade Reserve at Les Brebis. Relief completed by 12 midnight.	
LES BREBIS	25		In Reserve Field unable to carry out drill owing to proximity of enemy's observation balloon 1 day of shelling. Sp Lieut Phipps Ferry arr. four Officers arrived from England with draft of 10 men	

1577 Wt. W10791/1773 500,000 1/15 D. D. & L. A.D.S.S./Forms/C. 2118.

18 LON REGT Army Form C. 2118.

WAR DIARY
or
INTELLIGENCE SUMMARY.
(Erase heading not required.)

Place	Date	Hour	Summary of Events and Information	Remarks and references to Appendices
ASTERLUS	June 25		from Bac.	
	26		Reserve billets. Riggings of shelter trap proceeded with.	
	27		Reserve billets. Riggings of Splinter proof proceeded with.	
	28		Batt. Relieved 20 Batt Lon Regs in W3 in evening. Relief completed 12.30 PM	
W 3			A B & D in front line C in Reserve.	
	29		Quiet day. Slight shelling by enemy but no damage done. Work commenced on B LINE.	
"	30		Enemy shelled Batt. H.Q & neighbourhood with H.E. Shell. No casualties. Considerable damage done to hostile observation Station. Work on B line continued.	

SECRET

REPORT ON
ADVANCED SECOND LINE FROM M.I.D to BULLY-GRENAY-RUTOIRE. RD (exclusive)

Nature of Trench

From point A, to point half way between point F and point H. trench is about 4 feet deep, 2 ft 6 inches wide with a parapet 9 inches high. The whole trench is cut out of chalk throughout the line. From point half way between F and H to K, trench is somewhat shallower: from K to N, trench is again 4 feet high. The whole front is protected by an entanglement about 2 ft 6 inches to 3 foot high and about 12 to 15 feet broad.

Position of 2 Companies

Suggested disposal of Companies is as follows.

Left Company

From point K to point N where trench is 4 foot deep, on right of this company at point K is a dugout suitable to contain Headquarters. A good field of fire is obtainable throughout this line. The company could keep in touch with broken line of fire trench on the other side of the LE RUTOIRE road.

Right Company

From half way between H and K, to point A on the GRENAY-VERMELLES road

As in the case of the left company there is a good field of fire. Also this company would cover the road mentioned above. and would also cover the guns of the R.I.A. which are in position about 100 yds in rear.

The Centre

This, it is suggested should be left unoccupied.
(1) Owing to the nature of the trench
(2) Because below easy range mark of the mining village unnamed.
(3) Because field of fire is not so good as the contour runs in close to the village.

Means of Approach

It is suggested that both companies should approach by day time by the track marked O.

P.T.O

Means of Approach (cont'd) Left Company
(1) Alternative approach by the communication trench in front of FOSSE is dangerous.
(a) It is under observation from the double tower near LOOS. also the communication trench does not cross the LE RUTOIRE ROAD.
(2) Alternative approach by TRACK.N is also under observation.

Right Company
Alternative approach via GRENAY VERMELLES ROAD and point A. This is somewhat exposed troops use small trench running parallel with road. also considerably more time would be taken than when using suggested approach.

Suggested Approach
Both companies just by TRACK.O.
Left Company Would turn into unnamed village and use second track in village turning down short communication trenches H. I. J.
Right Company would turn into unnamed village and use first track in village leading down to fire trench via point G and short communication trench point G to point E.

It is suggested that these means of approach would obviate any portion coming under observation by day. Companies would however have to move at necessary intervals

By night.
Right Company could move as above.
Left Company could use the TRACK.M. and enter trench by short communication trench at point L.

J H Nuder Capt.

NOEUX-LES-MINES.
15/6/15.

H. M. Healy
Major
London Irish Rifles

Report on
Roland 3

141st Inf. Bde.
47th Division.

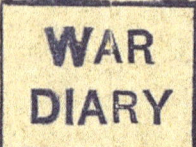

18th LONDON REGT.

JULY

1915

On His Majesty's Service.

Army Form C. 2118.

WAR DIARY
or
INTELLIGENCE SUMMARY.
(Erase heading not required.)

Instructions regarding War Diaries and Intelligence Summaries are contained in F. S. Regs., Part II. and the Staff Manual respectively. Title pages will be prepared in manuscript.

Place	Date	Hour	Summary of Events and Information	Remarks and references to Appendices
MARCC	July 1st		Enemy shelled neighbourhood H.Q. at intervals throughout day. Only damage done to No 11 Observation Station. Work continued on 13 line. Repairs to their Station.	
	2		ditto	
	3		Enemy shelled CRAISIER heavily all afternoon did extensive damage to both observation Stations 9 compelled withdrawal of observers. Work continued on 13 line. No 14 faces no damage. Trevor's Howitzer Battery reported for duty in Section.	
	4		Heavy shelling round Reserve boys splinter proofs in afternoon 1 man killed 7 wounded (Carried on repairs to observation station damages on 13 line	
	5		In trenches Heavy shelling all day, men wounded	
	6		In trenches good deal of shelling during day, relieved by 15 Batt at night	
	7		In Brigade reserve. Enemy sent one shell into town one evening wounding 2 men	
MAZINGARBE	8		In Brigade reserve. C.O. & Capt Beauish left for England on 7 days leave	
			" " Lieut J.H. Jelly carried on	APP1

CH Redfield Major

Army Form C. 2118.

WAR DIARY
or
INTELLIGENCE SUMMARY.
(Erase heading not required.)

Instructions regarding War Diaries and Intelligence
Summaries are contained in F. S. Regs., Part II.
and the Staff Manual respectively. Title pages
will be prepared in manuscript.

Place	Date	Hour	Summary of Events and Information	Remarks and references to Appendices
MAZINGARBE	July 10		In Bde Reserve - fine weather, posters during night	Appx
	11		" " " " "	Appx
	12		" " " " "	Appx
	13		" " " " "	Appx
	14		" " " " "	Appx
	15		12 noon XI Sect. to 21st Div LONDON R.E. - relief compltd 11pm	Appx
	16		In trenches quiet day. C.O Capt Bennett returned from leave	
	17		Adjutant left on two days leave to England. Batt relieved by 10th Batt	
FOSSE 7	18		In reserve. Quiet day	
	19		Two platoons Cameron attached for instruction quiet day	
	20		Quiet day. Returned to Batt on X1	
	21		In trenches. Wiring two lengths. 6 Cameron's attached for instruction	
	22		In trenches. 8 C/S recog. scouts & Assistant Officers	
	23		arrived. Quiet day. One C/S heavily bombed.	
			1 killed 2 wounded by German infantry 3 men	

[signature]

1577 Wt. W10791/1773 500,000 1/15 D. D. & L. A.D.S.S./Forms/C. 2118.

WAR DIARY
or
INTELLIGENCE SUMMARY

(Erase heading not required.)

Army Form C. 2118

Instructions regarding War Diaries and Intelligence Summaries are contained in F.S. Regs., Part II. and the Staff Manual respectively. Title Pages will be prepared in manuscript.

Place	Date	Hour	Summary of Events and Information	Remarks and references to Appendices
Fosse No 4	July 24		Enemy shelled Dulentin at intervals during day 2 C75 & 7" KRSB relieved Canns. O/c Adjut & M.O. attached for instructional also. Strongest officers + NCOS	
	25		Quiet day. Relieved by 20th Batt and brumis.	
Philosophe	26		Billets at Philosophe (Cellars & dugouts accommodation good. Enemy shelled area regularly	
	27		Quiet day. Enemy shell(?) area no war	
	28		Enemy sent a few shells into Fosse N°3 causing great damage apparently looking for batteries in rear.	
	29		ditto	
	30		Relieved by 1st Battalion. Went in to Billets & they up also in Divisional Reserve. Billets good.	
Mazingarbe	31		Carried out Training. Handling arms guard & close order drill	

Geo. F. Maye

141st Inf. Bde.
47th Division.

WAR DIARY

18th LONDON REGT.

AUGUST

1915

On His Majesty's Service.

Army Form C. 2118.

WAR DIARY
or
INTELLIGENCE SUMMARY.
(Erase heading not required.)

18 Batt London Regt
(London Irish Rifles)

Instructions regarding War Diaries and Intelligence Summaries are contained in F.S. Regs., Part II. and the Staff Manual respectively. Title pages will be prepared in manuscript.

Place	Date	Hour	Summary of Events and Information	Remarks and references to Appendices
MAZINGARBE	Aug 1		Enemy sent a few shells over & that fell short of Billets no damage	
	2		Training continued. Received orders that Battalion would take	
	3		up billets in — Day devoted to cleaning up.	
	4		Quiet Although 5 a.m. All men settled in Billets by 6 a.m. day devoted to resting men. Billets in some cases not very sanitary	
NOEUX LES MINES	5		beginning carried on	
	6		All men of Battalion bathed at Duehel Mines. Running school order & all carried out another Coy arrangements	
	7		Training generally by Coy arrangements carried on	
	8		Church Parade directly 13 Battalion arrangements	
	9		Battalion Route march in morning. Rifles inspected well	
	10		May to King Lucheley in afternoon	
	11		Training under Coy arrangements continued	
	12		ditto	
			Training continued	

Army Form C. 2118.

WAR DIARY
or
INTELLIGENCE SUMMARY.

18 Batt London Regt
(London Irish Rifles)

(Erase heading not required.)

Instructions regarding War Diaries and Intelligence Summaries are contained in F. S. Regs., Part II. and the Staff Manual respectively. Title pages will be prepared in manuscript.

Place	Date	Hour	Summary of Events and Information	Remarks and references to Appendices
ALLOUAGNE	Aug 13		All morning fatted.	
	14		Battalion drill in morning. Battalion sports in afternoon	
	15		Brigade Church Parade. Heavy rain broke up parade. Battalion	
			Y.M.C.A. entertainment in afternoon.	
	16		Brigade Route March. Further troubles not made marching easy	
	17		Training continued. Brigade sports in afternoon. Battalion	
			very successful.	
	18		Moved to Hocron-Les-Mines 12 noon arrived 3.30pm. Billets	
			good. Owing to guides of outgoing Battalion leaving before	
			arrival, men were not settled until about 4pm.	
NOFRIL(?) LES MINES	19		Digging parties provided for new Third line.	
	20		ditto	
	21		ditto	
	22		ditto	
	23		ditto	
	24		ditto	

Army Form C. 2118.

1st Batt Lon: Regt
(London Irish Rifles)

WAR DIARY
or
INTELLIGENCE SUMMARY.
(Erase heading not required.)

Instructions regarding War Diaries and Intelligence Summaries are contained in F. S. Regs, Part II. and the Staff Manual respectively. Title pages will be prepared in manuscript.

Place	Date	Hour	Summary of Events and Information	Remarks and references to Appendices
	Aug 25		Div: & divy boys seeing	
	26		Move to Lin Brebin at 8 PM arrived 9.20 PM	
	27		Whole Batt diggins out night in front of W3 section. New line to be constructed 200 yds in front of present line very moonlight. Enemy did not fire on party. Work commenced 9 pm	
	28		Diggins continued. Enemy shelled Batt: at intervals from 11 pm. MG Guns replies immediately on enemy front line. Enemy infantry did good deal of snipers. Our losses 1 kgld & 2 killed 3 wounded	
	29		Communication trenches out to new line finished to 6 feet depth & forming up commenced. Considerable shelling by enemy with 4.7 and Field guns both high explosive and shrapnel. 1 officer 6 men wounded one man dying after reaching hospital. Left us DRABIS by motor Bus for Bellek at Houchin	
HOUCHIN	30		Arrived HOUCHIN 4.30 am took over billets of 19th Batt slight rain falling Billets bad men very crowded. Men very tired & allowed to rest all day	
	31		Inspected by Brig Genl Thwaites who expressed himself as being very satisfied	CMB

Army Form C. 2118

18 Battⁿ. Regt.
London Irish Rifles

WAR DIARY
or
INTELLIGENCE SUMMARY
(Erase heading not required.)

Instructions regarding War Diaries and Intelligence Summaries are contained in F. S. Regs., Part II. and the Staff Manual respectively. Title Pages will be prepared in manuscript.

Place	Date	Hour	Summary of Events and Information	Remarks and references to Appendices
HOUCHIN	Aug 31 (contd)		and work done and with the appearance of the Battalion. Read message received from Major General Barter that C.R.E. had reported the excellent work done, especially remarked on the steadiness of the 18th who carried out sundry tasks triumphantly under considerable fire. The Major General chuck that report be communicated to all ranks & wished to express his complete satisfaction with the organization & work performed. Message from C.R.E. was also read thanking the officers & men of the Battalion for the good work done	

1875 Wt. W593/826 1,000,000 4/15 J.B.C. & A. A.D.S.S./Forms/C. 2118.

141st Bde.
47th Division

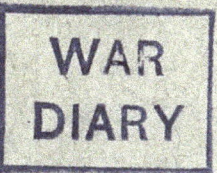

1/18th LONDON REGIMENT.

SEPTEMBER

1 9 1 5

Appendices attached:-

Preliminary Instructions.

Army Form C. 2118.

WAR DIARY
or
INTELLIGENCE SUMMARY.
(Erase heading not required.)

Instructions regarding War Diaries and Intelligence Summaries are contained in F. S. Regs., Part II. and the Staff Manual respectively. Title pages will be prepared in manuscript.

Place	Date	Hour	Summary of Events and Information	Remarks and references to Appendices
HOOCHIN	Sept 1		Battalion paraded 9.15 am and practised attack on devnol line trenches. No work in afternoon. Orders received 4 pm for 200 men to proceed to LES BREBIS work under orders of RE and Brig. MG officer. A & C Coys detailed marched off 6.30 pm under command of Capt Hobbs.	JH
"	2		Battalion parade 9 am attack practice continued	JH
"	3		C O & Adjt proceeded at 9.15 am to front line to reconnoitre ground in front. Zero hour 100 men sent off to 7 pm party working under RE.	JH
"	4		General Training	JH
"	5		General Work	JH
"	6		Working party returned from LES BREBIS	JH
"	7		Attack practice carried out by whole Battalion on lines marked to correspond with German Trenches. Brig. Genl Thwaites commented very favourably on the way it was carried out.	JH
(LES BREBIS)	8		Batt proceeded 9.30 for inspection - close order drill. Moved to Les Brebis by an Enemy for work in Trenches. Worked until 2 am & returns to Reillet at LES BREBIS.	JH

Army Form C. 2118.

WAR DIARY
or
INTELLIGENCE SUMMARY.
(Erase heading not required.)

Instructions regarding War Diaries and Intelligence Summaries are contained in F. S. Regs., Part II. and the Staff Manual respectively. Title pages will be prepared in manuscript.

Place	Date	Hour	Summary of Events and Information	Remarks and references to Appendices
LES BREBIS	Sep 9		Billets LES BREBIS worked on Trenches at night	
	10		ditto worked at night on Trenches	
	11		Moved by bus route to NOEUX LES MINES arrived 4 AM Billets good Billets over from 20th Batt. Men rested all day.	
NOEUX LES MINES	12		Billets NOEUX LES MINES. Drill & training carried on	
	13		ditto	
	14		ditto	
	15		ditto	
	16		ditto	
	17		ditto	
	18		ditto Moved by bus route to LES BREBIS 6 PM for everything in Trenches for went at night. Billets Batt'n over from 19th Batt	
	19		Billets at LES BREBIS men resting all day. Command of Battalion assumed by Maj. J.P. TREDENNICK. Dutch Trenches	
	20		Billets at LES BREBIS men resting all day.	
HOUCHIN.	21		Moved to HOUCHIN by Road from arrived 4 AM. Billets over crowded not good.	

WAR DIARY
or
INTELLIGENCE SUMMARY.
(Erase heading not required.)

Army Form C. 2118.

Place	Date	Hour	Summary of Events and Information	Remarks and references to Appendices
HOUCHIN / LES BREBIS	1/4/1915 22		Houchin. moved in Evening to LES BREBIS by Bus Route.	
"	23		LES BREBIS men resting all day.	
LES BREBIS	24		LES BREBIS. The Regiment went from LES BREBIS at 11.15am for the Trenches NW of Loos up a Comn. from to Maroc in the following day. All speak mention we u relieved during the day.	
LOOS	25th		Regt. 2 am the Regiment was accommodated in the Pd & Sukin Trenches between Copses 6 & 18 Rue Pondaming Instruction Sheet 2Y3. [The hour of Zero (commencement of our attack) was known for 5.50 am Time for assault 6.30 am. For Objective, Vide Op Order of Battle &C, See Pen Instruction. Sheet 1.] — Punctually at 5.50 am the gas & smoke attack Started & was seen answered by a heavy fire from the enemy, but very little enemy shells Reaching the Rd enemy & the Officers Trenches. The men escaped practically as casualties occurred during the 4/5 minute's gas & smoke attack. but a certain number of men suffered from the effect of gas. The twins & our Regt Zg.W. at the ensuing slightly & began to the opposing heavy lines in front of the two Trenches opposed by any heavy heavy fires. The enemy's lines. Heavy Infantry fire from our Own lines DRC MS it did not appear that the enemy fired on his for a considerable period. — At 6.30 am the leading platoon	spy

WAR DIARY
or
INTELLIGENCE SUMMARY.

(Erase heading not required.)

Army Form C. 2118.

Place	Date	Hour	Summary of Events and Information	Remarks and references to Appendices
LOOS	Sept 25-9		Cleared the parapet & rushed off in good line towards the enemy's front line although there were 300 yards away & Coys not to seen twenty yds before LCos's Garrards which it were envelopes it. On the open top, my Coy invaded the front Line, This reached the enemy's line, which was no and casualties but a heavy fight. The Garr Yeit heavy fire & held many convertible features. Which include among Coy 4 the officer commanding the Line and the 2d May checked the showers and brought back (covers quantity over the German Reserves pressing on towards Hill from their 2d Garrison Gun. They blew up [illegible] in a closely sector by the 2d, 3d, 4d & [illegible] a.m. the reserves line, each line suffering causalities at the German front line, as the line was crossed. I may say that it was good from there. final objective the enemy yet followed them for 3d May arrived. The two Coventry & Company also 2d Co. Troops & platoon of 2d The line, the mark of Han German Trench & a very short space of time. The Trench was clear of enemy & should had been Coventry french by 1.40. Organis on my right by 1.30. h. Severed in Telight. on the German line. The Coy in your line were pressing to the German 2 train from one Junior trench long hill line, as the enemy line, been taken copliany by surprise of had not to ourseen the 2 thus Trench west of LOOS.	A.R.

Army Form C. 2118.

WAR DIARY
or
INTELLIGENCE SUMMARY.
(Erase heading not required.)

Instructions regarding War Diaries and Intelligence Summaries are contained in F. S. Regs., Part II. and the Staff Manual respectively. Title pages will be prepared in manuscript.

Place	Date	Hour	Summary of Events and Information	Remarks and references to Appendices
LOOS	Sept 26		*[Handwritten entry — largely illegible. Partial reading:] They were known as being the Reserve in the Front but the enemy had it in sight & at 9:30 am on the right & at 10:45am on the left were seen approaching in a very broken line in the front line in the rear. The immediate flanks protected was the main & other trench in the rear faced throughout. Two & half of the company were employed as a Covering Party in front, but with the single exception of the platoon of the ??? who were about 300 yards from Hill 70 all ??? the Reserve Corps arrived within the boundaries of the objective district between ??? ??? the 10th Company ??? ??? inclusive 2am before dark & to the fact that had a careful reconnaissance of the ground has been made by all Officers when the regiments ?? the attack. The ??? for the attack, the positions at the company ??? were known by the advancing men & the ??? were equally known. The ??? ??? Capt [name] & the 12th Army Corps near [...] the Commander in Chief) ordered ??? to the ??? line where there was a [?] further. By 6:45am the Reserve Division had assembled in Puits ??? in the ??? had near to CEMETERY which was found unoccupied about a copy from the Commanding of 12 Officers & 820 File rank & two Platoons a line than the LENS ROAD running approximately S 25°C 65°F & front 80 yards North of the CEMETERY. Communication*	

Army Form C. 2118.

WAR DIARY
or
INTELLIGENCE SUMMARY.
(Erase heading not required.)

Place	Date	Hour	Summary of Events and Information	Remarks and references to Appendices
LOOS	Sept 25		The enemy's Field & Machine guns now got into position near the LENS Road. Regardless of enemy men & ammunition a superiority of fire was for a time attained. At first too much to stop was & the process of disposing it was not so difficult. The men on the R. of the Line trying to the South of Harry's trenches held. A note supply of Rifle ammunition during the afternoon & by night the trench was in a serviceable condition. During the night a large amount of work was done. The working parties were pushing underneath by the enemy but this. They poured enequateur on the front & the working parties near a factory Rifle Trenches lines fire from the enemy occupying Trench n. Casualties: Other ranks killed for the day. Officers killed & wounded 5. Other ranks killed 66 wounded 144 missing 27. A casualty list was compiled as soon as war situation serviced. A patrol of the Germans found been wounded of the line was caused, although the attacking line was about 1000 yards of them country source was of scenery too carefully guarded. It is difficult to estimate his resources. Enemy Casualties. Returns were presenting officers in the lines of the German 2 Bau von the CEMETERY by the Rev. had a large number of German were buried there on further in by addition to the Company & Orders of Germans Officers by the An caroled. No List of the Prisoners.	

WAR DIARY or INTELLIGENCE SUMMARY

Army Form C. 2118.

(Erase heading not required.)

Place	Date	Hour	Summary of Events and Information	Remarks and references to Appendices
Loos	27/9/15 26/9		Afterwards in a very threatening condition. Though it was now suffering from the French quite so. There appears there has been completely by surprise in Loos in a number of ???. Men were seen falling to the Cellars when the first troops entered. There ? few had escaped which our NCOs ??? in the ??? of the ??? ??? ???.	M.V.
		8am	As the new ground south of this town is going over our such ground and by & across between the ground N of the German posn. This was transferred across the French from us French Front.	
Loos	Sept 26		Night passed quietly, enemy's light artillery active during the early part of night but not as heavy as ???. Our much distressed troops managed to get a little food & obtain refreshing sleep during the morning. Between 9 am & 11am mild sniping ??? of ??? ??? ??? 70 men left front between our posns but on the enemy also saw seven Stretchers. The ground was seen occupied by our troops. At ??? a trench & redt. was seen up. Began had some ?? ??? at the VALLEY & CROS ROAD. About 300 yards between our ??? & German ??? was a pit in front of our line. This was taken from German OCH?????.	M.V.

WAR DIARY or INTELLIGENCE SUMMARY

Army Form C. 2118.

Place	Date	Hour	Summary of Events and Information	Remarks and references to Appendices
LOOS	5/10/15		Still in occupation of and consolidating German Trench west of LOOS. Fighting continues to our left front to possession of H11 c 7.0. LOOS Shelled during the night. We sent to a working party to consolidate Trench but machine gun fire through the day prevented us consolidating that position during the day. The Trench we were occupying was very shallow, & that perhaps accounts for our first casualty, Capt Lucas being killed and Tempey and 2/Lt Lowmen with two Territorians wounded & several men during the night. Germans shelled about H25. Lowmen was hit Territorians wounded & our first casualty during the night. German aircraft over trenches during the afternoon — 9 w 75 hr. German Artillery CM.4.9.T — 9 w 73 hr. 2 Offr 22 OR inspected line this afternoon with a view to taking over	All West
LES BREBIS	6/10/15		All quiet last night. 10 trench shelled the enemy fire during the day. Relieved by 29 Y Bn Leics Regt. [Relieve was necessary as the troop per cooks to very hot their war casualties about 7 officers & men exposed in 24 happy h/g in trench, but this was occupied. Passed at LES BREBIS supported Pay 9 pm. On relief was supposed nothing there Bn was offered from trench by 9.46 pm. On relief was supposed nothing there They tarry in the trench the Communication trenches in some places congestion as which was knee deep & made it were slow to get to them & when mid & badly In the open behind the trench. On relief two casualties on the open, who causing they then Bn killed at LES BREBIS. By 12.30pm the Bn reached HERSIN had reached Coy all around to billet at LES BREBIS.	Hersin

(9)

Army Form C. 2118.

WAR DIARY
or
INTELLIGENCE SUMMARY.
(Erase heading not required.)

Instructions regarding War Diaries and Intelligence Summaries are contained in F. S. Regs., Part II. and the Staff Manual respectively. Title pages will be prepared in manuscript.

Place	Date	Hour	Summary of Events and Information	Remarks and references to Appendices
LES BREBIS	Sept 29		Relieved rested during the day. [Brigadier Gen Thesiger meets Bn. during the morning.]	Appx
HESDIGNEUL	Oct 13	9 a.m.	Bn parades at LES BREBIS Church & marches off at 9.4 am to occupy billets at HESDIGNEUL arriving 12 noon. As billets could not be accessed till 4pm the Battalion did not get under cover till 4pm. Owing to the movement of the Convoy being by Interior routes, transport had horse by a circuitous route & did not arrive till 3.30 pm.	Appx

1577 Wt. W10791/1773 500,000 1/15 D. D. & L. A.D.S.S./Forms/C. 2118.

S E C R E T   Sheet 1

18th. BATTALION LONDON REGIMENT LONDON IRISH RIFLES

PRELIMINARY INSTRUCTIONS

BASED ON SECRET B M 36 RECEIVED FROM 141st INF. BDE. and ISSUED TO O.C.COYS.

(1) OBJECTIVE. The Battalion has been ordered to Capture the Hostile Second line of trenches from point 51 to point 63 and having done so to consolidate the captured position with the greatest possible speed.

(2) TROOPS. The following troops are under the orders of Officer Commanding London Irish Rifles for this purpose:

   London Irish Rifles
   2 Vickers light guns
   London Irish Grenadier Platoon
   2 Sections 19th Battalion Grenadier Platoon
   A party of 6 R.E.(for mine searching)

(3) INFANTRY ORDER OF BATTLE. The attack will be carried out on a three Platoon frontage from Sap 6 to Sap 18 both inclusive.

 A Coy will attack on the Right on a One Platoon Frontage
 C Coy will attack in the Centre on a One Platoon Frontage
 D Coy will attack on the Left on a One Platoon Frontage
 B Coy (less Two sections) in LOCAL RESERVE.

(4) OBJECTIVES of ATTACKING COYS.

 A Coy-- Hostile SECOND line from point 51 inclusive to Communication Trench at G 35 c 75 exclusive

 C Coy-- Hostile SECOND line from Communication Trench G 35 c 75 inclusive to S.W. Corner of CEMETRY exclusive.

 D Coy-- Hostile SECOND line from S.W. Corner of CEMETRY inclusive to point 63 inclusive.

(5) MACHINE GUNS   2 Vickers light guns will move with the LOCAL RESERVE.

SECRET   SHEET 2

(6) GRENADIERS   One Section from the Battalion Grenadier Platoon will
    and LEFT   be attached to each attacking Coy.(total 3 Sections)
    FLANK   and will move with the SECOND platoons of each Coy.
       GUARD.

                  No.8 Platoon under Lieut. Lane.
                  2 Sections 19th. Battalion Grenadier Platoon.

(8) FORMING
    UP PLACES   (a) In New Front Line
                  Leading Platoons of A Coy - between Sap 6 and Sap 8
                  as far North as the fire bay between short bays
                  70 and 71 inclusive (total 6 bays)

                  Leading Platoons of C Coy- from the First fire bay
                  immediately South of Sap 8 inclusive to Sap 12 but
                  NOT to include the fire bay into which Sap 12 leads
                  (total 4 long bays (fire) and 1 short fire bay)
                  Sap 13 will be now given to C.Coy.

                  Leading Platoon of D Coy. Two Sections 19th. Grenadier
                  Platoonsless one group (to form up from the right
                  in the orderenamed i.e,

                  Only the 36 foot bays are available for use there is
                  to be an Officer or an N.C.O.in each fire bay.

                  (b) In Trench Fifty Feet In Rear Of New Front Line
                  Second and Third Platoons of A Coy. Grenadiers
                  Sections attached.

                  Second & Third Platoons of C Coy. Grenadier Section
                  Attached.
                  Second & Third Platoons of D Coy. Grenadier Section
                  Attached.
                  2 men of the R.E. will be attached to each attacking
                  Coy as mine searchers_ these will move with the third
                  lines.
                  Same amount of frontage to be occupied as is alloted
                  to Companies in the New Front Line Trench.

SECRET   SHEET 3

(7)   (c) PRESENT FRONT LINE from trench 24 inclusive to Sap
       18 inclusive.

       4th. Platoon from A C and D Coys will be formed up in
       Old Front Line as follows—:

       A Coy Platoon from Sap 6 towards Sap 7
       C Coy Platoon from Sap 8 towards Sap 9 & 10
       D Coy Platoon from towards Sap 18

       Great care must be taken to see that all gangways are
       kept clear.
       The Officer or N.C.O. in charge of each of these Platoons
       will be at the head of his Platoon ready to lead into
       the Saps.

       EXACTLY 10 minutes before TIME these Platoons will move—
       A Coy into Sap 6
       C Coy into Sap 8
       D Coy into Sap 12
       The Officer or N.C.O. in charge of each Platoon will
       halt when he arrives at the junction of these Saps and
       the NEW TRENCH 50 feet behind the NEW FRONT LINE—
       Men will be spaced in the Saps at 4 paces interval and
       when halted in the Saps will kneel down and NOT close
       up.

(8) FORMING   (a) LOCAL RESERVE B Coy will form up in present front
UP OF LOCAL   line as in THREE Platoons the Centre Platoons being
RESERVE AND   named in these instructions as the CENTRE Platoons B Coy.
R.E.
                  RIGHT PLATOON B Coy.—Grenadier Group attached between
                  Saps 7 & 8 (Grenadier Group being nearest Sap 7).

                  CENTRE PLATOONS B Coy and two Vickers guns & 1 Section
                  Battn. Grenadier Platoon towards Sap 11.

                  LEFT PLATOON B Coy between Saps 11 & 12.

(9)   The following Trenches only will be used
COMMUNICATION   D Coy. Trench 26 and Sap 8
TRENCHES TO   A Coy. Trench 24 and Sap 6
BE USED BY   C Coy. Trench 26 and Sap 8
COMPANIES TO   B Coy. Trenches 24 & 26
REACH THE
FORMING UP   Coys will move in the above order but definate instruct-
PLACES.   ions will of course be published later.
                   O.C. Coys will ensure that every Officer and Platoon
                   Sergt. is thoroughly acquainted with the route laid
                   down for his Coy.

BN.HQ.   During the preliminary waiting for the attack and until
                   the attacking Coys have left our present system of Trench
                   Battalion Headquarters will be situated in Trench 26.

SECRET   SHEET 4

MOVE OF THE ATTACKING COMPANIES.

THE HOUR OF THE ASSAULT

(a) In accordance with Appendix 1 of Secret B.M. 36 the GAS and SMOKE attacks will take place for 40 minutes prior to the hour named for the ASSAULT.
This hour will be notified to all concerned later.
This hour (the actual time when the Assault is to commence) will be known in these instructions as "TIME" and all movements having relation to this word will be carried out at the VERY SECOND laid down.

(b) Exactly 5 minutes before TIME all men except those in the Saps will be ordered to fix bayonets but all men are to be cautioned against allowing any bayonet to show over the parapet.
At TIME the leading platoons of the attacking Coys will at once move forward — getting out of the Trench by scaling ladders provided (2 in each bay)

(c) Exactly 20 Seconds after "TIME the SECOND line will advance from their places of formation getting out by the footholds and hand pegs provided and will move forward in rear of the FIRST line doubling over the New Front Line Trench.

(d) Exactly 42 Seconds after "TIME" the THIRD line will advance from the same place of formation getting out in the same manner as the Second line and moving forward in rear of that line.

(e) IMMEDIATELY the THIRD line has left the Trenches the Platoons forming the FOURTH line at present in the Saps, will quickly file into their place of formation in the Trench 50 feet in rear of the New Front Line lately occupied by the Second and THird lines of their Coys and on arrival will at once fix bayonets and will advance in like manner as the THIRD line — distance in rear of the latter to be as nearly as possible 150 yards.

The SIGNAL for this advance will be given by the O.C. C Coy in the Centre of the Line by One Long blast on the Whistle but in default of this signal Platoons will move forward at TWO MINUTES 15 SECONDS after TIME.

SECRET   SHEET 5.

MOVE OF THE LOCAL RESERVE.

(13) Two minutes 15 Seconds after TIME the Platoons of B Coy
will move as follows—
RIGHT PLATOON preceded by the Grenadier Group attached
will move into Sap 7 and will debouch from there—men
extending to both flanks (except the Grenadier Group
who will extend to the RIGHT) and covering the exact
frontage laid down A Coy.

CENTRE PLATOON will move One Platoon through Sap 9 and
One Platoon through Sap 10, men extending immediately on
reaching the open and will cover the frontage laid down
for C Coy the Vickers Guns will follow closely the Platoon
moving through Sap 9.
The Section Battn. Grenadier Platoon will follow these two
platoons moving through Sap 10 (distance 50 yards)
LEFT PLATOON will move into Sap 11 and will debouch from
there—men extending to both flanks and covering the
exact frontage laid down for D Coy.
3 sharpshooters will be attached and moved with the
Centre Platoons B Coy.

SECRET   SHEET 6

ACTION ON ARRIVAL AT HOSTILE FRONT LINE TRENCHES.

(14)   (a)   All Platoons of Attacking Coys will lead straight
             forward over it.

       (b)   When the Local Reserve (B Coy) reaches the Hostile
             Front Line Trench - The RIGHT Platoon under Lieut
             BATEMAN with the Grenadier Section attached will
             immediately jump in to the Trench and will work
             South along it to connect with the 140th Bde at
             G 34 c 10 2.

             The LEFT platoons under Lieut.LANE on arrival at
             Hostile Front Line will immediately jump into the
             Trench and work NORTH up the front line from G 34
             G 34 a 65 to establish and maintain connection with
             the 44th. Bde.

             The Two Sections 19th. Grenadier Platoon less one
             group together with the leading Platoon.D Coy will
             be detailed to make straight for the Trench Juncture
             G 34 b 4. 5, The Grenadiers will work back from
             G34 b 45

SECRET   SHEET 7.

ACTION IF OPPOSITION IS ENCOUNTERED DURING ADVANCE

Energetic action must be taken at once -- The Platoons in rear, closing upon the leading platoons, the company reserve being also employed as rapidly as possible.

The Commanding Officer does not of course propose to lay down any instructions on the action to be taken - this must be entirely in the hands of Company, Platoon and even Section Commanders. He wishes to however remind Officers and N.C.Os that a rapidly executed attack on a Hostile flank is generally effective.

EXAMINATION OF LOCALITIES DURING THE ADVANCE

All buildings, low ground etc., passed during the advance must be rapidly examined---any men ordered to enter a cellar for purposes of examination must LOWER their smoke helmets.

INFORMATION DURING THE ADVANCE

Every effort must be made to keep Battalion Headquarters informed of the situation as often as possible. It is probable that during the early stages of the attack a good deal of the information will have to be sent back by Runners--Two men per platoon will therefore be told off as Runners within the Coy in addition to those detailed with BN. HQ. The value of NIL reports must be remembered.

DISTINGUISHING FLAGS!

Each attacking Platoon of the first Line of the attack will be issued with FOUR Divisional Discs (Yellow Color) with a Black Cross, and carried by each of the Two Platoons of B Coy detailed to work in the Front Line Trench.

These flags are to be carried by specially selected men and other selected men also told off to carry them on the event of the first men being casualties.

The Commanding Officer directs that these flags be looked upon for the time being as Battalion Colours and are therefore to be brought forward at all costs.

These flags are to be carried NOT planted and should be periodically waved to attract the attention of our Artillery.

It is notified for information that the 15th. Divisional Mark is a Yellow Flag.

SECRET   SHEET 8

ACTION ON ARRIVAL AT GERMAN SECOND LINE TRENCHES.

(a) No Officer, N.C.O. or man of the Battalion except the Grenadiers will on any account whatsoever proceed further forward than the GERMAN SECOND LINE. The big task of the Battalion is the CONSOLIDATION of the GERMAN SECOND LINE and this must be carried out as rapidly as possible.

FIRE AND WORK (b) O.C.Coys will make careful arrangements to ensure that one man in every THREE acts as lookout and carries on the pursuit by FIRE, all other N.C.Os and men will immediately commence the work of Consolidation --- the most careful supervision of junior Officers and of all N.C.Os is essential to see that labour is not wasted. The normal proceedure will be for the whole of the leading Platoons of the attacking Coys assisted by chosen men from the Second line to carry on the pursuit by fire until Coy Commanders are able to detail their best shots to take these mens places -- this should be done however as rapidly as possible in order to ensure greater fire effect.

GRENADIERS (c) Immediately on arrival Grenadier Sections attached to Coys will work down all Communication Trenches leading towards the enemy and also down the Second Line Trench itself to either flank to obtain and maintain communication with the Brigades on either flank.

Section of the Grenadiers attached to C Coy will be responsible for communication Trenches G 35 c 75 and G 35 c 78. Section of Grenadiers attached B Coy will be responsible for the triangle at point 63 and will work down the German Second Line towards point 96 to connect with 15th. Div.

In addition Grenadier Sections attached to Coys are responsible for any other Communication trenches in their Coy attack Sectors which may be found to exist and which are not enumerated above. Section of Grenadiers attached A Coy will be responsible for working SOUTH along German Second Line to gain trench with 140th. Brigade.

Grenadiers will only proceed sufficiently far down Communication trenches to ensure that the enemy are kept out of Bombing distance---barricades should NOT be built unless absolutely necessary to ensure safety.

O.C.Coys will make arrangements for all dead Germans to be immediately thrown out of the trenches. This is to be done at once.

Men are to be instructed that if wounded they are to immediately hand over their ammunition to the next man to them-- the collection of ammunition from casualties is to be done under Coy arrangements and Platoon Reserve Depots of ammunition provided from this source.

SECRET   SHEET 9

N O T E S.

(1) <u>Extensions.</u> All extensions are to be to 5 —this is most important and requires the utmost supervision.

(2) <u>PACE</u> This will be regulated to a certain extent by the GAS but the normal pace will be a quick rifle step varied by steady doubling if necessary to get rapidly out of a particular fire Zone but Platoon and Section Commanders are held responsible that men arrive at German Second Line Trenches not only capable of beating down any resistance that may be offered but also of commencing work at once.

(3) STRETCHER BEARERS will proceed in rear of the last Platoon of each Coy.
No attempt is to be made by stretcher bearers to evacuate wounded during the advance. These man should be made as comfortable as possible and placed in any cover such as shell holes etc., that can be discovered near by.
NO stretcher bearers of B Coy will accompany the Two Platoons working along the German First Line Trenches.

(4) SMOKE HELMETS The Two Platoons of B Coy and section of Grenadiers working along German First Line Trench and the Two Sections Grenadiers 19th. Battalion with the Two Sections B Coy as Flank guard will be most careful to have their smoke helmets lowered and tucked well into their jackets <u>Before</u> dropping into the trenches.

(5) German screens if any in captured trenches should not be pulled down as they are a signal to German Artillery not to fire on the trenches where they are placed.

(6) All men should be warned against the probable misuse of white flags and signs of surrender by the enemy.
The enemy have been known to sham death and then to shoot into the backs of our assaulting troops.
Officers are reminded of the proceedure of dealing with prisoners found with expanding or reversed bullets.

(7) <u>PRISONERS OF WAR</u> These will be sent back at once over the open with a very small escort under Coy arrangements this will normally be done by slightly wounded men—They will be handed over to an Officer of the Battalion in occupation of the New Front Line of our present system of Trenches. Officers taken prisoners will be sent seperately.

(8) Position of Battalion Aid Post will be notified later.

(9) <u>TRANSPORT</u> Cooks wagons will accompany the Battalion as far as NORTH MAROC.

No other Transport will accompany the Battalion. Special instructions re -transport have been issued to TPT Officer.

SECRET   SHEET 19/11.

(1)   PACKS   The following only will be carried in the Pack
                 1 Waterproof Cape-(at the bottom of the Pack)
                 2 Canteen
                 3 Service Dress Cap.
                 4 Towel, Washing & Shaving Materials.
                 5 Iron Rations-remainder of days rations & cheese
                        ration, if not already consumed.

(2)   SANDBAGS 3 sandbags willbe carried by each man. The method
                  of carrying these has been explained to O.C.Coys.

(3)   SMOKE HELMETS Allranks will WEAR their last issued helmets
                  The other being carried in the usual way. The
                  Helmets will be worn with the front rolled up above
                  the face ready to be lowered should troops enter trench
                  in which Gas is still hanging.

(4)   DRESS FOR OFFICERS Absolutely as for the men. All leather
                  cases must be properly covered. This can be done
                  by SERGT.HIGGINS. from Officers Hdkfs,etc.

        ORDERS & PLANS No orders or plans of our own trenches will
                  be taken into the trenches by any member of the
                  Battalion.

"B"

WIRE CUTTERS. 1 Wire Cutters will be distributed as follows

        Leading Platoon of each ATTACKING Coy.-
                 9 Pairs.per Platoon TotalPairs   27
        Second Platoon of each ATTACKING Coy
                 6 Pairs per Platoon Total Pairs 24
        All Sections Batt.Grenadier Platoon
                 2 pairs per Section Total "   8
        Right & Left Platoons "B" Coy
                 2 Pairs per Platoon Total "   4

                                   Total.----- 63 Pairs.

Wire Cutters are to be attached to the shoulders straps
and stuck in the belt. They will of course be distributed
amongst men who have received instruction in wiring, and
are thus familiar with their use. All men in possession
of Wire Cutters will wear a White patch on the right shoulder
strap. Rear Platoons will be responsible for the collection
of all the wire cutters from any men wearing these White
Patches who happen to be casualties.

SECRET   SHEET 12

PICKS & SHOVELS.

Picks and shovels will be carried by Companies as follows.-

	SHOVELS	PICKS	SHOVELS	TOTAL PICKS
First line of Platoon	---	---	---	---
Second " "	8	4	24	12
Third " "	8	4	24	12
Fourth " "	8	7	24	21
Centre Platoons B Coy	28	25	28	25
TOTAL			100	70

Tools will be drawn from the R.E. No Battalion tools except Wire Wire Cutters will be taken.

Company Commanders have been shown the correct manner of carrying these tools, and tools will not be carried in any other way.

All Sanitary men will carry shovels. These shovels will **NOT be** included in the Number arranged for above.

NOTE Men selected to carry Picks must be tall and strong.

141st Inf. Bde.
47th Division.

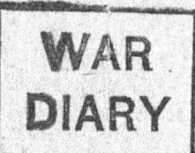

18th LONDON REGT.

OCTOBER

1915

Attached:

Appendix 1.

On His Majesty's Service.

WAR DIARY or INTELLIGENCE SUMMARY

Army Form C. 2118

18 London Regt.

Place	Date	Hour	Summary of Events and Information	Remarks and references to Appendices
HESDIGNEUL	1st Oct	10am	At 10am the Bn. paraded as strong as possible 14 Officers & 559 other ranks & were addressed by Brigadier Genl. W. Thwaites, Comdg. 141 Infantry Brigade. The General Congratulated the Battalion on their speed of march during the recent operations & the splendid discipline which carried the Battalion through a very trying period — all the end of his address three cheers were given for the General. — Remainder of day was spent in refitting & reorganizing Battalion. 2 Lt. J.A.O. MASON rejoined and was taken on strength of Battn.	A/4
"	2nd Oct		The day was spent on refitting &c. Each Company — in turn — during the day, the Padre Revd. G. Dinnen. M.C. to his Men held Kings & said a few words by grave of B. Copley on the Company parade ground. All ranks for known members sent in Kary.	A/4
"	3rd Oct	12 noon	Battalion paraded as strong as possible, now marching now withdrawing, from a brigade which served the lot of Jt. Duncan was presented his Service rifle. the Sergeant attam belied to break to break up this ranks & parades again until 12 the Transport stayed for a Short Time march. Route LABOURERE — HALLICOURT road to finish. Remainder returned by 1:20 pm	A/4
"	4th Oct		Battalion paraded in fighting order at 8 am for Brigade route march. Route HALLICOURT Length was much of march. Battalion got back to back by 11.30 am	A/4
HALLICOURT	5th Oct		Camps army & Battalion training was carried out during the morning. Reindeer parades at 4 pm at HALLICOURT recuping tent at the place. Battalion arrived at about 10am at 5pm, but shown Room on the same Most Kilok Perfus did not get in till after 7pm of various assaults throughout the Ypres to company front.	A/4

Army Form C. 2118

WAR DIARY
or
INTELLIGENCE SUMMARY
(Erase heading not required.)

18 LONDON REGT.

Instructions regarding War Diaries and Intelligence Summaries are contained in F. S. Regs., Part II. and the Staff Manual respectively. Title Pages will be prepared in manuscript.

Place	Date	Hour	Summary of Events and Information	Remarks and references to Appendices
HALLICOURT	6 Oct		Day spent in refitting men with equipment. Regimental Transport in billets. Arrival of new Cadres on strength 17/7 o.r.	
"	7 Oct.		Commanding Officers inspected parties in marching order at 10 a.m. and their boys at 167 minutes interval. The turn out was good considering the difficulty in getting equipment up to that order.	
"	8 Oct.		Battalion paraded at 8 a.m. to take part in a Brigade Route March and Outpost scheme. Battalion retn'd to billets at 2.30pm. Battalion re-placed on 6 hour notice from 5pm.	
"	9 Oct.			
"			Battalion paraded at 10.30 a.m. as taking over positions Thurs, marching men to inspection by Corps Commander. The Rt. Hon. Mr. Asquith paid both other Ranks were present on that occasion. Gen. De N. Richner after a short inspection of the troops addressed the parade & complemented all ranks on their achievement during the recent operation. Apl. M.	
"	10 Oct.		Corps Commander Ld. Lieut. Gen. Noel.... H.F. Burgess marched past Lord Plumer. Battn. restung. O/Lt. attended Voluntary Church Parades for C.E. Newcom formants & R.C. Or & a.c. Lt O/Lt attended a conference at Brigade HQ (141st) in connection with Op. O. No. 14. 141st Infty Bde.	P.M.
"	11 Oct.		Battn. paraded at 9 a.m. as strong as possible and practised opening to Artillery formation Lieuts P.M. and Eving & summer hours. The Brigadier Gen. visited the Battn. during the exercise. also Capt & Adjt H.P. Hamilton rejoined P.M. Leave. Staffs and Munro, joined and were taken strength of Battn. also Capt & Adjt H.P. Hamilton rejoined P.M.	
"	12 Oct.		Company training was carried out from 9 a.m. to 10 a.m. Remainder of morning preparing P.M. to move billets.	
MAZENGARBE	13 Oct.	8 P.M.	Battalion arrived and was billeted by 8.30 p.m. 1st line T.S.P. at NOEUX LES MINES. P.M.	
"			Battalion under orders to move at 2 & 1/2 hour's notice from 10 a.m. Men remaining in billets	

Army Form C. 2118.

18th LONDON REGT

WAR DIARY
or
INTELLIGENCE SUMMARY.
(Erase heading not required.)

Place	Date	Hour	Summary of Events and Information	Remarks and references to Appendices
MAZENGARBE	14 Oct		Draft of 100 O Ranks arrived from Base and were taken on strength. Transport taken from NOEUX LES MINES. Rear Head Qrs joined Battalion. Men confined to billets. Rear Qrs under orders to move at half an hours notice.	sketch map.
	15 Oct		At 5 pm orders received to move to lines of trenches G.30.d. (ref TRENCH MAP) (ref 36e N.W. 3.) to relieve APP. No 1. P.W. resting. Munster Fusiliers. Battn. moved at 6.45 pm and took over at 8 pm. Lieut Bircks + 2 O.R. wounded. P.W. at 8 pm.	P.W.
TRENCHES North of LOOS			Front line trenches in just condition except portion then in process of being dug out to occupy — Staff communicate trench to front line very shallow —	P.W.
	16 Oct		Line shelled by light H.E. f. direct Hill 70 + heavy H.E. f. direct HULLUCH. Not as our wire + defences of whole line concerned. Front line C B D Coys — Support A Coy. Support line shelled by light H.E. shells — retaliation by 18 pdrs on German first line — 2 LT. TIVY send f. HAVRE — 1 O.R. wounded	P.W.
	17 Oct		Quiet — 1 O.R. wounded — Co Quarts of reinforcement of front line trenches. Real salongs of arms + equipment collects + set down.	P.W.
	18 Oct		Shelling by 6 H light + heavy H.E. shells — wound D. Ollivantis Pioneer Battn. R. Welch Fusiliers carried new front line in f. f. PUITS 14 br.	P.W.
	19 Oct		Fairly quiet day — about 80 bodies buried Abs past 4 nights — wound. Alex Muff 3' R.H. Fusiliers completed new front line to a depth of four feet.	P.W.
	20 Oct		2 LT. HONYPENNY and 26 O.R. f. BASE — Battal. use to leave her relieved by	P.W.

WAR DIARY

Army Form C. 2118.

18 LON REGT

Place	Date	Hour	Summary of Events and Information	Remarks and references to Appendices
	20/4 (cont)		17 LON REGT had ors to prepare to attack. This was postponed until enemy informed Front Coy on our right as to means of covering their left flank shld attack attempt. Decided to move one Coy & one M. Gun to new front line. This was carried out at 6 p.m. Sentries ordered to especially highest Menin cliff of old front line by M.E. No attack was launched.	PN
	21N		Intermittent shelling of walls of Menin front line / heavy H.E. convenient bits. Men in flukes & intervening shells to light H.V. guns. Battn relieved by 17 Lon Regt. Relief cpltd 8 p.m. Battn marched to Reserve trenches at No 11 & SE of 2600 – plenty of digging at Accessory lines OR3, Wounds 10 OR. Men slept most of day – working party for work on CHALK PIT ALLEY at 6 p.m.	PN
	22N			
	23N		Men rested – Told over Ar Subrct (CHALK PIT and CHALK PIT WOOD) to 20 LON REGT at 7 p.m. – Front line A C D Coys – in support B Coy – 17 LON REGT on our Right – 19 LON REGT on our Left	PN

WAR DIARY
or
INTELLIGENCE SUMMARY

(Erase heading not required.)

Army Form C. 2118.

18 LONDON REGT

Place	Date	Hour	Summary of Events and Information	Remarks and references to Appendices
In trenches	24th		Slow in trench contact due to heavy shell - difficulty of commn between O.H. Hqrs & troops owing to b_n in CHAIN PIT which is unhealthy shelled all day - Wire continued - Pte of Sgt Coy - Wound Oth Rank 12.	P/
	25th		Intermittent shells all day - retaliate of our arty - chunk of held stiff - CITE ST ELIE and BOIS HUGO. Heavy & intense shell of whole subsect 2.20-4.30p.m - produced no answer owing to all shells fully sent shot. Wound O.R. 2.	P/
"	26/h		Patrols sent useful information re every work & after coln cut wire last night. Inform their wire - staff of subsect all day - Wound Oth Rank 5.	P/
	27/h		Vs heavy shell of whole subsect from 9am till dark - LTS G DALE & 2/7 F.H. BURY wounded. Killed O.R. 4. Wound Oth Rank 13. Retaken on 9.25 & heavy bombers.	P/

Army Form C. 2118.

WAR DIARY
or
INTELLIGENCE SUMMARY.
(Erase heading not required.)

18th LONDON REGT

Instructions regarding War Diaries and Intelligence Summaries are contained in F. S. Regs., Part II. and the Staff Manual respectively. Title pages will be prepared in manuscript.

Place	Date	Hour	Summary of Events and Information	Remarks and references to Appendices
In Trenches	6 Oct 28th		Battl. Shelling continues – 3 direct hits on B.N. H.Q. but no casualties. — Nuns of Str Paul 12.	P/
"	29th		Heavy shelling all day – Killed 1, Wounded 5. Hostile shelling seems hvy on our out-sects. Battal. Relieved by 19 LON REGT. – Relief complete 9.30 p.m. Battal moved to Reserve Trenches N. of LOOS. Battal. Rests in Reserve Trenches.	P/
"	30th		Battal. Rests in Reserve Trenches – Battal. moved to billets at MAZINGARBE bei relieved in Reserve Trenches by 6 LON REGT. Relief complete 10.35 p.m. – Brigade now in DIVISIONAL Reserve	P/
"	31st			

APPENDIX 1.

No 1

SKETCH MAP OF TRENCHES NE of LOOS. 14.10.15.

APPENDIX No 1.
Oct 1915 War Diary
18 LON REGT

CHALK PIT

Puits No 14 bis

Puits No 15

— British Trenches (in French)
— German —do—

Scale 1: 10,000
36 N.W.3 TRENCH MAP.

141st Inf. Bde.
47th Division.

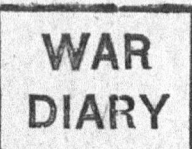

18th LONDON REGT.

NOVEMBER

1915

On His Majesty's Service.

Army Form C? 2118.

WAR DIARY
or
INTELLIGENCE SUMMARY. 18 London Regt.

(Erase heading not required.)

Instructions regarding War Diaries and Intelligence Summaries are contained in F. S. Regs., Part II. and the Staff Manual respectively. Title pages will be prepared in manuscript.

Place	Date	Hour	Summary of Events and Information	Remarks and references to Appendices
MAZANGARBE	1915			
Nov 1st	1		Reserve Billets. 1 Coy in strong post in old front German line.	ONC
	2		Reserve Billets - Billets bad - dirty	ONC
	3		ditto - ditto	ONC
	4		" "	ONC
	5		1 Coy in strong post in old German front line.	ONC
	6		3 Coys were inspected by Lord Mayor of London. Remainder of day rest this.	ONC
	7		In Trenches Section B2 1st line. Left Coy to Loos. Very quiet. Weather bad. Trenches in bad condition. 20th Lon Regt on Right; 19 Lon Regt on left.	ONC
	8		Quiet. 1.O.R wounded.	ONC
	9		Shelling of Communication Trench "Haymarket", HAIE ALLEY.	ONC
	10		Support trenches in Sect B2 wet.	ONC
	11		" "	ONC
	12		" "	ONC
	13		MAZANGARBE. Batt billeted in Bttn Corps of new huts. - Crowded but clean.	ONC
	14		Billets reached by train from NOEUX-LES-MINES at 3 pm. Batt billeted 6.5 pm very crowded. Fine bright day. in Corps Reserve	ONC

Army Form C. 2118.

WAR DIARY
or
INTELLIGENCE SUMMARY. 18 LON·REGT

(Erase heading not required.)

Instructions regarding War Diaries and Intelligence Summaries are contained in F. S. Regs, Part II. and the Staff Manual respectively. Title pages will be prepared in manuscript.

Place	Date	Hour	Summary of Events and Information	Remarks and references to Appendices
	1915			
RIMBERT	Nov 15		Arrived RAIMBERT. Billets good. In Corps reserve.	
"	16	10·40 am	Resting & cleaning up. Loitering	
	17/18			
"	19		Training of Bn. Commenced. Training coy consisting of first draft NCO's & junior officers.	
			Capt AP Hamilton to be attached to 19 Bn. Lon Regt. Training proceeded with - Bombing & musketry &c.	
	19		Training	"
	20		Training	"
	21		Training	"
	22		Training	"
	23		Training	"
	24		Training	"
	25		Training	"
	26		Training	Draft 18 O.R. joined men taken on strength.
	27		Training	"
	28		Training	"
	29	4·30 pm	Training	"

141st Inf. Bde.

47th Division.

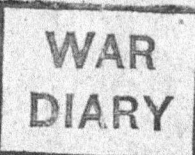

18th LONDON REGT.

DECEMBER

1915

On His Majesty's Service.

Army Form C. 2118.

Month of Dec, 1915

WAR DIARY

INTELLIGENCE SUMMARY.

(Erase heading not required.)

1/8 Lon Regt L.I.R

Place	Date	Hour	Summary of Events and Information	Remarks and references to Appendices
Rambert	Dec 1st		War Reminiscence Idea formulated by 4th Lon. Bn. Staff. Route march to have started today – postponed until tomorrow.	W.R.C
Rambert	2		Route Excercise – Left Rambert 8am arrived Rebecque – 5.30pm	W.R.C
Rebecque	3		Went into Billets – Left Rebecque 9.30am of the 3rd arrived Rambert 5.30 pm.	W.R.C
Rambert	4		Bn. at disposal of O.C. – One hour's steady drill – remainder of day resting	W.R.C
	5		Church parade.	W.R.C
	6		Training resumed – Range practice commenced.	W.R.C
	7		" " " – Senior officers outpost exercise	W.R.C
	8		Bathing (Sle..p) – Range practice	W.R.C
	9		Training Presentations	W.R.C
	10		ditto	W.R.C
	11		ditto	W.R.C
	12		Church Parade. – Sgts of Batt reunion dinner	W.R.C
	13		Entrained from Lillers 9.30am arrived Nouex les Mines 11am	W.R.C

Army Form C. 2118.

WAR DIARY
or
INTELLIGENCE SUMMARY
(Erase heading not required.)

8 Lon Regt L.I.R

Place	Date	Hour	Summary of Events and Information	Remarks and references to Appendices
MOEUVRES/MINDEC 13 LA BOURSE	Dec 13		Marched into Billets at LA BOURSE — Billets good — Resting in Div Reserve	JBC
	14		In trenches — relieved Black Watch in Sub Section known as "HAIRPIN".	JBC
	15		In "Hairpin Section. The Enemy made a small bombing attack on our Barricade in Essex Trench about 9pm this morning but were easily beaten off. About 6pm Enemy accounted for actively over their own Barricade in our rifle fire & were who were seen getting into the space between our cover & their cover screened by our barrier. It is difficult to say how many were killed by our bombs owing & nature of the ground but our fire has been extremely accurate & completely stopped the enemy up attack. Enemy Snipers were very active yesterday & today but have been silenced by our Snipers. The remainder of the day He every kept very quiet until 8 PM a German accounted in standing down SHIPKA SAP. as pointed for about 3 looked over He top appeared to be discovering He front, a small unemendeated bullet at him & he disappeared. This	JPC

1577 Wt.W10791/1773 500,000 1/15 D.D. & L. A.D.S.S./Forms/C. 2118.

Army Form C. 2118.

18 LON. REGT L.I.R.

WAR DIARY
INTELLIGENCE SUMMARY
(Erase heading not required.)

Place	Date	Hour	Summary of Events and Information	Remarks and references to Appendices
HAISNES Section.	(cont) Dec 15		together with the fact that the enemy had made no attack that morning led us to believe that the enemy was contemplating a further attack. A sharp lookout was kept and the presence of officer Lt Munro moved his two Vickers Indian Clara hill Sap. A patrol was sent out about 8 p.m. who reported our bombs had done considerable damage to the enemy's barricade in trench "H3" but the enemy did not appear to be doing any work on it. All was quiet till 11·45 p.m. when a German Officer suddenly appeared about midway between us & Shipka Sap. and fired 3 rounds from his pistol as a signal to attack at the same time the bomb attack commenced. Our bombers fell back a little at first to avoid the enemy bombs, which were well directed and were thrown from the right flank of the Sap, on reaching the front line from our bombers our bombers were reinforced by 6 from supports. In a few minutes their bombs fell as far as to the junction of our Right front flank some of their bombs fell as far as to the junction of our front line & Sap. About 12·20 a.m. it was decided to look for	A.J.C.

1577 Wt.W10791/1773 500,000 1/15 D. D. & L.   A.D.S.S./Forms/C. 2118.

WAR DIARY
INTELLIGENCE SUMMARY

Army Form C. 2118.

18 Div Regt L.I.R

Place	Date	Hour	Summary of Events and Information	Remarks and references to Appendices
Hurfrin Section of	August (continued)		(continued) Artillery support, what eye commands given. The conveying in rear of the enemy ceased. The enemy used rifle grenades during the attack, presumably with the idea of forming a barrage behind our trenches but the fire of these were badly directed exploded harmlessly in no mans land between Essex trench our Front line. The attack was of a determined nature was directed by an officer who could be seen observing as the bodies were Thrown. Their Stokes were to his party. He could not be seen any casualty were inflicted on the enemy owing to the darkness. They kept reasonably quiet for the rest of the night. At dawn any bombers became conspicuous a hundred of the same formation but received small encouragement from the Enemy and the affair died down.	R.C.
	16		Went into support	B.C.
	17		In support	B.C.
	18		Relieved by 4th Batt. marched to VERQUIN	B.C.

Army Form C. 2118.

WAR DIARY
or
INTELLIGENCE SUMMARY.
(Erase heading not required.)

18 Lon Regt L.I.R.

Place	Date	Hour	Summary of Events and Information	Remarks and references to Appendices
VERQUIN	Dec 19th		Batt billeted in "Chateau Verquin"	W.B.C.
	20		Resting in Verquin.	W.B.C.
	21		" " "	W.B.C.
	22		" " "	W.B.C.
	23		Relieved 23rd Batt Lon Regt in HOENSOLERN Section	W.B.C.
HOENZOLERN Section	24		4am British exploded own & German mine. 18th Batt occupied Crater 16 Killed 11 Wounded, heavy hostile shelling	W.B.C. W.B.C.
	25		Relieved by 19 Batt Lon Regt. Relief very difficult owing to terrible state of trenches, 2 feet of mud. Relief started 6 PM 25th relief effected 10 AM 26th Men very tired many Lewis Guns Boots had to be left in mud to enable men to extricate themselves from trenches.	W.B.C.
SAILLY	26		In Sailly. Men Resting	W.B.C.
	27		Resting in Sailly. Cleaning up proceeded with department in 200 guns &c/c.	W.B.C.
	28th		Relieved 19th Batt in Hoenzolern Section	W.B.C.
	29		In Section Hoenzolern.	W.B.C.

WAR DIARY
or
INTELLIGENCE SUMMARY.
(Erase heading not required.)

Army Form C. 2118.

18th Bn Royal L.I.R.

Place	Date	Hour	Summary of Events and Information	Remarks and references to Appendices
VERMELLES	Dec 30		Relieved by 19th Batt went into support in VERMELLES. Coy "A" in dome ashur trench Coy "C" in line. D Coy in junction keep & Coy in Vermelles.	J.P.C.
	31		Relieved at Vermelles by 8th Batt at 9 am marched to Billets at La Bourse.	J.P.C.

OFFICER COMMANDING
18th Bn. Co OF LONDON REGt

Army Form C. 2118.

WAR DIARY
or
INTELLIGENCE SUMMARY.
(Erase heading not required.)

Month of Jan 1916
1st Low Regt. L.I.R.

Instructions regarding War Diaries and Intelligence Summaries are contained in F.S. Regs., Part II. and the Staff Manual respectively. Title pages will be prepared in manuscript.

Place	Date	Hour	Summary of Events and Information	Remarks and references to Appendices
	JAN. 1916			
ABOURCE	1		In Billets at La Bourse, Billets good	A.P.C.
VERQUIN	2		Moved to Verquin. Great difficulty was experienced in obtaining open Billets.	A.P.C. A.P.C.
A.F.S. BRÉBIS	3		Marched to Les Brebis went into Billets by 1 P.M. Passed Corps Commander at Level Crossing in (L.14.c)	A.P.C. A.P.C.
Loos	4		Relieved the French in Loos Centre Sub Section. Relief commenced & effected between 6 P.M. & 10 P.M.	A.P.C. A.P.C. A.P.C. A.P.C.
	5		2 Officers wounded. Quiet. Supported by French Artillery.	A.P.C. A.P.C.
	6		Full day – Hostile heavy shelling in Craters	A.P.C.
	7		Quiet day.	A.P.C.
	8		Relieved by 17 Battn went into Support 2 Coys Loos 2 Coys MAROC	A.P.C. A.P.C.
	9		In Support	A.P.C.
	10		Relieved 10th Battn in Right Sub Section Loos	A.P.C.
	11		Quiet day.	A.P.C.
	12		Relieved by 8th Battn & went into Billets at Les Brebis	A.P.C.

Army Form C. 2118.

WAR DIARY
INTELLIGENCE SUMMARY.
(Erase heading not required.)

Month of Jan 1916

Instructions regarding War Diaries and Intelligence Summaries are contained in F.S. Regs., Part II. and the Staff Manual respectively. Title pages will be prepared in manuscript.

Place	Date	Hour	Summary of Events and Information	Remarks and references to Appendices
LES BREBIS	Jan 13		Battalion at Les Brebis	183 C.
"	14		ditto. ditto. Batt bathed.	183 C.
"	15		ditto " ditto " Resting	183 C.
MAROC Centre Sub-Sect.	16		Relieved 21st Batt in Maroc Centre Sub Section. Relief commenced 4.30 P.M. & 8.30 P.M. – 2 platoons 47th Div. Cyclists attached.	183 C. 183 C.
"	17		In Maroc Sub-Sect. – Information received that mining operation were in progress at Base of Southern Crassier	183 C. 183 C. 183 C.
"	18		Quiet day.	183 C.
"	19		Mining expert arrives to verify suspicion no mining – Experts decision "no hostile mining was in progress."	183 C. 183 C.
"	20		Relieved by 20th Batt. went into support.	183 C.
"	21		In Support – at 9 P.M. heavy hostile shelling of Maroc 2 killed	183 C.
"	22		Relieved 19th Batt in left sub Sect Maroc.	183 C.
"	23		At 2 A.M. Mine was exploded in Centre Sub Sect. Loos – Very slight retaliation on the part of the Enemy. Officer of 6th Batt came up to rec–	183 C. 183 C.

WAR DIARY
or
INTELLIGENCE SUMMARY
(Erase heading not required.)

Month of Jan 1916   Army Form C. 2118.

18 Lon Regt. L.I.R

Place	Date	Hour	Summary of Events and Information	Remarks and references to Appendices
	JAN 23 (Contd)		Commune Line	MC
	24		In Support Line. Batt HQ shelled intermittently during day – Relieved by 6th Batt went into Billets at BRAQUEMENT. House-tramines arrived 10-15 pm.	MC, 973.C
	25		In Billets at Braquement – Billets good	973.C
	26		In " ditto	973.C
	27		" Working party furnished 2 off – 100 men.	973.C
			ditto ditto ditto at 6.30 am	973.C
			Stand to. Enemy attempted attack on 15th Div – Stood bay 8-15 pm.	973.C, 973.C
	28		Relieved 22nd Batt in Left Sub Section LOOS – Col Frederick sick	973.C
	29		In Support Line G Craters - Shelled in the afternoon	973.C
	30		Normal disposition were assumed	MC
	31		Quiet	M.C.

J. Stevenson Stud
OFFICER COMMANDING
18th BN. Cᵒ OF LONDON REGT

Army Form C. 2118.

WAR DIARY
INTELLIGENCE SUMMARY.
(Erase heading not required.)

MONTH of FEB. 1916.

18. LON REG. (R^n IRISH RIFLES)

Place	Date	Hour	Summary of Events and Information	Remarks and references to Appendices
LOOS	1		3 doz. lead queek.	H.Q.H.
	2		Enemy observed doing little work	H.Q.H.
	3		Left by howitzer bombarded houses 4 seem to HPm also support line communication trench behind had coy	H.R.H.
	4		Quiet day	H.Q.H.
	5		Relieved by 6th Batt.	H.R.H.
	6		Rest billets.	H.Q.H.
LES BREBIS	7			H.R.H.
	8			H.R.H.
	9			H.R.H.
MAROC	10		Went into support to Trench Loheru	H.R.H.
	11		Quiet	H.R.H.
	12		ditto	H.R.H.
	13		2 Platoons to Coy went to reinforce 19th Batt. to left in the centre sub section	H.R.H.
	14		Enemy put a dark over day	H.R.H.
	15		Quiet	H.R.H.

Army Form C. 2118.

WAR DIARY
INTELLIGENCE SUMMARY.
(Erase heading not required.)

Month of FEB 1916   18 Lon Reg' (London Rifles)

Place	Date	Hour	Summary of Events and Information	Remarks and references to Appendices
	15		Proceeded to Les Brebis in the Evening, relieved by 2nd Regt	H.R.H.
			Fusrs	
	16		Marched to Mozur-les-Mines & entrained there for Lillers at 10.30am arrived Lillers 11.30am - Marched to Robeck in Corps Reserve	H.R.H.
Robeck	17		RIMBERT - very strong gale blowing - Billets good	H.R.H.
			Making & cleaning up - 2 hours mud night 17th to 18th night	
	18		Re-issue OHB, troops received 3 hours notice to entrain.	H.R.H.
			Cleaning up & deficiencies noted - issues of clothing &c made	
	19		6 hours Baths, Baths	H.R.H.
	20		Church Parade.	H.R.H.
	21		Individual training commenced	H.R.H.
	22		2nd day individual training	H.R.H.
	23		3rd - ditto - ditto -	H.R.H.
	24		Batt took March - Floringhem - Ferfay - Rambert	H.R.H.
	25		5th day individual training.	H.R.H.

WAR DIARY
-or-
INTELLIGENCE SUMMARY.
(Erase heading not required.)

Army Form C. 2118.
Month of FEB. 1916.
18 Battn Lon Reg. (Lon Irish Rifles)

Place	Date	Hour	Summary of Events and Information	Remarks and references to Appendices
RAIMBERT	26	—	6th day Range practice.	N.R.K.
	27	—	Church Parade.	N.R.K.
	28	—	Range practice 4th day individual training	N.R.K.
	29	—	Bde Route March 8-55 am Starting fm Raimbert — Route Auchel — Marles-les-Mines — Lozinghem — Auchel & turned to billets in Raimbert at 1 PM.	N.R.K.

Officer Commanding
Bn. Co OF LONDON

T.I.B. — Sounds for Dr. H. Ralph Hon — afternoon

Call H. Ralph 464-4040
or 702 or Dr. Jurow Ext 72411

WAR DIARY
INTELLIGENCE SUMMARY.
(Erase heading not required.)

Army Form C. 2118.

Month of MARCH 1916
1S Low. REGT (Bn. Ind. 12/4/16)

Instructions regarding War Diaries and Intelligence Summaries are contained in F. S. Regs., Part II. and the Staff Manual respectively. Title pages will be prepared in manuscript.

Place	Date	Hour	Summary of Events and Information	Remarks and references to Appendices
RAIMBERT	1	—	Range practice	H.Q.M.
"	2	—	— ditto —	H.Q.M.
"	3	—	— ditto —	H.Q.M.
"	4	—	Proceeded by bus to march to ERNY ST JULIEN (in First Army Training Area). Left Raimbert at 8.50am arrived 3.30pm. in heavy snow storm marched on – Estrée Blanche – Enguingatte went into billets in Erny St Julien – Barns good.	H.Q.M.
ERNY ST JULIEN.	5	—	Gen'l day field training – Artillery formation practiced – returned to Billets about 4.30pm.	H.Q.M.
"	6	—	Owing to severe weather, field training postponed – Lectures in Billets.	H.Q.M.
"	7	—	Defence à'Oline carried out – talca – defence of Erny St Julien	H.Q.M.
"	8	—	Field Exercise – The Attack.	H.Q.M.
"	9	—	Moved to Sachin. Rancy slippery – great difficulty in vehicles – great difficulty in getting attachments at Sachin at 3.30pm.	H.Q.M.
SACHIN.	10	—	Transport arrived. Marched from Sachin to BRUAY with 19th Batt	H.Q.M.

WAR DIARY / INTELLIGENCE SUMMARY

Army Form C. 2118.

MONTH of MARCH 1916.

18 Batt. Lon. Regt. (Lon. Irish. Rifles.)

Place	Date	Hour	Summary of Events and Information	Remarks and references to Appendices
BRUAY	10	(cont)	difficulty in finding billets during to Staff Capts. having received billeting representatives	HCM
	11		In BRUAY.	HCM
	12		Church Parade.	HCM
	13		Moved to Villers au Bois & Careney took over from 2nd North Hants.	HCM
CARENCY Section	14		Moved into left Sub Section Carency dist. relieved 1st Sherwood Foresters.	HCM
	15		Sig. dug. out blown in by aerial torpedo – Sgt Price D.C.M. Sig. Sgt. Sig. Riggs killed 3 others wounded. all of Sig Section. 1/4 Col Hornsby 17th Batt. arrived to reconnoitre trench.	M.M.
	16		Relieved by 14th Batt. 2 Coys proceeded to Carency & Coys to Villers au Bois.	HCM
	17		Supplied working parties.	HCM
Villers	19		Bn HQ was moved to Young Majors house in Villers au Bois	HCM

WAR DIARY
INTELLIGENCE SUMMARY.
(Erase heading not required.)

MONTH of MARCH 1916
18 Batt Lon Regt.

Army Form C. 2118.

Place	Date	Hour	Summary of Events and Information	Remarks and references to Appendices
VERDREL	20		Moved to Vedrel billets for men good difficulty for officers	M.C.
	21		Working party at Bouy 5 off 250 men for 138 Att Coy R.E.	M.C.
	22		Same working party furnished as the 21st.	M.C.
	23		Bathing at FRESNICOURT	M.C.
	24		Inspection of Coys by C.O. impossible to be carried out owing to snow.	M.C.
	25		Bde Assumed - Corps Commander Lt Gen H Wilson inspected the Brigade - snow very thick on ground.	M.C.
BOUVIGNY	26		Batt moved to Bouvigny huts - took over from 20nd Batt Relief completed by 11am - pelting rain.	M.C.
	27		Relieved by 19th Batt Lon Bouvigny huts relief completed by 6-30 pm. Still snowing - Took over the Lorette trenches from 24 Batt.	M.C.
LORETTE SECTOR	28		The Major Gun & Brig Gen & Bde Major came to B'n H.Q. at 4pm too dark for them to go round line.	M.M.
	29		C.O. sent to Gt Servins en route to France to England for his investiture.	M.C.

Army Form C. 2118.

WAR DIARY

INTELLIGENCE SUMMARY.

(Erase heading not required.)

MONTH OF MARCH 1916.

1/8 Batt Lon. Regt.

Place	Date	Hour	Summary of Events and Information	Remarks and references to Appendices
	30		Brig General G Bull Major went round line about 5.30 p.m.	H.R.H.
	31		Major Glen Barker & Lt Col Newton Taylor came to Bn HQ 10th & went round up to A Coy unable to proceed further owing to open ground.	H.R.H.

Officer Commanding
Bn. Co. of London Regt.

Army Form C. 2118.

1 Batt.n Row Regt
Lon Irish Rifles
141/45

WAR DIARY
or
INTELLIGENCE SUMMARY

(Erase heading not required.)

Instructions regarding War Diaries and Intelligence Summaries are contained in F.S. Regs., Part II. and the Staff Manual respectively. Title Pages will be prepared in manuscript.

Month of April 1916

Place	Date	Hour	Summary of Events and Information	Remarks and references to Appendices
LORRETTE RESERVE TRENCHES	1	—	In Reserve trenches (Lorette)	M.R.M.
	2	—	Villers au Bois	M.C.M.
	3			M.R.M.
VILLERS AU BOIS	4			M.C.M.
	5			M.R.M.
	6			M.C.M.

2449 Wt. W14957/M90 750,000 1/16 J.R.C. & A. Forms/C.2118/12.

Army Form C. 2118.

18. Batt. Lon Regt
Lon Irish Rifles

WAR·DIARY
or
INTELLIGENCE SUMMARY
(Erase heading not required.)

Month of April 1916

Instructions regarding War Diaries and Intelligence Summaries are contained in F. S. Regs., Part II. and the Staff Manual respectively. Title Pages will be prepared in manuscript.

Place	Date	Hour	Summary of Events and Information	Remarks and references to Appendices
Verdrel	7		Coy Resolsed - In Div Reserve	M.R.H.
	8		"	M.R.H.
	9		"	M.R.H.
	10		"	M.R.H.
	11		- D. Coy proceed to Isolation Camp.	
			Owing to Case of German Measles breaking out in their hut.	
	12		At Verdrel	M.R.H.
	13		"	M.R.H.
	14		Proceed to Gouy in Support	M.R.H.
	15		In Gouy - In Support.	M.R.H.
	16		" C Coy proceed to Evolution Camp.	M.R.H.
	17		"	
	18		" Supplies working & fatigue parties.	M.R.H.
	19		HQ Sigs & 19 OR A Coy proceed to Isolation Camp. In Support at Gouy. The Brig General Inspects New aircraft - Staff Sgt arrives to Supervise Physical Training	M.R.H.

2449 Wt. W14957/M90 750,000 4/16 J.B.C. & A. Forms/C.2118/12.

Army Form C. 2118.

WAR DIARY
INTELLIGENCE SUMMARY

(Erase heading not required.)

18. Batt. Lon. Regt
Lon. Irish Rifles.

Month of April 1916

Place	Date	Hour	Summary of Events and Information	Remarks and references to Appendices
Gouy	19 (Cont.)		– For one day only	N.C.H.
	20		Took over A Subsection night of 20/21st from 21st Batt. with 2 Coys together with 1 Coy 20th Batt & L.M. Gunners. Relief very slow owing to slippery mud. Relief complete 2.30 A.M.	N.C.H.
A Sub Section	21		Very quiet – arrangements made for patrolling – passed alert on Brig. came up at 5 PM. No Trench Stores arriv.	N.C.H.
"	22		Quiet – very wet day – Front line trench occupied by Right Coy. full of water in several places – pumping resorted to. – No patrolling possible. – Arrangements for artillery strafe cancelled.	N.R.H.
	23		Quiet	N.R.H.
	24		Dry weather – Trenches improve – Left Coy strafed enemy with Rifle grenades – Enemy replied with heavy Trench Mortars on Cuthbert Front. – Support line & Communication	N.C.H.

Army Form C. 2118.

WAR DIARY
INTELLIGENCE SUMMARY
(Erase heading not required.)

1st Batt. Lon Regt
Lon Irish Rifles

Month of April 1916

Place	Date	Hour	Summary of Events and Information	Remarks and references to Appendices
A Sub Section	24 (contin)		Trenches damaged - 10 casualties - 1st Coy sent Artillery retaliation which was given on Enemy front line - Patrol out from midnight till 2 am. Enemy apparently relieved at 12.30 am night of 24/25	H.P.H.
	25		At 3.30 am mine was exploded on right of Coy on our Right. Enemy at once began consolidation of Crater. At 3.35 am a second mine was sprung about 180 yards to left of 1st. At 4 pm a mine exploded on right of Batt. front. At 6 pm L 18 R Supported by opening rapid rifle fire on our left.	H.P.H.
	26/24		Quiet. Relieved by 4th Batt. at 1.20 am (when relief was completed)	H.P.H.
	24		Arrived in Billets in Mauricel Bourde at 4.30 am.	H.P.H.
	28		In support at Mauricel. The Major General inspected the Batt.	H.P.H.
	29		At Maurieul Bourde	H.P.H.

Army Form C. 2118.

18 Batt Lon Regt
Lon Irish Rifles

WAR DIARY
or
INTELLIGENCE SUMMARY
(Erase heading not required.)

Month of April 1916

Place	Date	Hour	Summary of Events and Information	Remarks and references to Appendices
MAISNIL	30	—	L Maisnil Bouché	MCR.

OFFICER COMMANDING
18 Bn. Co. OF LONDON REGT.

Secret

18 Bath
Dev Regt
L.I.R.F

Month of May 1916

Vol 14

Army. Form C. 2118

WAR DIARY
INTELLIGENCE SUMMARY
(Erase heading not required.)

Instructions regarding War Diaries and Intelligence Summaries are contained in F. S. Regs., Part II. and the Staff Manual respectively. Title Pages will be prepared in manuscript.

Place	Date	Hour	Summary of Events and Information	Remarks and references to Appendices
MAISNIL BOUCHÉ	May 1	—	Maisnil Bouche — In Reserve.	WD
	2		Moved to Bourecq — Bourecq Huts in Support.	WD
	3		In Bourecq Huts.	WD
	4		"	WD
	5		"	WD
	6		"	WD
	7		Moved to Villers — Neufport — Went into Billets for night.	WD
S.13 Centre Calor	8		Relieved 10th Batt Hants — Enemy Q.13 entire sector — Quiet. 3 Craters in line — In close touch with our artillery.	WD
	9		Trench mortar activity rather considerable on right front. 4.15 PM mine explodes 80 yds right of New Cut — thereby it fell of being enfiladed from enemy lip of new cut. — Trenches damaged — work continued. V	WD
	10		Little work possible by day — R.E. tunnelling — no word until 11 Batt. 10.9 P.M. Nothing of particular importance. New cut of trench together with — Both replied hotly with heavy gun — Enemy has	WD

WAR DIARY
or
INTELLIGENCE SUMMARY
(Erase heading not required.)

Army Form C. 2118

1st Batt. Lon Regt.
O. J. R.
Month of May 1916

Place	Date	Hour	Summary of Events and Information	Remarks and references to Appendices
	10 (Contd)		Huns called on his Artillery - We retaliated with Trench Mortars. Artillery barrage - Some fierce fighting - Quietens about 9.15 PM. - Much worth in repairing trenches & in consolidating them	W.D.
	11		Work continued on trenches by day - At night operations commenced on new Old Crater as Enemy supposed to be mining circle ".	W.D.
	12		Enemy Trench Mortars very active especially on right. Mine is supposed on Front & of Dunera in our right. - Work at night progressing well. Except on Sap between French Crater Work & Old Crater.	W.D.
	13		Line Sap pushed 25ft forward during night.	W.D.
	14		Very quiet day. Proceed to Maisnil Bouché night of 14/15.	W.D.
	15		In Billets at Maisnil Bouché in Reserve (Bde in Reserve)	W.D.
	16		"	W.D.
	17		"	W.D.

Army Form C. 2118

18 Batt Lon Regt
P.B.R.
Month of May 1916

WAR DIARY
INTELLIGENCE SUMMARY
(Erase heading not required.)

Instructions regarding War Diaries and Intelligence Summaries are contained in F. S. Regs., Part II. and the Staff Manual respectively. Title Pages will be prepared in manuscript.

Place	Date	Hour	Summary of Events and Information	Remarks and references to Appendices
Maroeuil Bouch	18	—	In Maroeuil Bouch (Bde in reserve)	W.T.A
	19	—		W.T.A
	20	—	Moves to Cabaret Rouge	W.T.A
	21	—	Heavy Enemy bombardment commenced at 3 PM. Orders to move up to Bapolle line received at 3.50 PM. Enemy attacks at 4.45 PM.	W.T.A
	22		at 2.10 am A Coy counter attacks — 2 offs & 35 OR missing. Counter attack not successful. Kept observing. at 9.20 pm A D & B Coy were relieved. (20 men C Coy + Lewis Guns & Bombers alone remain in Line) Returns to Villers attack up Bde H Q Bde + 2nd London arranged for	W.T.A
	23		Attack next arranged for 8.25 PM — at 8 PM the German heavy + field arty y barrage commenced. This lifted at 8.20 pm (ours began) but this of the time attackers met the result that they had before. Owing to heavy loss & change of orders operation suspended. Loss of Range — 2 Coy O I H 35 OR w/hts remain at Cabaret Rouge.	W.T.A
	24		A Y C remain at Cabaret Rouge.	W.T.A

Army Form

WAR DIARY
or
INTELLIGENCE SUMMARY

(Erase heading not required.)

1st Batt Lon R^t   F.1.R
for Month of May 1916

Place	Date	Hour	Summary of Events and Information	Remarks and references to Appendices
	24 (continued)		dug outs at 2 am A.V.C. moved down to Villers	W.D.A.
	25		13 L.D. Lewis guns & bombers relieved — moves to Cambrai "Abbe"	W.D.A.
	26		141st Inf Bde proceeds to Corps reserve 18th Batt billeted in Mareuil near Pernes. Maj. Trinder proceeded on leave Capt. Mahin in command of Regt.	W.D.A.
	27		"	W.D.A.
	28		"	W.D.A.
	29		"	W.D.A.
	30		"	W.D.A.
	31		In Mareuil in Corps reserve	W.D.A.

[signature]

SECRET

Army Form C. 2118.

18 Batt Lin Regt
Month of June 1916
Vol 15

WAR DIARY
or
INTELLIGENCE SUMMARY
(Erase heading not required.)

Instructions regarding War Diaries and Intelligence Summaries are contained in F. S. Regs., Part II. and the Staff Manual respectively. Title Pages will be prepared in manuscript.

Place	Date	Hour	Summary of Events and Information	Remarks and references to Appendices
MOREST.	1st		In Corps reserve. Morest.	ws
"	2		ditto — ditto.	ws
"	3		ditto — ditto	ws
"	4		ditto — ditto	ws
"	5		ditto — ditto. Draft of 75 arrived.	ws
"	6		ditto — ditto Draft of 31 arrived.	ws
"	7		Bate. Ceremonial Parade	ws
"	8		In Corps reserve Morest.	ws
"	9		ditto — ditto	ws
"	10		ditto — ditto Major Arnold resumes command of Batt.	ws
MOREST & COOIGNY	11		Moved to Barlin by train & thence by march route to billets in Coigny.	ws
"	12		Moved into line. A Sub section (Calonne Sector) - Quiet	ws
"	13		In Line — Quiet	ws
"	14		In Line — ditto	ws
"	15		ditto — ditto	ws
"	16		ditto — ditto	409

SECRET.

Army Form C. 2118.

WAR DIARY
INTELLIGENCE SUMMARY
(Erase heading not required.)

18 Batt Div Regt
Month of June 1916

Place	Date	Hour	Summary of Events and Information	Remarks and references to Appendices
ANGRES Cabaret Sector &	17		Moved to Bouvigny Huts. In Divisional Reserve	W.D.
BOUVIGNY.	18		In Bouvigny huts. Major W. Parker, 24th Bn. temporarily took over command.	W.D.
	19		ditto – ditto	W.D.
	20		ditto – ditto	W.D.
BULLY.	21		Moved into Support in Bully. – B.H.Q. in Bully Coys in Support trenches.	W.D.
	22		ditto – ditto	W.D.
	23		ditto – ditto	W.D.
	24		ditto – ditto	W.D.
ANGRES, Cabaret Sector.	25		Moved into A Sub Section. Calonne Section. Auper.	W.D.
	26		In Line ditto – ditto – Ouest.	W.D.
	27		In Line. In accordance with arrangements a bombardment of Enemy's front line system at Hoy Points began at 11.14 P.M. The bombardment was a preliminary to a Box Smoke attack under cover of which raids were to be made. The object of the raid was to cause loss to the Enemy to obtain identification of Enemy troops & further to destroy or capture any Rifle Grenade batteries, Trench Mortar Machine Guns or ammunition which may be found, also to locate Dugouts to These Shafts. — Two minor operation was	

SECRET.

Army Form C. 2118.

WAR DIARY
INTELLIGENCE SUMMARY

(Erase heading not required.)

18 Batt. Lin Regt.
North of June 1916

Place	Date	Hour	Summary of Events and Information	Remarks and references to Appendices
	27 (contd)		part of a system of roads at present carried along the British front. At 11.15 PM the gas & smoke attack was delivered on front of A.M.P.E.22. Section which continued for 2 hours. The raiding party consisting of part of the 19" Batt. & 11 Bombers 18"/13" H. then entered the Enemy trenches, remained there 15 minutes & then returned to own lines after carrying out the object held in view. — One prisoner was captured.	M.M.
Stirs	28"		Still in line. — Quiet.	W.M.
	29"		Moved to Sinis. HQ V2 Corps – 2 Coys Bombers & M6 Section in Bully. H 13 Bde Reserve.	W.M.
Bully	30.		ditto — ditto	W.M.

William Parker
Major
Cmdg 18 Lin Reg.

141st Brigade.
47th Division.

1/18th BATTALION

THE LONDON REGIMENT

JULY 1916

"A" Form. Army Form C. 2121.

MESSAGES AND SIGNALS. No. of Message_____

Prefix...*..Code..........m.	Words	Charge	This message is on a/c of :	Recd. at.............m.
Office of Origin and Service Instructions.		Sent		Date...14/
Secret		At............m.	..................Service.	From...
Confidential		To............		4
		By............	(Signature of "Franking Officer.")	By..........

TO { 141st Inf Bde

Sender's Number	Day of Month	In reply to Number	
DRT 95.	31/8/16		AAA

Herewith War diary for the month of July 1916.

From One Eighteen Lon Regt

Place
Time

The above may be forwarded as now corrected. (Z) 6/18 Lon batt

Censor. Signature of Addresser or person authorised to telegraph in his name.

WAR DIARY of INTELLIGENCE SUMMARY.

Army Form C. 2118.

Month of July 1916
1/8 Batt. Gen. Regt.

No 16

Place	Date	Hour	Summary of Events and Information	Remarks and references to Appendices
FOSSE 10.	1		At Fosse 10 in Bde Reserve	W.D.
	2		ditto	W.D.
Bouvigny	3		Moved to Bouvigny in Div. Reserve	W.D.
	4		In Bouvigny – Div. Reserve	W.D.
	5		ditto	W.D.
	6		ditto Draft of 99 O.R's arrived.	W.D.
Souchez	7		Moved to Line Souchez (1) Trenches Lad.	W.D.
	8		In Line – Quiet.	W.D.
	9		Enemy shelling Hauxrval – 22nd Batt. Res. Regt. attacked our left, got attack visited on Angres 2 section the relief accepted our Bn. Front – Enemy reply not severe – Our Bn Casualties 1 O.R. killed 10 wounded – not recovered.	W.D.
	10		In Line Souchez (1) Quiet	W.D.
	11		ditto	W.D.
	12		ditto	W.D.

WAR DIARY or INTELLIGENCE SUMMARY.

Army Form C. 2118.

Month of July 1916
1st Bn. 4th Bedf. Regt.

(Erase heading not required.)

Place	Date	Hour	Summary of Events and Information	Remarks and references to Appendices
SOUCHEZ (O)	13		In line – Souchez (O) – Quiet – Relieved by 14th Batt. & moved to SOUCHETTE HEIGHTS. met BHQ in ABLAIN.	WD
	14		In support. Quiet.	WD
ABLAIN	15		ditto – Quiet	WD
LOETTE HTS	16		ditto – Quiet	WD
"	17		ditto – Quiet	WD
"	18		ditto – Quiet	WD
"	19		ditto – Quiet – Relieved by DRAKE Batt.(RND)	WD
			proceeded to Huts in BOUVIGNY.	
			In Reserve – Lt Col JN TREDENNICK took command of Batt.	WD
BOUVIGNY	20		ditto. Brigadier General Commanding	WD
	21		ditto	
	22		Inspected Batt.	WD
			In Reserve – BOUVIGNY.	WD
	23		ditto – ditto.	WD
	24		ditto – ditto.	WD
	25		ditto – ditto	WD
	26		ditto – ditto	WD

Army Form C. 2118.

WAR DIARY
or
INTELLIGENCE SUMMARY.

(Erase heading not required.)

Month of July 1914
1/8 Bat. of Lon. Regt.

Place	Date	Hour	Summary of Events and Information	Remarks and references to Appendices
BUVIGNY	28		Move by March Route to Divion. Reveille 6.0am. Move off 7.30am. Yarrived Divion 12.15pm. In Corps Reserve.	WD
DIVION.	29		In Divion.	WD
			a.m. Major J.R. Minchin took over command of Batt. vice Lt. Col. Spedabrick to Hd Qrs. Dir School Pernes (a) command	WD
	30		Move by March Route to MAISNIL ST POL. Left Divion 7am arrived MAISNIL 7.30pm.	WD
	31		In MAISNIL ST POL.	WD

J M Linder Major
OFFICER COMMANDING
1/18th. Bn. Co OF LONDON REG[T]

141st Brigade.
47th Division.

1/18th BATTALION

LONDON REGIMENT

AUGUST 1 9 1 6

Army Form C. 2118.

WAR DIARY
or
INTELLIGENCE SUMMARY.
(Erase heading not required.)

1/18 Batt Lon Regt
Month of August

Vol 17

Place	Date	Hour	Summary of Events and Information	Remarks and references to Appendices
FORTEL	1		Moved by march route to FORTEL	W.R.S.
	2		Fortel	W.R.S.
	3		Ditto	W.R.S.
NOUELLY le DIEN	4		Moved by march route to Nouelly le Dien	W.R.S.
GAPENNES	5		Moved by march route to Gapennes	W.R.S.
"	6		In Gapennes Training procedure	W.R.S.
"	7		Ditto	W.R.J
"	8		Ditto	W.R.J
"	9		Ditto	W.R.J
"	10		Ditto	W.R.J
"	11		Ditto	W.R.J
"	12		Ditto. Role Operation practice attack on front system of trenches	W.R.J
"	13		In Gapennes Training	W.R.J
"	14		Ditto	W.R.J
"	15		Role operation Wood fighting in Crecy Wood (practice)	W.R.J

Army Form C. 2118.

1/18 Batt Lon Regt

Month of August 1916

WAR DIARY
or
INTELLIGENCE SUMMARY.

(Erase heading not required.)

Instructions regarding War Diaries and Intelligence Summaries are contained in F. S. Regs., Part II. and the Staff Manual respectively. Title pages will be prepared in manuscript.

Place	Date	Hour	Summary of Events and Information	Remarks and references to Appendices
Gapennes	16		Bn Operation practice attack on enemy front line system of trenches.	WD1
"	17		In Gapennes. Training	WD1
"	18		Ditto. Ditto	WD1
"	19		Ditto. Ditto	WD1
"	20		Bde practice Operation. Rear Guard Action after withdrawal.	WD1
ERNIES			moved by March Route to ERNIES (HQ & 2 Coys Bombers, 2 Blocks) 4 GORENFLOS (2 Coys).	WD1
GORENFLOS	21		Moved by march Route by FLESSELLES	WD1
FLESSELLES	22		Moved by March Route to MOLLIENS - au - Bois.	WD1
MOLLIENS	23		Moved by March Route to BRESLE. - Bde practise Regt operation.	WD1
BRESLE	24		In BRESLE. Training.	WD1
"	25		Ditto. Ditto.	WD1
"	26		Ditto. Ditto.	WD1
"	27		Ditto. Resting & Sports.	WD1

Army Form C. 2118.

WAR DIARY
INTELLIGENCE SUMMARY.

(Erase heading not required.)

1/18 Batt Lon Regt

Month of August 1916

Place	Date	Hour	Summary of Events and Information	Remarks and references to Appendices
BRESLE	28		Bresle - Training	W.21
"	29		Ditto	W.22
"	30		Ditto	W.23
"	31		Ditto Batt Operations practice attack	W.23.

J M Schrader Major
OFFICER COMMANDING
1/18BN, C? OF LONDON R

Army Form C. 2118.

Month of September 1916

1/18 BATT. LON REGT. L.I.R

VOL 18

WAR DIARY
INTELLIGENCE SUMMARY.
(Erase heading not required.)

Instructions regarding War Diaries and Intelligence Summaries are contained in F. S. Regs., Part II. and the Staff Manual respectively. Title pages will be prepared in manuscript.

Place	Date	Hour	Summary of Events and Information	Remarks and references to Appendices
BRESLE	1st		Bresle Training	J.J.
	2		Ditto - Ditto	J.J.
	3		Ditto - Ditto	J.J.
	4		Ditto - Ditto	J.J.
	5		Ditto - Ditto	J.J.
	6		Ditto - Practice Air Attack	J.J.
	7		Ditto - Training	J.J.
	8		Ditto - Practice Air Attack at 10am	A.J.
	9		Ditto - 6am	A.J.
	10		Ditto -	J.J.
	11		Moved to support area J.	
	12		In Support Area	A.J.
	13		Ditto Ditto	J.J.
	14		Ditto Ditto Moved into front line. Bn was on the left, with 14th on right, 19th & 20th being in support. No casualties during relief or up to midnight.	A.J.
	14			H.

WAR DIARY or INTELLIGENCE SUMMARY

Army Form C. 2118.

Month of September 1916

1/18 BATT. LON REGT. L.L.R.

Place	Date	Hour	Summary of Events and Information	Remarks and references to Appendices
HIGH WOOD	15	—	Batt attacked at 6.20 am. There was no barrage & being apparently hoped that the 3 tanks attacking through the wood would keep down the machine gun fire. This they entirely failed to do, and in consequence the first attack was to columns and there were heavy casualties from machine gun fire. Pl's C & D. Hamilton of the 9 H.L.I. immediately organised a number of men in a stampede as soon & this was killed together with every man who went over and I know after a consultation it was decided to bomb round the flanks — word was sent to B.C. H.Q. asking the situation & asking for Artillery support. These tactics proved highly successful & at noon 9.40 am the enemy all along the Batt front abandoned the trenches in a long new Strong Point behind the German line — These caused a number of casualties in detecting Major JR Trench who was shot though the head whilst reporting & being the removal of German prisoners. As soon as snipers had been located	

Army Form C. 2118.

Month of September 1916

1/18 Batt Lon Regt L.S.R.

WAR DIARY
or
INTELLIGENCE SUMMARY.
(Erase heading not required.)

Place	Date	Hour	Summary of Events and Information	Remarks and references to Appendices
HIGH WOOD	15th		up the Batt. pushed through the wood & consolidated a line beyond. In the afternoon Major B McMahon came up & took over command of a new line was dug out 150 yards clear of the wood. Total casualties were 223 all ranks. The wood was heavily shelled at 8 p.m. for about 2 hours without causing heavy casualties.	A.1.
	16th		Spent in digging new line 200 yds further forward which on the left connected with the 50th Division. Owing to heavy shelling on the right flank, a continuous line was not dug - to connect up the 14th Batt on our right, this was protected by a concentration of machine guns & was constantly patrolled. The shelling in front of the men constantly patrolled but were seen causalties.	A.1.
NAMPIZ	17th		Relieved about 4 p.m. by 24 Batt & moved to Mametz Wood. Draft of 96 OR's joined unit. Orders were received at 4 p.m. to move up at 4 p.m. & relieve 24th Batt.	

R.E.J.
Army Form C. 2118.
Month of September 1916
1/8 Bath Lan Regt L.F.J.R.

WAR DIARY
or
INTELLIGENCE SUMMARY.
(Erase heading not required.)

Instructions regarding War Diaries and Intelligence
Summaries are contained in F.S. Regs. Part II.
and the Staff Manual respectively. Title pages
will be prepared in manuscript.

Place	Date	Hour	Summary of Events and Information	Remarks and references to Appendices
HIGH WOOD	14th		In lines in front of High Wood. Relief effected at 10 P.M. without any casualties.	A.1.
	18th		Very heavy rain, impeding all work. - Trenches in very bad condition - shelling heavy - casualties slight	A.1.
	19th		In same position - heavy enemy shelling - slight damage.	A.1.
ALBERT	20		Relieved by 1st Cameron Highlanders at 2 P.M. marched to ALBERT arriving there about 7 P.M.	A.1.
BRESLE	21st		Moved to BRESLE	A.1.
	22		In Bresle.	A.1.
	23		Ditto. Ditto	A.1.
	24		Ditto. Ditto. Draft of 150 O.R's arrived.	A.1.
	25		Ditto. Ditto. Bde ceremonial	A.1.
	26		Ditto. Ditto. Training	A.1.
BECOURT	27		Moved to Becourt. Left Bresle 1.30 P.M arrived Becourt 5.20 P.M.	A.1.
	28		Moved to Bazentin and Bath in 13de reserve.	A.1.

Army Form C. 2118.

Month of September 1916
1/18 Batt London Regt

WAR DIARY
or
INTELLIGENCE SUMMARY.
(Erase heading not required.)

Place	Date	Hour	Summary of Events and Information	Remarks and references to Appendices
BAZANTIN	29th		In Bde Reserve. — at 1 pm. A Coy moved to High Wood. B. Coy moved to "Switch" line at 4 pm. A Coy moving to FLAG line	A.1. A.2.
	30th		Rest of Batt did not move. In Reserve.	

OFFICER COMMANDING
1/18 LONDON REGT

Vol 19

Mr Gray
18 L͟t͟ London Rd
October 1916

Army Form C. 2118.

11th Bn Hdrs Lincoln Regt

WAR DIARY
or
INTELLIGENCE SUMMARY.
(Erase heading not required.)

Bank of October 1916

Place	Date	Hour	Summary of Events and Information	Remarks and references to Appendices
High Wood to Eaucourt l'Abbaye	1st		Bn moved to position of assembly as foll:— A Coy M.34.c.88 to M.35.a.59. Bombers in Flag Lane less those attacked 19th Bde. B. Coy Starfish to Coy Prue Trench. D. Coy Cough Drop, Lewis Gunners, Flag Lane, H.Q. Starfish. Batn reach assembly position by dawn. Signal Officer had got communication by wire to A, B & C Coys by 10.30 am — D Coy was fast in a position to observe and were not laid on. By 12 noon all Coys had reported their reconnaissance complete & were ready to move up to take over from in co-operate with either of the three front line Batns. At Zero report received & sent back that Bde H.Q all correct on front. Zero + 10 report received troops gone over in good order, Yleurs Line taken. Zero + 15. Report all troops "smoke so thick that little can be seen — troops so if held up on left or centre. Conflicting reports during following 4 hours. Final order from Bde received upon which following order issued to Coys:— Bn will move to position vacated by 14th 4.30 a² Batts from A.25.b.88 to M.29.a.9.3. Order of Coys from right to left A.D.B.C. A & D Coys will move via sunken trench B & C via Sunken Rd to their new positions	

WAR DIARY or INTELLIGENCE SUMMARY

Army Form. C. 2118.

1/18 Batt
London Irish Rifles
Month of October 1916

Place	Date	Hour	Summary of Events and Information	Remarks and references to Appendices
			Coy frontage roughly 200 yards. Report at once when in position. Bn. HQ remain present position. Zero H 7pm (confirmation received from Bde 4.25) On moving Coys found considerable confusion. 17th 19th & 20th having elements back in the trench O.O.1. Runners from two left Coys had difficulty in finding their way back in the dark to HQ of exact position not known till 8.30pm. A Coy first in position at 6.30pm. D Coy was delayed by 19th Battn who thought them a re-inforcement but Coy reported in position at 7.30pm. B & D in position roughly at 6.30. Right very dark, early morning misty. Information received thro' Bde at midnight that our front or support lines were held in places by us but in parts enemy had strong points. Orders received to send 2 platoons of bombers to dislodge enemy from a strong point about M.23 c.8.1. Two platoons from B Coy & 1 section of Bn Bombers attacked at 3.0 am & succeeded in taking this point which was double blocked or held. Communication very bad also ground. No operations before dawn. Patrols reported enemy holding pont of Years line so far as our double block.	
O.B.I.	2/10/16	6.45am	22nd Batt attacked but without success. Orders received about 7.0am to attack us	And.

Army Form C. 2118.

11th Battn First R/f/Bs

WAR DIARY
or
INTELLIGENCE SUMMARY.
(Erase heading not required.)

Month of October 1916

Place	Date	Hour	Summary of Events and Information	Remarks and references to Appendices
	3/10/16		soon as possible. Objectives (1) Hun front & support line Lt Abbé along Lonkin Rd. (2) Line running NW of Eaucourt L'Abbé along Lonkin Rd. Message subsequently received to suspend attack. Condition of O.B.3 very bad & overcrowded. Sniping very active apparently from derelict tank. In the afternoon the 18th Batt closed up in waves but attack postponed. Patrols reported during night Hun line still occupied & remained confirmed this. Preliminary order 18th Batt would attack. Objectives (1) Hun front & support line M.23.c.0.5 M.23.c.6.0 (2) a line west corner Eaucourt L'Abbé to M.23.a.5.3 where joint 19th & 20th was still holding a position in touch with Anzac Division on right. Patrols reported Huns lightly held and a patrol was sent out at 11.30 am & on hearing from them that they penetrated Hun line without opposition authority was asked to push forward without barrage which was granted verbally at 1pm & at 3 pc There coys of the Batt went across in attack order. The fourth coy sent up Crescent Alley at 3 pc to form defensive flank. At first there was slackness Lewis fire which ceased as advance developed and about 40 enemy prisoners themselves	Ans.

WAR DIARY
or
INTELLIGENCE SUMMARY.
(Erase heading not required.)

Army Form C. 2118.

11th Batt
Kings Royal Rifles

Month & Year: Nov/Rifles/October 1916

Place	Date	Hour	Summary of Events and Information	Remarks and references to Appendices
BECHCOURT L'ABBAYE			up to 50 O.R. The enemy put barrage along those line which caused some casualties but both lines where occupied by 3.45. The two recr waves stayed here to consolidate & at 4 pm the 1st & 2nd waves moved forward through the village. No opposition offered there and by 4.10 the objective had been reached. Consolidation was carried on at once. Our line was formed up well that of 20th on right. Patrols were at once sent forward & established connection with 50th Div about M.22.b.2.1. The flew front & support line had been evacuated by enemy and sent back to Bde at 5.0 pm asking for gap to be filled. 2 Coys of the 17th Bn arrived at about 12.45 am. Heavy shelling by enemy all night.	
	4/10/16		Enemy seen in large numbers on Butt de Warlincourt. Barrage called for well satisfactory results & again at 7 pm their movements were suspicious & barrage put on satisfactorily.	am
	5/10/16		Battn was relieved by 6th Batt at 2.45 am & moved in to Bde reserve in BECHOURT	am
	6		Left Bechourt for MAMETZ WOOD.	am

WAR DIARY
INTELLIGENCE SUMMARY

11/8 Baft
2nd Army Rfs.
Month of October 1916

Army Form C. 2118.

Place	Date	Hour	Summary of Events and Information	Remarks and references to Appendices
FRANVILLERS	7		Left MAMETZ wood & Arrived travellers by march route started at 2.30 pm & arrived in billets at 11 pm. Capt S.B Stevington & 300 ORS were left behind attached to 17th Batt. as a working party.	A.M.
	8		For Corps reserve travellers in billets	A.M.
	9		Ditto	A.M.
	10		Ditto	A.M.
	11		Ditto	A.M.
	12		Ditto	A.M.
	13		Ditto	A.M.
	14		Ditto	A.M.
	15 AM		Left travellers by march route for Albert. & entrained there at 9 pm. for Longpres-les-Corps-Saint arriving there about 8 pm night of 15th & marched to Bussus.	A.M.
	16		Billets at Bussus - Left Busses by march route at 11 pm. for Longpres les Corps Saint Station	A.M.
	17th		Entrained at 6 am for Northern Area. arriving at.	A.M.

178

Army Form C. 2118.

1/18 Batt
Lon Irish Rifles
Month of October 1916

WAR DIARY
or
INTELLIGENCE SUMMARY
(Erase heading not required.)

Instructions regarding War Diaries and Intelligence Summaries are contained in F. S. Regs., Part II. and the Staff Manual respectively. Title pages will be prepared in manuscript.

Place	Date	Hour	Summary of Events and Information	Remarks and references to Appendices
WAGENBRUGE	17		CAESTRE Station ad 9 p.m. & marched to Billets in WAGENBRUGE (near STEENVOORDE) arriving there about 11.30 pm.	A.M.
STEENVOORDE	18		In WAGENBRUGE. Drill. Kits.	a.m.
	19		Drill. Kits.	a.m.
SCOTTISH CAMP	20		Left WAGENBRUGE at 4.30 AM. & moved over the frontier into Belgium arriving at Scottish Lines (near OUDERDOM) at 7 pm. In Divisional Reserve.	a.m.
	21		In Div. Reserve. Training of Specialists carried on except Lee at 10 o'clock.	a.m.
	22		In Div. Reserve.	a.m.
	23		Ditto	a.m.
	24		Ditto	a.m.
	25		Ditto	a.m.
	26		Ditto	a.m.
	27		Ditto. Service held & new Colours were consecrated.	a.m.
	28		Inspection by GOC 2nd Army at 12 noon. In Div. Reserve.	a.m.

74

1/8 Batt.
Lon. Irish Rif.
Army Form C. 2118.

WAR DIARY
or
INTELLIGENCE SUMMARY.
(Erase heading not required.)

Month of October 1916

Instructions regarding War Diaries and Intelligence Summaries are contained in F. S. Regs., Part II. and the Staff Manual respectively. Title pages will be prepared in manuscript.

Place	Date	Hour	Summary of Events and Information	Remarks and references to Appendices
Bois Leauy	29		Battalion in Bde Reserve. BnHQ & one Coy in WOODCOTE HOUSE. C Coy in strong points. One Coy in Café Belge & one Coy Coy "A" dug outs.	AML
	30		" " "	AM AM
	31		" " "	

A M Wattaght
for OFFICER COMMANDING
1/18 Bn. Co OF LONDON R.C

14/45

Vol 20

War Diary

1/18th B. London Regt.

November 1916

Secret

Army Form C. 2118.

WAR DIARY
INTELLIGENCE SUMMARY.
(Erase heading not required.)

Month of November 1916.

1/18th Battn. London Irish Rifles

Instructions regarding War Diaries and Intelligence Summaries are contained in F. S. Regs., Part II. and the Staff Manual respectively. Title pages will be prepared in manuscript.

Place	Date	Hour	Summary of Events and Information	Remarks and references to Appendices
	1.		Battn. in Reserve - BNHQ at WOODCOT HOUSE	WRJ
	2.		Ditto	WRJ
	3.		Ditto 4 Officers 160 ORs under Lt. Col Mackay proceeded to VLAMENTINGHE	WRJ
	4.		In Reserve and were reviewed by H.R.H. The Duke of Connaught	WRJ
	5.		In Reserve	WRJ
	6.		Ditto	WRJ
	7.		Ditto	WRJ
	8.		Ditto – until evening when Battn	WRJ
	9.		moved into the line (Left Sub-Sector)	
	9.		In Line Left Sub-Sector. — quiet	WRJ
	10.		Ditto	WRJ
	11.		Ditto	WRJ
	12.		Ditto	WRJ
			Enemy TMs active. Brikest wounded	
	13.		In Artillery Hill	WRJ
	13.		In Line Left Sub-Sector — Enemy TMs active during afternoon	WRJ
	14.		Ditto	WRJ

Army Form C. 2118.

WAR DIARY
OR
INTELLIGENCE SUMMARY.
(Erase heading not required.)

Instructions regarding War Diaries and Intelligence Summaries are contained in F.S. Regs., Part II. and the Staff Manual respectively. Title pages will be prepared in manuscript.

Month of November 1916
1/18th Battn London Scottish Rifles

Place	Date	Hour	Summary of Events and Information	Remarks and references to Appendices
YPRES	15		In Line	WDY
LEFT SUB-SECTOR	16		Ditto	WDY
	17		Ditto	WD
	18		Ditto	WD
SCOTTISH LINES	19		Battn was relieved by 23rd Battn night of 18/19 and proceeded by tram from YPRES to Breilen Area arriving about 4 am 19th inst. Lt Col A.M. Tralew proceeded on leave Major S.O Skevington took over temp. command. In Div. Reserve – Scottish Lines.	WD
	20		Ditto	WM
	21		Ditto	WM
	22		Ditto	WD
	23		Ditto	WD
	24		Ditto	WD
	25		Ditto	WD
	26		Ditto	WD
	27		Ditto	WD
	28		Moved into Bole Avenue in (Chalfont Camp) In Reserve Reinfort Camp.	WD
	29 & 30			WD

(signature)
Lt. Col.

T.134. Wt. W708—776. 500000. 4/15. Sir J. C. & S.

Vol XI
4/11

War Diary

1/18th London Regiment

December 1916

WAR DIARY

for month of December 19[..]

Army Form C. 2118.

Instructions regarding War Diaries and Intelligence Summaries are contained in F. S. Regs., Part II. and the Staff Manual respectively. Title pages will be prepared in manuscript.

INTELLIGENCE SUMMARY.
(Erase heading not required.)

Stamp: 1/18th BATTN. LONDON REGT. 1st LONDON IRISH RIFLES 2.1.17

Place	Date	Hour	Summary of Events and Information	Remarks and references to Appendices
	1st		In Brigade Reserve, Spezifax Camp.	ApdI
	2		do	ApdI
	3		Relieved 19th Battn in Left Sub-Sector. Held 60 sector.	ApdI
	4		In the Line	ApdI
	5		do	ApdI
	6		do	ApdI
	7		do	ApdI
	8		do	ApdI
	9		Relieved by 19th Bn 66 and moved to support with HQ at Railway Dugouts with one Coy & Coy at Belgian Chateau and one Coy at Battersea Farm.	ApdI
	10		In support.	ApdI
	11		do	ApdI
	12		do	ApdI
	13		do	ApdI
	14		Relieved 14th Battn in Left Sub-sector. Held 60 sector	ApdI
	15		In the Line. Heavy bombardment by hostile trench mortars and	ApdI

WAR DIARY
or
INTELLIGENCE SUMMARY.
(Erase heading not required.)

Army Form C. 2118.

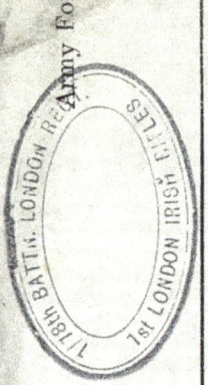
1/18th BATTN. LONDON REGT
1st LONDON IRISH RIFLES

Instructions regarding War Diaries and Intelligence Summaries are contained in F. S. Regs., Part II. and the Staff Manual respectively. Title pages will be prepared in manuscript.

Place	Date	Hour	Summary of Events and Information	Remarks and references to Appendices
	15		artillery from 9am till 10 am. A second heavy bombardment by hostile artillery and trench mortars from 4.10 pm till 5 pm. S.O.S. signal put up by Battn. on the left. Enemy came over but were driven back.	RWJ
	16		In the line, quiet.	RWJ
	17		do	RWJ
	18		do	RWJ
	19		In the line. Camouflet sprung by Australian Tunneling Company at 2 am. No action followed. Relieved by 53rd Battn. at 10pm	RWJ
	20		Went back to Scottish Lines, by train from YPRES.	RWJ
	21		At Scottish Lines	RWJ
	22		do Camp inspected by General Sir Douglas Haig	RWJ
	23		At Scottish Lines	RWJ
	24		do	RWJ
	25		do	RWJ
	26		do	RWJ

WAR DIARY
or
INTELLIGENCE SUMMARY.

(Erase heading not required.)

Army Form C. 2118.

Place	Date	Hour	Summary of Events and Information	Remarks and references to Appendices
	26		At Scottish Lines	
	27		do	
	28		do	
	29		Moved into Reserve with A Co. and two Coys at Swan Chateau and two Coys at Chateau Segard	
	30		do	
	31		do	

for OFFICER COMMANDING
1/18th Bn. Co. of London Regt.

Vol 22

141/47.

Confidential.
War Diary.

1/18th London Regiment.

from 1st January 1917 to 31st January 1917.

Army Form C. 2118.

WAR DIARY
INTELLIGENCE SUMMARY.
(Erase heading not required.)

MONTH of JANUARY 1917.
1/18 Bn L.N. Regt.
1st Dn Irish Rifles

Place	Date	Hour	Summary of Events and Information	Remarks and references to Appendices
Bluff Sector	1st		In Bde Reserve. HQ at Swan Chateau	QMJ
	2nd		Relieved 14th Batt. in Left Subsector (Bluff) In Line	QMJ
	3		In Line Quiet	QMJ
	4		Ditto	QMJ
	5		Ditto	QMJ
	6		Ditto	QMJ
	7		Ditto relieved by 14th Batt moved	QMJ
"			into support with HQ & 1 Coy Woodcote House 1 Coy Bluff Tunnels	QMJ
"			1 Coy Ravine Wood 1 Coy Strong Post.	QMJ
"	8		In Support	QMJ
"	9		In Support	QMJ
"	10		In Support.	QMJ
"	11		In Support.	QMJ
"	12		Relieved 14th Batt moved into Line (Left Sub Sector Bluff.	QMJ
			Sector	QMJ
	13		In Line.	QMJ

Army Form C. 2118.

WAR DIARY
INTELLIGENCE SUMMARY.
(Erase heading not required.)

MONTH of JANUARY 1917
1/18 Battn Lon Regt
1st Lon Irish Rifles

Place	Date	Hour	Summary of Events and Information	Remarks and references to Appendices
Bluff Sector	14	–	In Line.	
	15	–	In Line. Lt Col B.M. MAHON admitted to Hos. Lt. Col. Mayer	
			D.B. PARRY took over command of Batt.	
	16	–	In Line. Heavy bombardment of the German front line	
			system. Enemy reply weak.	
	17	–	In Line.	
	18	–	In Line. Relieved by 21st Bn night of 18/19	
			Moved by Train to Sir Reserve Area.	
SCOTTISH LINES.	19		In Div Reserve at Scottish Camp.	
	20		In Div Reserve.	
	21		Ditto	
	22		Ditto	
	23		Ditto	
	24		Ditto	
	25		Ditto. Batt inspected by 2/Army Commander	
	26		Moved to Halifax Camp. Relieved 15th Batt.	

WAR DIARY

INTELLIGENCE SUMMARY

(Erase heading not required.)

Army Form C. 2118.

MONTH of JANUARY 1917
1/18 Batt. Lon. Regt.
London Irish Rifles

Place	Date	Hour	Summary of Events and Information	Remarks and references to Appendices
HALIFAX CAMP	27		In Bde Reserve (Halifax Camp).	
"	28		Ditto	
"	29		Ditto	
"	30		Ditto relieved 14th Batt. Lon. Regt.	
HILL 60	31		Subsector Hill 60 Sector In line	
			In line.	

C.W. Salberg Lt
for O/C Commanding
1/18 Batt. Lon. Regt

SECRET.   1/17th London Regiment.   Copy No. 1

OPERATION ORDER No. 17.

Ref.Map. BELGIAN Sheet 28.N.W. 1/20000.   6/4/17.

1. **RELIEF.** The Battalion will be relieved on the night 6/7th
   April 1917, by the 11th SHERWOOD FORESTERS. Order of relief
   as follows :- B - C - D - A Companies.

   B.Company 11th Sherwood Foresters will relieve B.Company.
   C.   C.Company.
   D.   A.Company.
   A.   D.Company.

   On completion of relief, platoons will proceed independently
   to BELGIAN CHATEAU via SHRAPNEL CORNER - KRUISSTRAAT. Coys will
   assemble at BELGIAN CHATEAU, where soup will be issued. *Proceeding*
   DRYGROWEN JAGER & DOMINION CAMP

2. **GUIDES.** One guide per platoon, except for Posts, will be at
   TRANSPORT FARM at 7/45 p.m.

   The relieving garrisons of GLASGOW - LONE TREE and
   FORGE WOOD POSTS are reporting at TRANSPORT FARM at 4 p.m.
   Guides from BATTERSEA FARM will be provided at TRANSPORT FARM
   at that hour.

   2/Lt.G.F.PALMER will be in charge of guides.

3. **LEWIS GUNS.** Lewis Guns will come up with their Companies,
   and will take over from us 20 magazines per gun. B.Coy.
   guns will assemble at JACKSONS DUMP for loading on limber -
   C. and A. Coys ammn at ZILLEBEKE DUMP. Limbers will be at
   respective dumps at 10/30 p.m. and 11 p.m. They will collect
   20 magazines per gun of 11th Sherwood Foresters from TRANSPORT
   FARM on return journey. 2/Lt. G.F.PALMER will superintend
   the loading of these magazines on wagon.

4. **COOKS, MESS GEAR ETC.** Company Cooks, Mess Gear etc., will be
   ready for loading as follows:-
   1 limber will be at JACKSONS DUMP for "B" Coy Mess Gear at
   10 p.m., and will proceed to ZILLEBEKE DUMP at 10/30 p.m.
   for "A" and "C" Coys Gear. Cart for "B" Coy will be
   at TRANSPORT FARM at 9 p.m. Mess Cart for Mess Gear
   and Medical Officer's Cart for Medical Gear, will be at
   JACKSONS DUMP at 10 p.m.

   Two Cookers will be at BELGIAN CHATEAU at 12 p.m. One cook
   from each Company will report there to the Sergt.Master Cook
   (Sgt J.Buck) at 10 p.m., to prepare soup for the Battalion.
   Remaining two cookers will proceed to DOMINION CAMP and prepare
   tea for the Battalion on arrival, under the supervision of the
   A.C.M.S.
   One limber will await the arrival of the Adjutant at BELGIAN
   CHATEAU.
   The Quartermaster will allot huts to each Company, with the
   required number of blankets in each.

5. **CHARGERS.** Chargers for the Commanding Officer and Adjutant will
   be at SHRAPNEL CORNER at 12 midnight; for Major O DREW O
   at TRANSPORT FARM at 10 p.m., and for Company Commanders at
   BELGIAN CHATEAU at 11 p.m.

6. **TRENCH STORES.** All Defence Schemes, Maps, Air photographs,
   Trench Stores, Bombs, Ammunition etc., will be handed over
   and receipts taken in duplicate. Lewis Very Lts & Pistols
   will NOT be handed over.
   Receipts to be forwarded to B.H.Q. .... to 1 ct.

2.

7. **CLEANLINESS OF BILLETS.** All Billets, dugouts and latrines will be handed over in a clean and sanitary condition. Special attention will be paid to this, and certificates to the effect that this has been will be forwarded to Bn.H.Q., with receipts for Trench Stores.

8. CODE WORD for Relief Complete -- "EASTER".

E A Morkey
Lt A/Adjt.,
1/17th London Regt.

```
Copy No. 1. - File.-
        2.   O.O.
        3.   A.
        4.   B.
        5.   C.
        6.   D.
        7.   R.T.O.
```

Vol 23

Confidential
War Diary.
1/18th London Regt
February 1917.

Army Form C. 2118.

WAR DIARY
or
INTELLIGENCE SUMMARY.

For Month of February 1917

(Erase heading not required.)

Instructions regarding War Diaries and Intelligence Summaries are contained in F. S. Regs., Part II. and the Staff Manual respectively. Title pages will be prepared in manuscript.

Place	Date	Hour	Summary of Events and Information	Remarks and references to Appendices
	1st		In left Sub-Sector. Hill 60 Sector — Quiet.	6R)
	2nd		In the line — quiet.	4R)
	3rd		In the line — quiet.	4R)
	4th		Relieved by the 14th Battn. and moved to support with H.Q. and 2 Companies at Railway Dug-outs and 2 companies at Belgian Chateau	6R)
	5th		In support.	5R)
	6th		do	5R)
	7th		do	4R)
	8th		Relieved 14th Battn. in Left Sub-Sector Hill 60 Sector	6R)
	9th		In the line — quiet.	4R)
	10th		do	4R)
	11th		Relieved by 24th Battn. London Regt. and went into Divisional Reserve at Ottawa Camp.	4R)
	12th		In Divisional Reserve	6R)
	13th		do	4R)
	14th		do	4R)

T-2131. W₁. W708-776. 500000. 4/15. Sir J. C. & S.

Army Form C. 2118.

WAR DIARY
of
INTELLIGENCE SUMMARY.
(Erase heading not required.)

Instructions regarding War Diaries and Intelligence Summaries are contained in F. S. Regs., Part II. and the Staff Manual respectively. Title pages will be prepared in manuscript.

Place	Date	Hour	Summary of Events and Information	Remarks and references to Appendices
	15th		In Divisional Reserve	WD1
	16th		do	WD2
	17th		do	WD3
	18th		do	WD4
	19th		Relieved 6th Battn. London Regt. in Brigade Reserve to Canal Sub-sector at Canal Reserve Camp	WD5
	20th		In Reserve	WD6
	21st		do	WD7
	22nd		do	WD8
	23rd		Relieved 17th Battn. in left Sub-sector Canal sector	WD9
	24th		In the line - quiet	WD10
	25th		do	WD11
	26th		do	WD12
	27th		do	WD13
	28th		Relieved by 14th Battn. went into support with Bn. H.Q. and 1 Company at Swan Chateau, 1 Company at Chateau Segard, 1 Company Canal Dug-outs, and 1 Company Strong Points 7 & 8.	WD14

FB Pawley
Lt Col Commanding
1/8th Batt. London Regt.
1st London Rifle Brigade.

T2134. Wt. W708—776. 500000. 4/15. Sir J.C. & S.

Confidential. Vol. 24.

War Diary

1/18th London Regt.

March 1917.

Army Form C. 2118.

WAR DIARY
or
INTELLIGENCE SUMMARY.
(Erase heading not required.)

For month of March 1917

[Stamp: 1/18th BATTN. LONDON REGT. 1st LONDON IRISH RIFLES A29/247 3-4-17]

Place	Date	Hour	Summary of Events and Information	Remarks and references to Appendices
	1		In Support	W.R.I.
	2		"	W.R.I.
	3		"	W.R.I.
	4		In Support. Relieved 19th Battalion in Left Selvin Canal Sub-Sector in evening	W.R.I.
	5		In the line - quiet	W.R.I.
	6		"	W.R.J.
	7		In the line - quiet. Relieved by 21st Battalion and went into Divisional Reserve at Scottish Lines.	W.R.I.
	8		In Reserve	W.R.I.
	9		"	W.R.I.
	10		"	W.R.I.
	11		"	W.R.I.
	12		"	W.R.I.
	13		"	W.R.I.
	14		"	W.R.I.

Army Form C. 2118.

WAR DIARY
OF
INTELLIGENCE SUMMARY.
(Erase heading not required.)

Instructions regarding War Diaries and Intelligence Summaries are contained in F. S. Regs., Part II. and the Staff Manual respectively. Title pages will be prepared in manuscript.

Place	Date	Hour	Summary of Events and Information	Remarks and references to Appendices
	15		In Reserve. Relieved 6th Battalion in Left Section Hill 60 Sub-Sector	A.R.S.
	16		In the line - quiet	W.T.S.
	17		do	W.T.S.
	18		do	6.O.S.
	19		do	W.T.S.
	20		Relieved by 4th Battalion and moved into Brigade Reserve at Halifax Camp	W.T.S.
	21		In Reserve	W.T.S.
	22		do	W.T.S.
	23		do. Commenced special training	W.T.S.
	24		do	W.T.S.
	25		do	W.T.S.
	26		do	W.T.S.
	27		do	W.T.S.
	28		do	W.T.S.

Army Form C. 2118.

WAR DIARY
or
INTELLIGENCE SUMMARY.
(Erase heading not required.)

Instructions regarding War Diaries and Intelligence Summaries are contained in F. S. Regs., Part II. and the Staff Manual respectively. Title pages will be prepared in manuscript.

Place	Date	Hour	Summary of Events and Information	Remarks and references to Appendices
In Reserve	29		Corps Commander visited Battalion at training	W.N.
	30		" " " " "	W.N.D.
	31		Brigadier General visited Battalion at training	W.N.D.

S S Peery
Lt. Col. Commanding
1/18th Battn. London Regt.
1st London Irish Rifles.

Operation Orders No 3
by
Major E Brereton
Commanding "C" Battalion

In the Field
17/8/17

SECRET
Copy No 1

1. **Move:** The Battalion will parade in Marching Order in the SQUARE at 8.45 a.m. to move to the YPRES-SWAN CHATEAU area.

Battalion will report to R.T.O. WIZERNES at 9 a.m.

Capt. W. R. O'BRIEN will act as detraining Officer for the Battalion at OUDERDOM.

Haversack Rations and all waterbottles will be carried.

2. **Billeting Party:** 2/Lt. H. J. CHAPPELL + 5 C.Q.M.S. and 1 N.C.O. from Stores will report at ESQUERDES Church at 7.30 a.m. and proceed by bus to HALIFAX Camp reporting to Area Commandant.

3. **Transport:** Drag ropes will be provided by Units.

Two lorries are allotted to this Battalion all stores must be carried. Any surplus, including ammunition drawn for training purposes, will be handed over to the Area Commandant.

Orders for Transport which proceeded to NOORDPEENE last night will be issued direct to Senior Officer of Divisional Train, who will be in charge of all Transport moving by road.

B.T.O. will supervise entrainment and detrainment of Transport.

4. **Billets:** Particular attention will be paid to cleanliness of billets and certificates rendered to Bn HQ that they have been left in a clean + sanitary condition

(signed) Major
E. Brereton

P.T.O.

Confidential

War Diary

1/8th London Regiment.

April 1917

Vol 25

Army Form C. 2118.

WAR DIARY
–or–
INTELLIGENCE SUMMARY.   For the month of April 1917.

(Erase heading not required.)

Instructions regarding War Diaries and Intelligence Summaries are contained in F. S. Regs., Part II. and the Staff Manual respectively. Title pages will be prepared in manuscript.

Place	Date	Hour	Summary of Events and Information	Remarks and references to Appendices
	1		Training at Halifax Camp.	W.R.S
	2		do	W.R.S.
	3		do	W.R.S
	4		do	W.R.S.
	5		Training at Halifax Camp. Major General visited the Battalion at training	W.R.S
	6		Relieved 8th Battalion London Regt in the Left Sub section of the Canal Sub sector.	W.R.S
	7		In the trenches. The Battalion carried out a minor operation Zero hour being 8 pm. All objectives were gained successfully, but there was delay owing to the extraordinary bad state of No man's land. and the ground between the enemy's front and Support lines. The withdrawal was carried out successfully, but very slowly owing to heavy enemy barrage. A stubborn resistance was met with, and many of the enemy were killed, eighteen prisoners were taken. Several emplacements and dug-outs were destroyed, and one heavy machine gun.	W.R.S
	8		Relieved by 15th Battalion London Regt at 5-30 a.m. and went into Reserve at Halifax Camp.	W.R.S.

2353 Wt. W2544/1454 700,000 5/15 D. D. & L.   A.D.S.S. Forms/C. 2118.

Army Form C. 2118.

WAR DIARY
or
INTELLIGENCE SUMMARY.
(Erase heading not required.)

Instructions regarding War Diaries and Intelligence Summaries are contained in F. S. Regs., Part II. and the Staff Manual respectively. Title pages will be prepared in manuscript.

Place	Date	Hour	Summary of Events and Information	Remarks and references to Appendices
	9		At Watford Camp.	W.R.S
	10		do	W.R.S
	11		Moved by march route to Steenvoorde	W.R.S
	12		At Steenvoorde	W.R.S
	13		Started training.	W.R.S
	14		training	W.R.S
	15		do	W.R.S
	16		do	W.R.S
	17		do	W.R.S
	18		do	W.R.S
			The Army Commander visited the Battalion at training	W.R.S
	19		At Steenvoorde - training	W.R.S
	20		do	W.R.S
	21		do	W.R.S
			The Army Commander visited the Battalion at training.	
	22		training	W.R.S

Army Form C. 2118.

WAR DIARY
or
INTELLIGENCE SUMMARY.
(Erase heading not required.)

Instructions regarding War Diaries and Intelligence Summaries are contained in F. S. Regs., Part II. and the Staff Manual respectively. Title pages will be prepared in manuscript.

Place	Date	Hour	Summary of Events and Information	Remarks and references to Appendices
	23		Training	WD1
	24		do	WD1
	25		The Divisional Commander presented medal ribbons to men who had been awarded the Military Medal.	WD1
	26		Moved by march route to Ontario Camp.	WD1
	27		At Ontario Camp 500 men per day out on working party.	WD1
	28		do	WD1
	29		do	WD1
	30		do	WD1

Brig. M. Mahon Major
Commanding
1/18th Bn. London Regt.
1st London Irish Rifles.

SECRET   Copy No. 13

OPERATION ORDERS No. 155 by
- Lt. Col. D. B. PARRY -
Commanding 1/18th Battn. London Regt.,
1st LONDON IRISH RIFLES

April 1st 1917

REFERENCE. Attached Maps:-
  (a) Objectives.
  (b) Company dispositions by Platoons.
  (c) Barrages
  (d) Minor objectives in detail.

1. **INTENTION** THE LONDON IRISH will carry out a minor operation against the German Salient in I.34.b. and d.

2. **OBJECTS**
  (a) To kill or capture as many Germans as possible.
  (b) To capture or destroy war material.
  (c) To destroy Machine Gun and Trench Mortar emplacements and dugouts.

3. **OBJECTIVES** As shown in Map (a)

4. **INFORMATION** The objective contains a Front Line, an Intermediate Line and a strong Support Line. The Front Line was reported on 20th February to consist of a breastwork with frequent traverses but a weak and very broken parados. The Intermediate Line was little used at that time and nearly ruinous, but since then a good deal of work has been noticed in progress on it. The Support Line was strong and

4. INFORMATION (Continued)

probably has been thoroughly restored.

No Mans Land is irregular in width varying from a possible 100 yards to a minimum of 35. It slopres uniformly upwards towards the German Lines. The soil is light and dries quickly. There is a double crater opposite the top of LOVERS LANE which touches both British and German Front Lines.

The enemy's wire is fairly thick on the Front Line (but very close to the parapet) weak on the Intermediate Line - and strong on the Support Lines.

The whole area of the Operation is under observation from HILL 60, THE CATERPILLAR, and the CANAL BANKS.

Emplacements for Machine Guns and Trench Mortars also Dugouts are believed to be sited as shown on the attached Map.

Dummy raids will be carried out at ST. ELOI and on the HILL 60 Sub-sector.

A Mine will be exploded on the HILL 60 sector at ZERO - 5 minutes.

THE ROYAL FLYING CORPS will co-operate by low-flying, dropping lights etc.

5. DETAIL OF ASSAULTING TROOPS

4 Companies - THE LONDON IRISH
6 Lewis Guns - THE LONDON IRISH
1 Officer and 10 Other Ranks - 517th Company ROYAL ENGINEERS.

6. TRENCH GARRISON

8 Lewis Guns)
8 Groups of 4)
men each to)
be detailed)
later.)

Capt. A. TOTTON will be in general charge of the Front Line during the Operation, assisted by 2/Lieut. J.F. BURKE, who will be in command from HEDGEROW to THE RAVINE (inclusive)

Garrison as per margin.

7.	ASSEMBLY	A., D., and C., Companies in Line as follows:-

                      C. Company - HEDGEROW to RAVINE

                      D. Company - RAT ALLEY to 30 yards North of THORNE STREET

                      A. Company - 30 yards North of THORNE STREET to 60 yards left of point of SALIENT.

                      B. Company - will assemble behind the centre of D., and A., Companies.

LEWIS GUNS

    Nos. 9 & 11 - With C, Company
    Nos. 5 & 8 - With B. Company
    Nos. 2 & 3 - With A. Company

1 extra Lewis Gunner will be detailed from the Teams left to garrison the line to carry extra magazines for each of the above.

Detachment Royal Engineers

2 Sappers will be attached to each Company, the remainder will act under the R.E. Officer attached. One specially trained rifleman will be attached to each Sapper and act under his orders.

8.	DATE, ZERO HOUR & PASS WORD	Will be notified later.
9.	THE ASSAULT	(a) before ZERO

The assaulting troops will move in small bodies to the Front Line. This will be commenced at ZERO - 2½ hours and completed by ZERO - 30 minutes. The normal Front Line garrison will be doubled during the night previous to the operation.

A hot meal will be arranged for ZERO - 3 hours

9. **THE ASSAULT**
(Continued)

and a tot of rum and a biscuit will be served out to each man at ZERO - 2 hours.

Every effort will be made to preserve the normal appearance of the Line, during the time of assembly.

(b) after ZERO

The attack will be carried out in 4 Waves :-

<u>1st Wave</u> - Nos. 11, 12, 13, 14, 1 & 2 Platoons.
<u>2nd Wave</u> - Nos. 15 & 16 Platoons.
<u>3rd Wave</u> - Nos. 9, 10, 5, 6, 4 & 3 Platoons
<u>4th Wave</u> - Nos. 7 & 8 Platoons.

<u>LEWIS GUNS</u> will move as follows:-

Nos. 2 & 11 Guns follow 1st Wave. The remainder follow 3rd Wave

The advance will be made as follows:-

<u>AT ZERO + 2 minutes 20 seconds</u> the troops of the 1st wave occupying the re-entrants of the Front Line will leave the parapet and get into line.

<u>AT ZERO + 3 minutes.</u> The first wave will advance. The 2nd wave will follow the first as closely as possible. The remaining waves will conform and follow at <u>distances</u> of 75 yards.

The R.E. detachment will act under the orders of the Officers Commanding Companies to which they are attached.

<u>BOMBING GROUPS</u> - composition as per margin will block all trenches to the flanks and front of the area of the operation.

---

1 N.C.O.)
2 Bayonet Men)
  who will also)
  act as Cover-)
  ing Party)
1 Thrower)
1 Carrier)
1 Rifle Grena-)
  dier)
2 Reserve Men)

Total 8

10. "MOPPERS UP"   1 N.C.O and 10 men will be detailed in each platoon to act as "Moppers Up".   It must be clearly understood that these parties are responsible for the clearing of dugouts and the collection and destruction of material while the remainder of the platoon acts as garrison of the captured trenches. They must also fully realize that the enemy must be allowed to surrender as the success of the operation will be judged by the number of prisoners taken.

11. DISTINGUISH-ING MARKS   Will be worn by all Ranks as follows both on back and chest:-

        1st Wave - White Circle

        2nd Wave - White Triangle

        3rd Wave - White Cross

        4th Wave - White Square.

12. CASUALTIES   It must be clearly understood by all ranks that no man must check his advance to give assistance to wounded men. The Stretcher Bearers only will collect and attend to these until the withdrawal is commenced when every effort will be made by all ranks to bring wounded and dead back, using scaling ladders and traversor mats for this purpose.

13. WITHDRAWAL   The advanced troops will commence to return at ZERO + 40 minutes and the German Support Line will be cleared by ZERO + 45 minutes. The Intermediate Line will then be evacuated and at ZERO + 60 minutes the withdrawal will be complete.

The word "RETIRE" must on no account be used. All Ranks must be warned that the use of this word is a frequent German ruse and any man using it will be

13.	WITHDRAWAL (Continued)	treated as an enemy.

Rockets (colours to be notified later) will be sent up from STRONG POINT 8 at intervals of 1 minute from ZERO + 40 minutes.

All movements will be by time - but French Horns will be carried by all Officers of B. Company which will be used as an additional signal.

On withdrawal Companies will resume their morning dispositions, a roll call by platoons will at once be carried out, and reports furnished to Battalion Headquarters as soon as possible.

14. WIRE

2/Lieut. T. I. JONES will be responsible that sufficient gaps are cut in our own wire. These will be made diagonally and so arranged that the enemy do not detect them.

The same Officer will also be responsible for marking and preparing sortie points in our own parapet

In case the enemy's wire is not sufficiently cut by the bombardment 3 traversor mats per platoon will be carried.

15. CONTROL POSTS

One man will be posted at each of the following points:-

        Top and Bottom - PETTICOAT LANE
        Top and Bottom - DEANS GATE
        Top and Bottom - LOVERS LANE
        Top of - RAT ALLEY
        Junction of - RAT ALLEY & RESERVE

These will be under the orders of the Provost Sergeant.

16. DETAIL OF OFFICERS

Battalion Headquarters (COMMANDING OFFICER
(ADJUTANT

Trench Garrison (CAPT A. TOTTON
(2/LIEUT. J. F. BURKE

In charge of Operations (CAPT. C. P. WATSON
(- assisted by -
(2/LIEUT. T. I. JONES

A. Company	B. Company
Lieut. C.E.ASHBY	Capt. P.E.FAIRLEIGH
2/Lieut. D.S.WHYTE	2/Lieut. S.W.HAYLOCK
2/Lieut. C.H.I.STEWART	2/Lieut. R.SHERIDAN
2/Lieut. L.G.DOMINY	2/Lieut. L.R.DUBOIS
	2/Lieut. H.S.TUGHAM

C. Company	D. Company
Lieut. G.P.FLETCHER	Capt. J.TIERNEY
2/Lieut. H.B.WILSON	Lieut. F.S.MACKENZIE
2/Lieut. C.F.BURNAY	2/Lieut. H.STUBBING
2/Lieut. W.D.J.LYSAGHT	2/Lieut. H.C.TYSON
2/Lieut. P.O.KNOWLES	

Supervision of Advance Communications, 2/Lt. R.A.MALLET

Prisoners collecting Post - 2/Lt. P.F.KEANE

CAPT. C. P. WATSON will establish his Headquarters by the POWER BUZZER STATION (See Schedule B. Communications).

8th [Mavoon?] Sep 1917

17.	MEDICAL ARRANGEMENTS	THE 4th LONDON FIELD AMBULANCE will be responsible for all arrangements behind the Front Line system and will establish an advanced Dressing Station in the present Regimental Aid Post SUNKEN ROAD.

The 32 Battalion Stretcher Bearers now under training will collect wounded from No Mans Land and the German Trenches   32 Bearers detailed from other units who clear our own Front Line system. Capt. A. S. HEBBLETHWAITE R.A.M.C. will be in general charge and will establish his Headquarters in the British Front Line.

For details of arrangements see Schedule A.

18. DRESS

(a) OFFICERS

Service dress with trousers and puttees, web equipment.
Rifle and Bayonet and 20 rounds S.A.A.
2 Bombs in breast pocket of tunic
Box Respirator.

(b) OTHER RANKS

Skeleton Drill Order.
Rifle and Bayonet
Box Respirator at the alert position.
S.A.A. - 110 rounds in pouches and 10 in magazine.
2 Mills Bombs in breast pockets.

(c) BOMBERS AND RESERVE MEN

No equipment
Box Respirator in alert position.
50 rounds S.A.A. in bandolier.
Rifle and Bayonet, No Sandbag
16 Mills Hand Grenades in bomb buckets
Entrenching Tool.

18. DRESS
(Continued)

(d) RIFLE GRENADIERS

(As in (b) except blank ammunition in pockets.
50 rounds S.A.A. in canvas bandolier.
No Sandbag
16 Rifle Grenades in buckets
Entrenching Tool

(e) LEWIS GUN TEAMS

As in (b) with the exception of the Sandbag.
All will be armed with revolvers and will not
carry rifles, but will carry entrenching tools.

(f) RUNNERS

Rifle, bayonet and 50 rounds S.A.A. in canvas
Bandolier.
Box Respirator in the alert position.

Assaulting troops will move to THE RAVINE sub-sector without Caps, Greatcoats or packs. All will wear leather jerkins and carry waterproof sheets strapped to the waist belt.

19. LETTERS PAPERS MAPS IDENTITY DISCS ETC

Will not be carried but left in haversacks in the Trenches. Each man will write his name and number on a piece of paper and carry it in his right breast pocket otherwise no printed or written matter will be carried. No regimental buttons or badges of any sort will be worn.

20. EXTRA EQUIPMENT

Will be carried as follows:-

20.	EXTRA EQUIPMENT (Continued)	Wire Cutters, Turnover	... 90 per Company
		Wire Cutters, Hand	... 12 per Company
		Rope 15' lengths	... 8 per Company
		Torches, electric	... 16 per Company
		Traversor Mats ...	... 12 per Company
		Axes, Small Hand	... 3 to each "Mopping Up" Party
		Scaling Ladders...	... 16 B. Company
		" " ...	... 8 A. Company
		" " ...	... 8 D. Company
		" " ...	... 5 C. Company
		Tear Bombs M.S.K..	... 25 per Company
		P. Bombs ...	... 32 per Company
		(Carried by "Mopping Up" parties)	

Explosives will be carried by R.E. Detachment

The Traversor Mats and ladders will be placed in the Front Line during the night preceding the operation and great care must be taken that the enemy do not detect them.

21. **PRISONERS**

A collecting post for prisoners will be arranged in the CORD LANE Dugouts.

2/Lieut. P. F. KEANE will be responsible for sending prisoners on under escort to STRONG POINT 8 and will arrange to have each one searched and all arms and ammunition taken from them. Personal belongings, money, clothing or equipment will on no account be touched. All slightly wounded men will be used as escort for prisoners both from the area of operation to this point and from it to STRONG POINT 8.

2/Lieut. P. F. KEANE will report to Battn. Headquarters by Runner as to numbers. The Battalion

21.	PRISONERS (Continued)	Sergeant-Major will assist 2/Lieut. P. F. KEANE in these duties and will also supervise the Captured Material Dump.
22.	CAPTURED MATERIAL	Will be brought back from the German Lines during the withdrawal. All Maps, documents and letters found in dugouts must be placed in sandbags and sent as soon as possible to 2/Lieut. P. F. KEANE at CORD LANE dugouts. Other Material will be handed over to the Battalion Sergeant-Major at the same place.
23	COMMUNICATIONS	See Schedule B. 1 Battalion Observer will be attached to each Company Commander and 2 to Capt. C. P. WATSON to act as Runners.
24.	SYNCHRONISATION OF WATCHES	Orders will be issued later.
25.	BOMB DUMPS	Will be established during the night previous to the operation in our Front Line as follows:-

        Top of   -   PETTICOAT LANE
        Top of   -   DEANS GATE
        50 Yards -   RIGHT OF LOVERS LANE

12 men from each Company will each carry a bucket containing 12 No. 5 Mills Bombs and 4 No. 23 Mills. - and with these will establish dumps in the German Front Line at points marked X in Map (d)

26.	HAVERSACKS MESS TINS WATERBOTTLES & ENTRENCHING TOOLS	Will be left by the Front Line Garrison in Shelters, by the remainder of the assaulting party in their normal positions. They will be packed into sacks by platoons and labelled. Company Commanders will arrange to have 4 full water tins available for their Companies on returning from the operation.
27.	ARTILLERY ETC	Arrangements will be communicated separately.
28.	INTERPRETERS	6573 Rfn. J. M. GOLDBERG attached to 2/Lieut. P. F. KEANE.
29.	BATTALION HEADQUARTERS	Will be in the present Commanding Officer's dug out by the bottom of PETTICOAT LANE. Capt. A. TOTTON will establish an advanced Headquarters at the advanced Report Centre and will be generally responsible for the communications and reports between the area of operations and Battalion Headquarters.

(Sgd) W.R. STRAHAN
Lieut. & Adjt.
1/18th Battn. London Regt.
1st LONDON IRISH RIFLES

Issued as under:-

```
Copy No. 1.    Commanding Officer
         2.    Second-in-Command
         3.    O/C. A. Company
         4.    O/C. B. Company
         5.    O/C. C. Company
         6.    O/C. D. Company
         7.    Lewis Gun Officer
         8.    Bombing Officer
         9.    Signalling Officer
        10.    O/C. Detachment R.E.
        11.    Brigade Headquarters )
        12.    Brigade Headquarters )
        13.    O/C. Right Flank Battalion
        14.    O/C. Left  Flank Battalion
        15.    O/C. Strong Points 7 & 8.
        16.    Senior Artillery Liaison Officer
        17.    O/C. Right Artillery Group
        18.    War Diary
        19.    Retained
        20.    Retained
```

SCHEDULE A.

DETAIL OF MEDICAL ARRANGEMENTS

1. **PERSONNEL**

    Medical Officer, 1/18th Battn., London Regt., 1 Corporal, 1 Runner, 32 Stretcher Bearers of 1/18th Battn. London Regt.

    32 Extra Stretcher Bearers to be detailed later from other units.

    THE 4th LONDON FIELD AMBULANCE will establish an advanced Dressing Station at the Battalion AID post in the SUNKEN ROAD.

2. **OBJECTIVES**

    (a) To evacuate wounded from our Front Line and Communication Trenches to AID POST in SUNKEN ROAD.

    (b) To evacuate wounded from area between our Front Line and German Front Line - and from German Trench System.

    For objective (a) the 32 extra Stretcher Bearers will be detailed.

    For objective (b) the Medical Officer 1/18th Battn., London Regt., 1 Corporal, 1 Runner and 32 Stretcher Bearers of the 1/18th Battn., London Regt., will be detailed.

3. **DISPOSITION**

    FOR OBJECTIVE (a)

    There will be two relays of Stretcher Bearers arranged as follows:-

    A. 1 Party of 4 Stretcher Bearers in Front Line at head of PETTICOAT LANE.

    B. 1 Party of 4 Stretcher Bearers in Front Line at head of THORNE STREET.

1.

4. Two parties consisting of 1 N.C.O and 4 men will leave the BRITISH FRONT LINE at I.34.b.60.34 and I.34.d.21.92 in rear of the last wave of assaulting troops each carrying a D.III instrument and laying a double metallic line of D.II cable. They will establish stations outside the German Front Line at I.34.b.60.20 and I.34.d.38.72. Each Party will carry sufficient cable for 4 spare lines and on their lines being cut will at once run a new pair across NO MANS LAND.

5. A Party consisting of 1 N.C.O and 3 men will leave the BRITISH FRONT LINE at I.34.b.28.10 and establish a POWER BUZZER Station just outside the German Front Line at I.34.b.43.07 An Amplifier will be placed in the dugout at I.34.b.10.90 (approximately)

6. The REPORT CENTRE in PETTICOAT LANE will be manned by 1 Sergeant, 3 Operators, 1 Lance-Corporal and 4 Linesmen and 4 reserves to act as runners if necessary.

7. All communications by telephone will be SPOKEN to avoid jamming the Power Buzzer Signals. All signals will be in attached code except where no code exists for the desired message.

8. Communication will be maintained between Signal Headquarters by 4 reserve Signallers and two Battalion Runners - the party acting under the direction of L/Cpl. E. J. Oldfield. Two Battalion Runners will also work between the Power Buzzer dugout and Battalion Headquarters.

9. Communication in advance of the German Front Line will be

by runner solely. One Battalion Observer will be allotted to each Company Commanded and two to the Officer directing operations.

10. Company Commanders will carry flags as follows:-

        A. Company - GREEN
        B. Company - RED
        C. Company - YELLOW
        D. Company - BLUE

These will be put up and kept flying as soon as Companies have gained their objectives.

All Signals will report instantly these are shown.

11. Three Battalion Observers will man two Observation Posts
    (a) At the EIFFEL TOWER
    (b) At the junction of 32 SUPPORT and THE RAVINE
and will report progress by runner at intervals of 5 minutes direct to Battalion Headquarters. The remainder of the Battalion Runners will be divided between these posts.

12. Company Commanders will establish Headquarters at convenient spots in the centre of the main objective of their Companies where all reports will reach them. Should they find it necessary to leave these Headquarters a responsible Officer must replace them.

13. It must be impressed upon all leaders that reports must reach Battalion Headquarters continuously throughout the operation and that the maintainence of communication is vital.

SCHEDULE B.

COMMUNICATIONS

1. Communication will be maintained between the German Front Line and Battalion Headquarters via an Advanced Report Centre by two D.III telephone sets and direct from German Front Line to Battalion Headquarters by Power Buzzer.

2. The Report Centre will be situated in the left Company Headquarters in PETTICOAT LANE. An alternative Report Centre will be prepared in the Company Headquarters lower down PETTICOAT LANE.

3. On the morning before the raid metallic circuits of D.V. cable will be laid as follows and stapled down to the side of the trench 6 inches from the ground.

   1. REPORT CENTRE to Front Line at I.34.b.60.34 via PETTICOAT LANE.

   2. REPORT CENTRE to Front Line at I.34.d.21.92 via PETTICOAT LANE, RESERVE TRENCH, RAT ALLEY and FRONT LINE.

   3. Armoured "quad" from REPORT CENTRE to BATTALION HEADQUARTERS

   4. D.V. pair from E.S.43 office to Battalion Headquarters. This line will run direct from Commanding Officer to General Officer Commanding.

   5. D.V. pair from E.S. 43 (exchange) to Battalion Headquarters. This line will be the working line to BRIGADE HEADQUARTERS and will have a No. 2 telephone and D.III in Battalion Headquarters.

3. DISPOSITION (Continued)

FOR OBJECTIVE (a) (Continued)

    C.   1 Party of 4 Stretcher Bearers in Front Line at head of DEANS GATE

    D.   1 Party of 4 Stretcher Bearers in Front Line at head of LOVERS LANE.

Each Party will have 2 Stretchers. This is 1st relay of 16 men.

    A.   1 Party of 4 Stretcher Bearers at junction PETTICOAT LANE - RESERVE TRENCH

    B.   1 Party of 4 Stretcher Bearers at junction THRONE STREET - CORD LANE.

    C.   1 Party of 4 Stretcher Bearers at junction DEANS GATE - CORD LANE

    D.   1 Party of 4 Stretcher Bearers at junction LOVERS LANE - CORD LANE.

Each Party will have 2 Stretchers. This is 2nd relay of 16 men.

ACTION. 1st Relay will exchange an empty stretcher for a loaded stretcher at Front Line and carry it to 2nd relay.

2nd Relay will exchange an empty stretcher for a loaded stretcher and carry it to AID POST at SUNKEN ROAD - returning to posts with an empty stretcher.

There will be a store of 4 stretchers in the Front Line with each of the 1st relay squads.

FOR OBJECTIVE (b)

32 Stretcher Bearers divided into 8 groups of 4 men per stretcher.

AT ZERO. Stationed in SUPPORT TRENCH.

3. DISPOSITION (Continued)

FOR OBJECTIVE (b) (Continued)

ACTION. The Medical Officer 1/18th Battn., London Regt., 1 Corporal, and 1 Runner x above 8 groups will follow the last wave of the attack into No Mans Land collect wounded and carry them to our Front Line - exchanging them with 1st Relay for an empty Stretcher. When this area is cleared they will proceed to clear German Front Line and Trench system of wounded.

These Bearers will be the last to leave the German Trenches at end of Raid to ensure no wounded being left behind.

No treatment except shell dressing will be attempted. No splints to be applied - a bandage will be used for a tourniquet. Each bearer will carry 5 shell dressings.

(Sgd)   A. STUART HEBBLETHWAITE
Captain R.A.M.C., T.
Medical Officer.
1/18th Battn., London Regt

SCHEDULE C.

DISPOSITIONS PRIOR TO THE ASSEMBLY

On taking over THE RAVINE Sub-sector the Battalion will be disposed as follows:-

<u>A. Company</u>
1 Platoon left of THE SNOUT
1 Platoon WINDY CORNER to top of THORNE STREET
1 Platoon WOOLEY WALK
1 Platoon RESERVE TRENCH

<u>B. Company</u>   (Reserve) CORD LANE DUGOUTS

<u>D. Company</u>
2 Platoons Front Line THORNE STREET to RAVINE
1 Platoon SUPPORT
1 Platoon RESERVE (Ravine Tunnels)

<u>C. Company</u>
2 Platoons FRONT LINE
1 Platoon SUPPORT
1 Platoon RESERVE

<u>Lewis Guns</u>
2 Guns - C. Company - Front Line
2 Guns - D. Company - Front Line
2 Guns - A. Company - Front Line
2 Guns - Support Line - (WOOLEY WALK)

The 6 Guns detailed for the Operation - RESERVE TRENCH

<u>Headquarters</u> Normal dispositions

<u>R.E. Detachment</u> With attached riflemen - RAVINE TUNNELS

War Diary

C O D E

First Wave gained Objective ...	ARTHUR
Second Wave gained Objective ...	BERTRAM
Third Wave gained Objective ...	CHARLES
Fourth Wave gained Objective ...	DOUGLAS
Few Casualties	SMALL ERNEST
Heavy Casualties	BIG ERNEST
No Resistance	FRANK
Slight Resistance	GEORGE
Stubborn Resistance	HENRY
Prisoners	ISAAC (with numbers)
Machine Guns taken	JAMES
Minenwerfers taken	KENNETH
Emplacements destroyed ...	LEONARD
Dugouts destroyed	MATTHEW
Enemy surprised	NORMAN
Enemy surrendering	OSCAR
Withdrawal commenced... ...	PATRICK
Withdrawal going on well ...	QUENTIN
Withdrawal complete ...	ROBERT
Killed	SAMUEL
Wounded (Severely)	THOMAS
Wounded (Slightly)	ULICK
Missing	VINCENT
Enemy's machine guns active ...	WILLIAM

"A" Form.
MESSAGES AND SIGNALS.

(in pads of 100).
No. of Message _____

Prefix _____ Code _____ m. | Words | Charge | This message is on a/c of: | Recd. at _____ m.
Office of Origin and Service Instructions.
SECRET | Sent | _____ Service. | Date _____
At _____ m. | | From _____
To _____ | |
By _____ | (Signature of "Franking Officer.") | By _____

TO { E @ U 20

| Sender's Number. | Day of Month. | In reply to Number. | AAA |
| EST 644 | 4/4 | | |

On the night of 7/8"
April no traffic for WOODCOTE
or LANKHOF is to arrive
before 1 AM aaa Acknowledge aaa
Please arrange as regards return
xxx

From   E   O   15
Place
Time   JS Thompson
The above may be forwarded as now corrected.   (Z)
                Censor.   Signature of Addressor or person authorised to telegraph in his name.
* This line should be erased if not required.

contd.

~~Thursday morning~~

Log. 7/4/17

8.14 pm German Shrapnel over King St
8.15 pm One flare breaking into 2 green and red.
8.19   C Coy fairly quiet
8.20   O.K. B Coy
   21   C Coy occasional heavy
8.12   Shrapnel
8.22   C Coy wire gone
8.29   Heavy shelling round E.55.3
8.31   Blg Gun knocked out
8.34   C Coy O.K.
8.37   Very lights apparently ours front line
8.42   B Coy O.K.
8.50 (pm) One Rocket bursting into 2 Red   134 - 132
8.52   C Coy Germ Rocket breaking into 2
8.55   B Coy may I send for gun from reserve

9.45 Hun fire stopped   "C" Coy

9.48 Hun apparently coming back

9.45 Enemy sending very lights over towards Ravine.

9.48 Capt Maynard is trying to get a report from front line

9.54 A normal night despatches received.

~~9.6~~ ~~All in order~~ to Front line all in order
10.6 No casualties 18th went over very well

10.7 Mine up

10.25 Door "B" Coy

10.28 Door "C" Coy

7 contd.   the remaining

9-0pm Considerable retaliation in 'A' but
quiet in 'B' also retaliation in WYND
'B' Coy

9.3 German artillery less active ('C' Coy)

9.4 O.K. 'C' Coy

9.7 O.K. do

9.9 do do

9.11 do do

9.15 do do

9.16½ B Coy, beating O.K. more severe King St WYND

9.21 Machine Gun fire in front line 'C' Coy

9.24 C Coy O.K.

9.24½ All right in beatie

9.30 fire slackened considerably B Coy

9.30½ O.K. ~~~~ Right Batt.

9.37 Been King and B myself chit
uncomfortable (C Coy)

"C" Form.

MESSAGES AND SIGNALS.

Army Form
(In books of 100).
No. of Message

| Prefix SM | Code HRD | Words 13 | Received. From B Coy By B.7 | Sent, or sent out At m. To By | Office Stamp. ARMY L.F.B. 7 APR 1917 TELEGRAPHS |

Charges to collect £ s. d.

Service Instructions.

Handed in at E551   Office   m. Received 8.53 m.

TO E 020

Sender's Number	Day of Month	In reply to Number	A A A
HO 172	7		

May I send for gun from reserve aaa

FROM PLACE & TIME   E551 (B Coy)

* This line should be erased if not required.

(6334). Wt. W7496/M357. 500,000 Pads. 10/16. D. D. & L. (E 489). Forms C/2123/3.

(56925) W+ W 10-80 M1071. 2/17. 100,000 pads. J.C.&S. E 685 Forms/C2122,6.

"B" Form.
MESSAGES AND SIGNALS.

Army Form C 2122
(In pads of 150)

No. of Message ......

Prefix .... Code ..... m.		Received	Sent	Office Stamp
Office of Origin and Service Instructions.	Words	At 852/ ......m.	At .... m.	ARMY L.F. 7 APR 1917 TELEGRAPHS
		From	To	
		By	By	

TO

*	Sender's Number.	Day of Month.	In reply to Number.	AAA
	Rocket	rading		
	green			

From			
Place			
Time			

* This line should be erased if not required.

(56923). Wt W 10.80/M1071. 2/17. 100,000 pads. J E & S. **E 685** Forms/C2122/6.

Army Form C 2122
(In pads of 150)

"B" Form.

MESSAGES AND SIGNALS. No. of Message ......

Prefix ... Code .... m.		Received	Sent	Office Stamp
Office of Origin and Service Instructions.	Words	At .... m.	At ....m.	
		From	To	
		By	By	

TO

* Sender's Number.	Day of Month.	In reply to Number.	AAA

From

Place

Time

* This line should be erased if not required

"C" Form.
Army Form C. 2123.
(In books of 100).

MESSAGES AND SIGNALS. No. of Message...........

Prefix SM Code HHP Words 13 | Received. From B Bay By ...... | Sent, or sent out. At ...... m. To ...... By ...... | Office Stamp. 7 APR 1917

Charges to collect
Service Instructions. ES1

Handed in at .... Office .... m. Received 8.46 p.m.

TO   EU 20.

Sender's Number	Day of Month	In reply to Number	AAA
HO 171	4		

ALPHAGUN out aaa Rfn.

RUSHTON wounded aaa

FROM PLACE & TIME   ES 51 (B Bay)

"B" Form.
MESSAGES AND SIGNALS.

Army Form C 2122
(In pads of 150)

No. of Message ......

Prefix ... Code .. m.		Received	Sent	Office Stamp
Office of Origin and Service Instructions.	Words	At .... m.	At .... m.	7 APR 1917
		From	To	ARMY TELEGRAPHS
		By	By	

TO

* Sender's Number.	Day of Month.	In reply to Number.	AAA

From			
Place			
Time			

* This line should be erased if not required.

(56925.) Wt W 10-80 M1071. 2/17. 100,000 pads. J.C. & S. E685 Forms/C2122.6.

"B" Form.
MESSAGES AND SIGNALS.

Army Form C 2122
(In pads of 150)
No. of Message ......

Prefix	Code	...m.	Received	Sent	Office Stamp
Office of Origin and Service Instructions.		Words	At .... m.	At .... m.	ARMY L.F.B.
			From	To	7 APR 1917
			By	By	TELEGRAPHS

TO		E020		

*	Sender's Number.	Day of Month.	In reply to Number.	AAA
	One	light	breaking	
	into	two	red	I 34
	1			

From	C Coy		
Place			
Time			

* This line should be erased if not required.

(56823). W t W 10.80 M107f. 2/17. RG.996 pads. J. C. & S. E 685 Forms/C2122 6.

Army Form C 2122
(In pads of 150)

"B" Form.
MESSAGES AND SIGNALS.   No. of Message ......

Prefix .... Code .... m.		Received	Sent	Office Stamp
Office of Origin and Service Instructions.	Words	At .... m.	At .... m.	ARMY S.T.B. 7 APR 1917 TELEGRAPHS
		From	To	
		By	By	

TO

*	Sender's Number.	Day of Month.	In reply to Number.	AAA
	Very	lights	apparently	
			front line	

From				
Place				
Time				

* This line should be erased if not required.

BM/ Secret   6 Bn
                    15 B:

(1) Ref raid by 18 Bn on night April 7/8
15th Bn. will arrange to send up
RED rockets from the neighbourhood
of strong point 8 at intervals of 1
minute, 8.40 P.M until 9.0 P.M
as a signal for the withdrawal of the
infantry.

(2) 6 Bn will send up 3 Green
particoloured rockets from 3 Coy
Quarters at Zero plus 6 to indicate 9
= zero plus 15
Zero is 9.2 P.M

(3) Runner will arrange to carry necessary
rockets or stores from staff captain

Acknowledge

                                    [signature]

BM/434B.
6 - APR. 1917

(56925). W.W. 10580 M1071. 2/17. 100,000 pads. J.C.& S. E 685 Forms/C2122.6.

"B" Form.   Army Form C 2122
MESSAGES AND SIGNALS.   (In pads of 150)
No. of Message ......

Prefix ... Code	m.	Received	Sent	Office Stamp
Office of Origin and Service Instructions.	Words	At .... m.	At .... m.	ARMY L.B. 7 APR 1917 TELEGRAPH
		From	To	
		By	By	

TO

* Sender's Number.	Day of Month.	In reply to Number.	AAA
	7		

DOOR

From			
Place			
Time			

* This line should be erased if not required.

"C" Form.
MESSAGES AND SIGNALS.

Army Form C. 2123.
(In books of 100).

No. of Message

Prefix SM	Code KDP	Words 7	Received. From	Sent, or sent out At	Office Stamp.
	£ s. d.				APR 1917
Charges to collect			By	To	
Service Instructions. ES51				By	

Handed in at _____ Office _____ m. Received 10·25 p m.

TO _____ EV20

Sender's Number	Day of Month	In reply to Number	A A A
110180	7	—	

DOOR aaa

FROM ES51
PLACE & TIME B Coy.

"C." Form.
MESSAGES AND SIGNALS.

Army Form C. 2123.
(In books of 100).
No. of Message ....

Prefix SM Code SP Words 11

Received. From R.Boy By [illegible]

Sent, or sent out. At ......m. To ...... By ......

Office Stamp. [ARMY TELEGRAPHS -7 APR 1917]

Charges to collect

Service Instructions. ESSI

Handed in at .... Office ...... m. Received 10.5 p.m.

TO	EO10.		
*Sender's Number	Day of Month	In reply to Number	A A A
HO 179	7		

A NORMAL NIGHT disposition resumed aaa

FROM
PLACE & TIME   ESSI   (R. Boy)

* This line should be erased if not required.
(6334). Wt. W7496/M857. 500,000 Pads. 10/16. D. D. & L. (E 489). Forms C/2123/3.

(56925). Wt W 10580 5/1071. 2/17. 100,000 pads. J.C. & S. - E 685 Forms/C2122/6.

"B" Form.
MESSAGES AND SIGNALS.

Army Form C 2122
(in pads of 150)
No. of Message ......

Prefix ... Code ... m.		Received	Sent	Office Stamp
Office of Origin and Service Instructions.	Words	At................m.	At................m.	
		From..............	To..............	
		By	By	

TO		E020		

*	Sender's Number.	Day of Month.	In reply to Number.	AAA
		7		

Front	line	all	in
order	no.	casualties	
18th	went	over	very
well			

From: O. C. C. Coy
Place:
Time:

* This line should be erased if not required.

(5692?). W. W 10.80 M1071. 2/17. 100,000 pads. J. C. & S. E 685 Forms/C2122.6.

"B" Form.
MESSAGES AND SIGNALS.

Army Form C 2122
(In pads of 150)
No. of Message ......

Prefix ... Code ... m.	Received	Sent	Office Stamp
Office of Origin and Service Instructions.	Words	At .... m.	At .... m.	
		From	To	7 APR 1917
		By	By	

TO

Sender's Number.	Day of Month.	In reply to Number.	AAA

Capt Maynard is trying
to get a report
from front line

From	C C C C
Place	
Time	

* This line should be erased if not required.

(56923). Wt W 10580/M1071. 2,17. 100,000 pads. J.C.&S. E685 Forms/C2122,6.

"B" Form.   Army Form C 2122
MESSAGES AND SIGNALS.   (In pads of 150)
                                  No. of Message ......

Prefix Code m.	Received	Sent	Office Stamp
Office of Origin and Service Instructions.	Words At .... m.	At .... m.	ARMY L.F.B. 7 APR 1917 TELEGRAPHS
	From	To	
	By	By	

TO

Sender's Number.	Day of Month.	In reply to Number.	AAA
Him track	approaching		coming

From
Place
Time

* This line should be erased if not required.

"B" Form.

MESSAGES AND SIGNALS.

Army Form C 2122
(In pads of 150)

No. of Message ......

Prefix ... Code ... m.		Received	Sent	Office Stamp
Office of Origin and Service Instructions.	Words	At .... m.	At .... m.	7 APR 1917
		From	To	
		By	By	

TO

*	Sender's Number.	Day of Month.	In reply to Number.	AAA

From

Place

Time

* This line should be erased if not required.

"G" Form. Army Form C. 2123.
MESSAGES AND SIGNALS. No. of Message

Prefix SM Code EPm Words 9 | Received. From P.K. By Baily S | Sent, or sent out. At To By | Office Stamp. 7 APR 1917

Charges to collect

Service Instructions. ES51

Handed in at _____ Office _____ m. Received 9.27 m.

TO EU20

Sender's Number	Day of Month	In reply to Number	A A A
HO 196	7		

Fire slackened considerably

aaa

FROM ES51 (B Coy
PLACE & TIME

(56925). Wt W 10580 M1071. 2/17. 100,000 pads. J. C. & S. **E 685** Forms/C2122 6.

Army Form C 2122
(In pads of 150)

"B" Form.
MESSAGES AND SIGNALS.
No. of Message ......

Prefix ... Code ... m.		Received	Sent	Office Stamp
Office of Origin and Service Instructions.	Words	At .... m.	At .... m.	
		From	To	7 APR 1917
		By	By	

TO

EU 20

*	Sender's Number.	Day of Month.	In reply to Number.	AAA
	~~			
	Machine	Gun	fire	
	on the	front	line	

From
Place
Time

* This line should be erased if not required.

"G" Form.
MESSAGES AND SIGNALS.

Army Form C. 2123.
(In books of 100).

Prefix **Sm** Code **IBP** Words **14**

Received. From **B Bay** By **Bailey**

Sent, or sent out. At ___ m. To ___ By ___

Office Stamp: **APR 1917** ARMY TELEG

Charges to collect

Service Instructions. **FS51**

Handed in at ___ Office ___ m. Received **9.14 p**m.

TO **EU20**

Sender's Number	Day of Month	In reply to Number	AAA
HO 17#	7		

CRATERS OK aaa MORE severe KING STREET Wynds aaa

FROM PLACE & TIME: **FS51 (B Bay)**

* This line should be erased if not required.

Secret

"O.C. 6 N:

Ref. 18th N: orders for Raid:-

(1) Zero is at 8 P.M.

(2) Please inform tunnelers.

(3) Clear trenches by 7.30 PM.

(4) Keep Lewis gun posts in front line.

(5) Reoccupy line as soon as possible after completion of operations - which should be 9 P.M.

(6) Inform this office when normal positions have been resumed.
acknowledge.

W Parker Major Bde
140" 2/ ave

BM/430B.
6 APR 1917

"A" Form.
MESSAGES AND SIGNALS.

Army Form C.2121

TO: OC D Coy

Sender's Number: HQ 720
Day of Month: 7

AAA

Send one gun and team up to B Coy via North St aaa

Gun has [illegible] will [illegible]

From: E H 20
Time: 8-55 pm

SECRET.   **140th. INFANTRY BRIGADE ORDER No.152.**   Copy No. 4

4th. April 1917

Reference:- ZILLEBEKE, 1/10,000.

1. 18th. Bn. London Regt. will carry out a Raid in Left Section, CANAL Sub-Sector on night of 7/8th. April.

2. (a) 8th. Battalion will be relieved in Left Section by 18th. Battalion on night of 6/7th. April.
   (b) Details to be arranged between Officers Commanding concerned.
   (c) On relief, 8th. Battalion will move to HALIFAX CAMP.

3. On night of 7/8th. April
   (a) 15th. Battalion will relieve 18th. Battalion in Left Section. No guides will be provided by 18th. Battalion. Officer Commanding 15th. Battalion will have the Line reconnoitred by Platoon Commanders during 7th. April so that Troops can move direct to their position in the Line.
   (b) 8th. Battalion will move into Support at SWAN CHATEAU as soon as 15th. Battalion move forward.
   (c) Above moves will take place on receipt of message "O.K." from Brigade, Battalions being in a state of constant readiness from 9. 0 p.m. onwards.

4. (a) On night of 6/7th. April, G.O.C, 141st. Brigade will take over command of Left Section on completion of relief by 18th. Battn.
   (b) On night of 7/8th. April, G.O.C, 140th. Brigade will re-assume command of Left Section on completion of relief by 15th. Battn.

ACKNOWLEDGE.

R.H. Foster
Major,
Brigade Major,
140th. Infantry Brigade.

Issued to Sigs. at:-

Copy No. 1. War Diary
2. File
3. 47th. Division
4. 6th. Bn. London Regt.
5. 7th. Bn. London Regt.
6. 8th. Bn. London Regt.
7. 15th. Bn. London Regt.
8. 140th. M. G. Coy.
9. 140th. T. M. B.
10. Brigade Observers
11. B. T. O.
12. B. B. O.
13. No. 4 Sec. Signals.
14. 520th. Coy. R.E.
15. 2nd. Aus. Tun. Coy.
16. Right Group
17. 456th. Coy. A.S.C.
18. Supply Officer
19. 141st. Infantry Brigade
20. 142nd. Infantry Brigade
21. Brigade on Right
22. Lt. Ry. Control Offr.
23. G. O. C.
24. S. M.
25. S. C.
26. B. I. O.
27. 141st. T. M. B.

Secret

Administrative Instruction No. 1 in connection with 140th.
Infantry Brigade Operation Order No. 153.

1. SCOTTISH and OTTAWA CAMPS will be vacated by all details of the 140th. Infantry Brigade by 11.0 a.m., 8th. instant.

2. The above details including Machine Gun Coy. Depot will be accommodated in East End of DOMINION CAMP under arrangements to be made between the Units concerned and the Central Area Commandant.

                                          Major,
                                  Staff Captain,
                          140th. Infantry Brigade.

Officer Commanding,
   6th. Bn. London Regt.
   7th. Bn. London Regt.
   8th. Bn. London Regt.
  15th. Bn. London Regt.
 140th. M. G. Company.
Central Area Commandant.

Jan 1916

Vol 26.
1st/4th

Confidential

War Diary

1/18th Bn London Regt.

May 1917

Army Form C. 2118.

WAR DIARY
— or —
INTELLIGENCE SUMMARY.
(Erase heading not required.) MONTH of MAY 1914.

1/8 BATT. Lon REGT

Place	Date	Hour	Summary of Events and Information	Remarks and references to Appendices
RENINGHELST	1		In Reserve at RENINGHELST.	WRJ
	2		ditto	WRJ
	3		ditto	WRS.
	4		ditto	WRJ
	5		ditto	WRJ
	6		ditto	WRJ
	7		ditto	WRJ
	8		ditto	WRJ
	9		ditto	WRJ
	10		ditto	WRJ
SPOIL BANK	11		Relieved 4th (Seventh) Batt in the Spoil Bank Subsector	WRJ
	12		In Line Spoil Bank Subsector. — Quiet	WRJ
	13		ditto	WRJ
	14		ditto	WRJ
	15		ditto	WRJ
	16		ditto	WRJ

Army Form C. 2118.

WAR DIARY
or
INTELLIGENCE SUMMARY.
(Erase heading not required.)

MONTH of MAY 1917

1/18 Batt. Lon. Regt

Instructions regarding War Diaries and Intelligence Summaries are contained in F. S. Regs., Part II. and the Staff Manual respectively. Title pages will be prepared in manuscript.

Place	Date	Hour	Summary of Events and Information	Remarks and references to Appendices
SPOIL BANK	17		In Line Spoil Bank Subsector.	WD
"	18		ditto	WD
"	19		Relieved 14th Batt. in Support at "SWAN" CHATEAU.	WD
SWAN CHATEAU	20		ditto	WD
"	21		ditto	WD
"	22		ditto	WD
"	23		ditto	WD
"	24		ditto	WD
"	25		ditto	WD
"	26		ditto	WD
"	27		ditto	WD
"	28		Relieved 14th Batt. in Spoil Bank Subsector.	WD
SPOIL BANK	29		In Line Spoil Bank. Great activity by our Arty.	WD
"	30		ditto	WD
"	31		ditto	WD

Wm Kaye
Lieut Col.
Comdg 1/18 London Regt.

copy

Report of Work done by 1/18th Battn London Regt., in Spoil Bank Sub-Sector 12th – 20th May 1917.

Front Line. Strengthening and raising parapet and building new traverses.

Drainage Trench. Digging out to a depth of 4 ft and planting mustard seed.

New Support. Clearing out old trench and making new Support Line.

West Terrace. Building new dugouts under R.E. supervision.

Norfolk Lane. Raising and making parapet bullet proof.

Estaminet Lane. Clearing trench where blown in, raising parapet and repairing trench boards. Clearing drain at lower end.

Old Kent Road. Clearing where necessary and building new cut to front line.

Digging new trench to cut off corner of Estaminet Lane.

Making new cut from Estaminet Lane to an old Reserve Trench.

Making new beds in Infantry Tunnels under R.E. supervision.

Building new Dumps in
1. Norfolk Lane (completed)
2. Estaminet Lane (begun)
3. Spoil Bank (begun)
4. Two in Front Line (begun and completed)
5. Three in Front Line (begun)

Repairing damaged Dumps in Spoil Bank.

Clearing cellars in Norfolk House.

Work under R.E. supervision in Eclose 8.

Carrying parties for R.E.

Men supplied to Australians
1 Officer and 35 Other Ranks nightly and 4 shifts of 18 Other Ranks – each shift working 6 hours.

21st May 1917.

(Sd) D.C Perry
Lt. Colonel Commdg
1st London Irish Rifles.

Confidential. 141/47   Vol 27

War Diary.

1/18th Bn. Lon. Regt:

JUNE 1917

Army Form C. 2118.

S E C R E T

Instructions regarding War Diaries and Intelligence Summaries are contained in F. S. Regs., Part II. and the Staff Manual respectively. Title pages will be prepared in manuscript.

WAR DIARY for month of JUNE
or
INTELLIGENCE SUMMARY. 1/18th Battn. London Regt.

(Erase heading not required.)

Place	Date	Hour	Summary of Events and Information	Remarks and references to Appendices
SPOIL BANK	1		In SPOIL BANK Sub-Sector. Our Artillery very active	ws
"	2		Do	ws
"	3		Do	ws
"	3/4		Battalion carried out a small raid on night 3/4th. Party consisted of	ws
"	"		1 Officer (2/Lt. T.I.JONES), 1 Sergeant and 19 Other Ranks. No enemy	ws
"	"		seen. Our casualties 1 Other Rank Wounded.	ws
"	4		Relieved by 8th Battn London Regt., and moved to DOMINION LINES	
DOMINION LINES	5		At DOMINION LINES. Moved to DICKEBUSCH VILLAGE in the evening	ws
DICKEBUSCH	6		At DICKEBUSCH. Moved in to reserve position in ECLUSE TRENCH in the	ws
			evening.	
ECLUSE TRENCH	7		ZERO hour 3.10 a.m. when 2nd Army offensive started. Battalion stood	ws
"	"		to in ECLUSE TRENCH. No casualties. At 7.0 a.m. the Battalion moved	
OLD FRENCH TR.	"		forward in Artillery formation to OLD FRENCH TRENCH. Very slight casualties	ws
"	"		Remained in OLD FRENCH TRENCH.	
"	8		In OLD FRENCH TRENCH. Little shelling few casualties. Warned to move	ws
"	"		to front line at 10.0 p.m. Move subsequently cancelled.	ws

T.J.134. Wt. W708—776. 500000. 4/16. Sir J. C. & S.

Army Form C. 2118.

WAR DIARY for Month of June
or
INTELLIGENCE SUMMARY.
(Erase heading not required.)

1/18th Battn. London Regt

Instructions regarding War Diaries and Intelligence **SECRET** Summaries are contained in F. S. Regs., Part II. and the Staff Manual respectively. Title pages will be prepared in manuscript.

Place	Date	Hour	Summary of Events and Information	Remarks and references to Appendices
OLD FRENCH TRENCH BLUE LINE	9		In OLD FRENCH TRENCH night 9/10th. Relieved 23rd & 24th in the BLUE LINE and TRIANGULAR SPOIL BANK North of CANAL. Battalion Headquarters established in O.G.2. A small raiding party sent out by C. Company consisting 2/Lt. C. F. BURNAY and 30 Other Ranks. Enemy met and smart fight ensued in which many of the enemy were killed. Many dugouts were bombed. Our casualties were very slight consisting of 3 Other Ranks wounded and 1 Other Rank missing.	
"	9/10			
"	"			
"	"			
"	"			
"	"			
"	10		In the line. Battalion Headquarters moved to O.G.1 Intermittent shelling all day.	
"	11		Do Do Do	
"	12		Do Do Do	
"	13		Do Enemy kept up continuous bombardment all day & night 13/14t	
"	13/14		Battalion Headquarters and two advanced Companies relieved by Company of 8th BUFFS and moved to BLUFF TUNNELS.	
BLUFF TUNNELS	14		Remaining two Companies moved to BLUFF TUNNELS. Attack by 24th Division at 7.30 p.m. Entirely successful. Battalion stood to in TUNNELS but	
"	"			
"	"			

2353 Wt. W2514/1454 700,000 5/15 D. D. & L. A.D.S.S. Forms/C 2118.

Army Form C. 2118.

WAR DIARY for Month of June

or

INTELLIGENCE SUMMARY

SECRET

(Erase heading not required.)

1/18th Battn. London Regt

Instructions regarding War Diaries and Intelligence Summaries are contained in F.S. Regs., Part II. and the Staff Manual respectively. Title pages will be prepared in manuscript.

Place	Date	Hour	Summary of Events and Information	Remarks and references to Appendices
	14		was not required.	wng
HEKSKEN	15		Battalion moved to Camp at HEKSKEN – left BLUFF TUNNELS at 4.0 a.m.	wng
"	"		Motor Lorries took Battalion from KRUISTRAAT HOEK to CAMP.	wng
CAESTRE	16		At HEKSKEN. Battalion moved by march route to billets at CAESTRE.	wng
RACQUINGHEM	17		Battalion moved by march route to billets at RACQUINGHEM, arrived 12.30 a.m. 18th inst.	wng
"	"		In RACQUINGHEM	wng
"	18		Do	wng
"	19		Do	wng
"	20		Do	wng
"	21		Do	wng
"	22		Do	wng
ST. MARTIN-AU-LAERT	23		Left RACQUINGHEM by march route and arrived ST. MARTIN-AU-LAERT	wng
	24		In ST. MARTIN-AU-LAERT near ST. OMER. Battalion carried out Musketry Course TILQUES	wng
	"			wng
	25		Do Do	wng
	26		Do Battalion carried out Field Firing	wng

2353 Wt. W2544/1454 700,000 5/15 D. D. & L. A.D.S.S. Forms/C 2118

SECRET

Army Form C. 2118.

WAR DIARY for Month of June
or
INTELLIGENCE SUMMARY

(Erase heading not required.)

1/18th Battn. London Rgt

Instructions regarding War Diaries and Intelligence Summaries are contained in F. S. Regs., Part II. and the Staff Manual respectively. Title pages will be prepared in manuscript.

Place	Date	Hour	Summary of Events and Information	Remarks and references to Appendices
SERCUS	27		Left ST. MARTIN-AU-LAERT by march route for SERCUS	
"	28		In SERCUS	
"	29		In SERCUS	
GODEWAERS-VELDE	30		Left SERCUS by march route for Neighbourhood of GODEWAERSVELDE and billeted near MONT DES CATS	

W.H. Matthew Lt.Col
for O.C. 18 London Regt

2353 Wt. W2514/1454 700,000 5/15 D. D. & L. A.D.S.S. Forms/C. 2118.

Vol 28

Confidential.

War Diary.

1/18th Lon. Regt.

for

month of

July - 1917.

WAR DIARY / INTELLIGENCE SUMMARY

Army Form C. 2118.

1/18 Batt. London Regt. Rifles
1st Lon. Irish Rifles

Month of July 1917

Place	Date	Hour	Summary of Events and Information	Remarks and references to Appendices
MONT des CATS GOEDEWAERSVELDE	1		Left Mont des Cats by march route & arrived at Camp situated in M.A.O (near La Clytte) in our Reserve Area	W/TM
	2		In Camp M.A.D	W/TM
RIDGEWOOD	3		Batt moved into Reserve at RIDGEWOOD	W/TM
"	4		at RIDGEWOOD	W/TM
"	5		— Ditto —	W/TM
"	6		— Ditto —	W/TM
"	7		— Ditto —	W/TM
"	8		— Ditto —	W/TM
"	9		Batt moved into Line - Right Sub Sector - N. of Canal relieving 20th Batt. Lon Regt. Division on Right advanced their line 10 P.M. - Heavy Enemy shelling on attacking divisional front - Heavy intermittent shelling on our Batt front during relief - Relief commenced 10 P.M. & Effected 2.30 A.M. 10th inst. Bn H.Q situated in O.C.2. - Casualties slight in	W/TM

Army Form C. 2118.

1/18 Batt Lon Regt Ir Irish Rifles
Month of July 1917.

WAR DIARY
or
INTELLIGENCE SUMMARY.
(Erase heading not required.)

Place	Date	Hour	Summary of Events and Information	Remarks and references to Appendices
RIGHT SUB-SECTOR M of CANAL	9/10		Comparidy with enemy shelling	wore
	10		- In Line -	wore
	11		- ditto -	wore
	12		- ditto -	wore
	13		- ditto -	wore
"	14		- ditto -	wore
"	15		Batt relieved by 24th Batt Lon Regt & moved into Camp M.G.D. near La Clytte	wore
M.G.D.	16		In Camp. Div Reserve M.G.D.	wore
	17		- ditto -	wore
	18		- ditto -	wore
	19		- ditto - Brigadier General inspects Batt in Camp	wore
	20		In Camp M.G.D. G.O.C. Div inspects Bath in Camp expresses pleasure at cleanly state of Camp	wore

Army Form C. 2118.

1/18 Batt. Lon. Irish Rifles

WAR DIARY
or
INTELLIGENCE SUMMARY. Month of July 1917.
(Erase heading not required.)

Place	Date	Hour	Summary of Events and Information	Remarks and references to Appendices
M.G.D.	21		In Camp M.G.D.	WOR
	22		-ditto- Major M.H. MURPHY	WOR
			joined Batt. & assumed Second-in-Command	WOR
			of Batt. - Lt.Col Parry returned from Leave	WOR
	23		In Camp M.G.D.	WOR
	24		-ditto-	WOR
	25		-ditto-	WOR
	26		-ditto-	WOR
	27		-ditto-	WOR
	28		-ditto-	WOR
	29		-ditto-	WOR
"	30		Batt. moved into position at RIDGE WOOD at the	WOR
			disposal of 41st Div. for impending operations	WOR
"	31		41st Div. in conjunction with Divisions on Right & Left	WOR
			attacked after extremely violent bombardment of	WOR
			enemy trench & defence systems Zero hour 3.50am	WOR

Army Form C. 2118.

1/18 Battⁿ Lond Reg^t
(London Irish Rifles)
Month of July 1917

WAR DIARY
or
INTELLIGENCE SUMMARY
(Erase heading not required)

Place	Date	Hour	Summary of Events and Information	Remarks and references to Appendices
RIDGEWOOD	31		Batt. stood to but did not move.	679m

W. Westbury
Major
18 London Regt

Vol 29

Confidential
War Diary
of
18th London Regt.
for
month of
August 1917.

Army Form C. 2118.

WAR DIARY for Month of AUGUST 1917
1/18th London Regt
INTELLIGENCE SUMMARY 1st LONDON IRISH RIFLES

(Erase heading not required.)

Instructions regarding War Diaries and Intelligence Summaries are contained in F. S. Regs., Part II. and the Staff Manual respectively. Title pages will be prepared in manuscript.

Place	Date	Hour	Summary of Events and Information	Remarks and references to Appendices
RIDGE WOOD	1		In Reserve to 41st Division – quiet – Weather very bad. Under ½ hours notice.	C.P.
	2		Do Do Do	C.P.
	3		Do Do Do	C.P.
	4		Do Do Do	C.P.
	5		In Corps Reserve. Under two hours notice.	C.P.
	6		Do Do	C.P.
	7		Received warning order to move back.	C.P.
	8		Moved back to Camp at M.6.d.5.8 (Sheet 28 N.W. 1 / 20000)	C.P.
M.6.d.5.8	9		Marched from M.6.d.5.8 to ABEELE thence by train to ST. OMER and marched to ESQUERDES. Inspected on the road by 2nd Army Commander Genl. Sir H.C.O. Plumer	C.P.
ESQUERDES	10		Training for the offensive in open warfare	C.P.
	11		Do Do	C.P.
	12		Church parade. Presentation of Bar to Military Medal to Sgt. BURTON by Brigadier Genl. R. MACDOUALL	C.P.

Army Form C. 2118.

WAR DIARY
or
INTELLIGENCE SUMMARY.
(Erase heading not required.)

Instructions regarding War Diaries and Intelligence Summaries are contained in F. S. Regs., Part II. and the Staff Manual respectively. Title pages will be prepared in manuscript.

Place	Date	Hour	Summary of Events and Information	Remarks and references to Appendices
ESQUERDES	13		Training	A.D.
	14		Battalion inspected by 2nd Army Commander General Sir H.C.O. PLUMER	A.D.
	15		Training	A.D.
	16		Training. Warning order to move	A.D.
HALIFAX	17		Moved to HALIFAX CAMP by tactical train and in the evening marched to YPRES. Battalion Headquarters at LILLE GATE. Lt. Col. D. B. PARRY D.S.O admitted to Hospital sick. Major W. H. MURPHY took over command of Battalion.	A.D.
IN LINE	18		Relieved 2nd NORTHANTS and 2nd SHERWOOD FORESTERS in line at WESTHOEK RIDGE. Battalion Headquarters JAFFA TRENCH. 2nd Lieut. E. D. R. PINKERTON Wounded	A.D.
	19		In line - shelling very heavy. Casualties - Wounded - 2nd Lieuts C.H.I. STEWART, S.A. THODAY and C.F. HAVORD. 2 Other Ranks killed and 9 wounded.	A.D.
	20		In line. Heavy shelling continues. 3 Other ranks killed, 2 missing and 13 wounded	A.D.
	21		In line. Heavy shelling. 3 Other ranks killed and 30 wounded. Relieved	

Army Form C. 2118.

WAR DIARY
or
INTELLIGENCE SUMMARY.
(Erase heading not required.)

Instructions regarding War Diaries and Intelligence Summaries are contained in F. S. Regs., Part II. and the Staff Manual respectively. Title pages will be prepared in manuscript.

Place	Date	Hour	Summary of Events and Information	Remarks and references to Appendices
IN LINE	21		by 20th Battn. LONDON REGT., Capt. M. B. O'BRIEN Wounded	P/D.
IN SUPPORT	22		In Support at BELLEWARDE RIDGE. Attacks launched by 14th and 15th Divisions	
	23		Zero hour at 4.45 and 7. O a.m. Patrols pushed forwards by 47th Division	P/S.
			Heavy counter attacks during the afternoon. Warned to "Stand to".	P/S.
			Lieut. R. E. A. MALLET Wounded. 7 Other Ranks killed 15 wounded and 1	
			Missing.	P/D.
			In support. 2 other ranks killed and 10 wounded	P/D.
	24		In support. Relieved by 21st Battn. LONDON REGT and moved back to SWAN	P/D.
			CHATEAU. In Divisional Support. 9 Other Ranks wounded.	P/D.
	25		At SWAN CHATEAU. 2 Other ranks wounded on Working party	
	26		Do Under ½ hours notice	
	27		Do Daily working party of 2 Officers and 80 Other Ranks	
			and work on repairing roads and paths round CHATEAU. Construction of	P/D.
			Rifle Range started	P/D.
	28		Do	
	31		Do	

Operation Orders
by
Lieut. Col. W.W. Hughes M.C.

SECRET

4/8/17

1. MOVE.
Battn. will parade on Coy. parade grounds at 8/45 A.M. for march to MURRUMBIDGEE Camp in the following order:- H.Q. A - B - C - D Coys.
Route via track to Light Railway hence by footpath along side of Light Railway to VIERSTRAAT - HALLEBAST CORNER Rd - HALLEBAST CORNER and LACLYTTE.
Distance of 200 yds will be maintained between Coys on the road.
H.Q. Coy will move off at 8/45 A.M.

2. TRANSPORT.
Coy Officers Mess gear will be ready for loading by D Coys H.Q. at 8 A.M. H.Q. Mess, H.Q. Coy dixies and Medical Stores will be ready for loading at entrance to H.Q. Compound by 8 A.M. Cookers and Water Carts to be ready for hooking in by 8 A.M.
One limber for water cans and one for Lewis guns will be at D Coys H.Q. for loading at 8 A.M.
The 8 pack mules at present with the Battn. will accompany the

(2)

Transport which will move via
KRUISTRAATHOEK - CAFE BELGE and
DICKEBUSCHE.

Chargers for H.Q. and Coy Officers
will be at the camp at 8/30 am

[signature]

Lieut & Adjutant
"D" Battalion.

SECRET.   Copy No............

                        AMENDMENT No. 1.
                              to
                      OPERATION ORDER No.17.

                                                  8/8/17.

Lewis Guns.   Reference para 5 of Operation Order No.17.
                   45 magazines per Lewis Gun will now be exchanged –
                   NOT 30 per Gun.

                                              Lt A/Adjt.,
                                         1/4-th London Regiment.

              Copy No. 1. – 2iC.
                   "   2.   O.C.
                   "   3.   A
                   "   4.   B
                   "   5.   C
                   "   6.   D.
                   "   7.   T.M.

Operation Orders No 2
by
Major C. Beresford
Comdg. O. Bn.

Secret.
Copy No. 3

In the Field
8·8·17

Ref Map. HAZEBROUCK 5A
1/100000

1. MOVE. The Bn will parade in Mass at 9.30 a.m. tomorrow 9th inst to march to ABEELE via RENINGHELST — ABEELE ROAD. Bn will entrain at ABEELE for WIZERNE Area. Band will march between B & C Companies. Drill Order – Fighting Order. All ranks will wear Shrapnel helmets.

2. BILLETING PARTY. Billeting Party, (2/Lt ABT BROWN and 5 C.Q.M.Ss) will report to RENINGHELST Church at 4 A.m. and Proceed by Lorry to take over billets in New Area.

3. RATIONS. All ranks will be in possession of Haversack ration and full waterbottles.

4. SURPLUS STORES. Companies Mess Gear and all officers Mess Gear will be stacked at entrance to Camp by 5.30 a.m. also any surplus stores etc. 2 runners will be detailed to report at RENINGHELST Church at 6 a.m. to guide 2 lorries to Camp.

5. LIAISON OFFICER. 2/Lt H. LINGE will act as Liaison Officer and will report to entraining officer (Major J. S. STOKES. DSO., M.C.) on arrival at the Station. He will obtain entrainment state from the Adjutant.

6. CLEANLINESS of CAMP. Particular attention will be paid to cleanliness of Camp. 2/Lt P. Carter will report to A/T/C at 9.30 a.m. that the Camp is clean & clear of all kit and stores.

E A Moby
A/Capt
A/Adjt O. Bn.

Issued through Signals to:–

1 C.O.
2 2nd i/c
3 Adjt
4 A Coy
5 B Coy
6 C "
7 D "
8 2/Lt B&T Brown
9 File

Operation Order No 4
by
Major C Y Beresford
Commanding & Bon

SECRET
Copy No
In the Field
17·8·17

Ref Map Sheet 28 N.W. 1/20000

1. RELIEF
The Bn will relieve 8th BORDER REGT tonight in the YPRES Area.
Bn will parade in Marching Order outside Coy billets ready to move off at 8pm. Route via DEN GROENEN JAGER CABARET & BELGIAN CHATEAU. Distance of 200 yards will be maintained between Coys.

2. GUIDES. Guides will be at KRUISTRAAT Road junction H.18.d.9.6 at 9pm

3. BILLETING PARTY:- One Officer and one NCO per Coy, and 2/Lt CHAPPELL & PALMER and Sgt ROLFE for HQ, will report to Orderly Room at 6.30pm to proceed to take over billets. They will report to 75 Inf Bde HQ in YPRES at I·8·d·0·1 and ascertain present position of 8th BORDER REGT

4. WATER: All waterbottles will be filled before moving off. Water Point East of OUDERDOM Road opposite Camp.

/5

-2-

5/ Transport:- Cookers will proceed with Coys. HQ Company Dixies will be carried on A and B Coy Cookers. HQ and Company Officers Mess Carts will be loaded by 8pm. Medical Cart will be loaded by 8pm. Chargers for HQ & Company Commanders will be at WINNIPEG Camp at 8pm.

6 Cleanliness of Billets:- All billets will be left thoroughly clean, and certificates to this effect rendered to Orderly Room by 7.30pm

7. Code Word for Relief Complete - "LIFE"

E. Mosley
H. Clagg
O. Bm

Copy No 1. File
       2.   C.O.
       3.   Adjt
       4.   A
       5.   B
       6.   C
       7.   D
       8.   8th Border Regt.

"A" Form.
MESSAGES AND SIGNALS.

Army Form C.2121
(in pads of 100).

SECRET
Runner

TO: ES61 ~~ES23~~

Sender's Number.	Day of Month.	In reply to Number.		AAA
SC877	8			
Refce	OO	No 160	AAA	Trains
for	units	of	this	Brigade
will	be	at	YPRES	STATION
as	follows	PETREL	12.30	midnight
GUISE	1.30AM	AAA	Train	will
await	units	if	late	AAA
PETREL	will	detail	one	officer
&	superintend	entrainment	and	one
officer	to	superintend	detrainment	of
both	units	AAA	Acknowledge	

From: EP 20

Signature: A F Topher
Staff Captain

SECRET

Operation Orders No.67
by
Lieut.Colonel.W.W.Hughes,M.C.,
Commanding "C" Battalion.

Copy No. 12

Ref. Map - Sheet 28.N.W., 1/20000.

In the Field,,
30/8/17.

1. **RELIEF.** The Battalion will relieve "A" Battalion in the Right Section tonight, in the following order:- H.Q.-D-A-C-B: "D" Company will relieve "D" Coy, "A" Bn on the Right.
   "A"   "   "   "   "A" "   " "   " Left.
   "C"   "   "   "   "C" "   " "   " in Support.
   "B"   "   "   "   "B" "   " "   " in Reserve.
   Battalion will parade in Fighting Order on Company Parade Grounds, ready to move off at 6/45 pm. Route via KRUISSTRAAT - YPRES - MENIN GATE - HELL FIRE CORNER. Distances of 100 yards to be maintained between platoons.
   Party remaining out of the line will parade under Captain K.R.O'Brien at 6/30 pm., West of the Camp.

2. **GUIDES.** One guide per platoon and two for Headquarters will be at HOOGE CRATERS at 8/30 pm.

3. **LEWIS GUNS.** Lewis Guns will be loaded on Limbers and proceed under Limber Corporal to point 500 yards West of HELL FIRE CORNER by 7/15 pm. Nos. 1 and 2 of teams will accompany the limbers, and will unload and be ready to join platoons as they pass.

4. **AMMUNITION.** In addition to 120 rounds per man, front line platoons of "A" and "D" Companies, and the garrison of Posts, will take two bombs per man. Right hand platoon of "C" Company will also take two bombs per man.

5. **SANDBAGS.** Three sandbags per man will be carried into the Line as far as Limber will allow.

6. **RATIONS AND WATER.** Rations for 31st inst and 1st prox will be cooked today and distributed INDIVIDUALLY to all ranks. All water-bottles will be filled before 6 pm.
   Two days water supply will be taken into the line. 18 tins per Company and 12 tins for H.Q. Company will be issued by water duty men at Duck-boards, HOOGE, tonight, and carried into the line. It must be impressed on all ranks that this will be the only water supply for two days, and every care must be taken to avoid loss of water in transit.

7. **TRANSPORT.** Lewis Gun Limbers in charge of Limber Corporal will be at point 500 yards West of HELL FIRE CORNER at 7/45 pm. Nos 1 and 2 of each team will accompany guns and unload ready to join platoons as they pass.
   18 full watercans per Company and 12 for H.Q. Company will be sent to Duck-boards, HOOGE by 6/30 pm., where they will be issued to Battalion by water Duty man. A Battalion Runner will act as guide. Medical Stores, and H.Q., and Company Officers' Mess Gear, will be ready for loading by 6/30 pm. Chargers for H.Q.Officers and Company Commanders will be at the Camp by 6/30 pm.
   Cookers and Water Carts will return to Transport Lines. All surplus H.Q. and Company Officers' Mess Gear will be loaded by 6/30 pm., for removal to Transport Lines. Officers' Valises and Orderly Room boxes will be ready for removal to Transport Lines by 5 pm.

8. **TRENCH STORES.** Receipts for Trench Stores taken over will be sent to Battalion Orderly Room by 10 am 31st inst.

9. **SANITATION.** Steps will be taken to ensure that the Camp is left in a thoroughly clean and sanitary condition, and certificates to the effect that this has been done, signed by the Officer taking over, will be sent to Battalion Orderly Room by 10 am 31st inst.

10. **CODE WORD** for Relief Complete - "LIGHTNING".

                                          Lieut. A/Adjutant.
                                          "Q" Battalion.

Issued through Signals to :-

Copy No. 1.   C.O.   ×
  " No. 2.   2nd i/c. ×
  " No. 3.   Capt. K.H. O'Brian. ×
  " No. 4.   Adjutant. ×
  " No. 5.   "A" Company. ×
  " No. 6.   "B"   "   ×
  " No. 7.   "C"   "   ×
  " No. 8.   "D"   "   ×
  " No. 9.   L.G.O.   ×
  " No. 10. T.O. & Q.M. ×
  " No. 11. "H" Battalion. ×
  " No. 12. File. ✓

1/4 1/8th London Regt Vol 30

War Diary

October 1917

Confidential

SECRET

Instructions regarding War Diaries and Intelligence Summaries are contained in F.S. Regs, Part II. and the Staff Manual respectively. Title pages will be prepared in manuscript.

Army Form C. 2118.

WAR DIARY 1/18th Battn. LONDON REGT. 1st LONDON IRISH RIFLES
or INTELLIGENCE SUMMARY.
(Erase heading not required.)

Place	Date	Hour	Summary of Events and Information	Remarks and references to Appendices
SEPTR. 1917				
SWAN CHATEAU	1		In Divisional Support. Relieved by 24th Battalion and moved to G.14.a.1.5 Belgium 28 1/40,000	A.D.
-				
G.14.a.1.5	2		In Divisional Reserve. Enemy Aircraft very active all night.	A.D.
MICMAC CAMP H.31.b.3.5	3		Do Battalion moved to McMac Camp. Enemy aircraft active and H.V. Guns at night.	A.D.
	4		Military Medal Ribbons *presented by Major L.H. Murphy* to PARRY D.S.O to 590142 Cpl. C.F. EASTHILL, 591527 Rfn. W. McNAMARA, 590293 Sgt. T.E. HATT and 591734 L/Sgt. W.J. MURPHY. Enemy aircraft active.	A.D.
DOMINION LINES	5		Battalion moved to DOMINION LINES at 10.0 a.m. Division came under orders of 1st ANZAC CORPS at 12 noon to-day. Enemy aircraft active.	A.D.
	6		Warning Order received probably moving into line 8/9th. Lt. Col. PARRY D.S.O. assumed command of the Battalion on return from Hospital	A.D.
	7		Company Commanders reconnoitre Line.	A.D.
	8		Battalion moved into line and relieved 9th Battn. LOYAL NORTH LANCS. *at WESTHOEK-YPRES* *Major W.H. Murphy Commanding.*	A.D.
	9		In Line. 5 O.Rs. Wounded	A.D.
	10		Do 2 O.Rs. Wounded	A.D.

WAR DIARY
or
INTELLIGENCE-SUMMARY.
(Erase heading not required.)

Army Form C. 2118.

Place	Date	Hour	Summary of Events and Information	Remarks and references to Appendices
LINE	11		WEST HOEK – GLENCORSE WOOD.	
			In Line. 3 O.Rs Killed and 6 O.Rs Wounded.	P.P.
	12		Do Battalion relieved by 17th Battalion and moved to Ramparts	P.P.
			YPRES. 2 O.Rs. WOUNDED 1 O.R. Missing. A Brigade Dump was set on	P.P.
			fire by hostile shell. 591481 Sgt. L.C.LOVELESS M.M. at great personal	P.P.
			risk put the fire out and saved an important position from being discovered	P.P.
			by the enemy. He was recommended for a Bar to his Military Medal.	P.P.
	13		In Brigade Reserve. Ramparts, YPRES. Working Party Found	P.P.
	14		Do DO	P.P.
	15		Do Do	P.P.
	16		Do Bombs dropped by Enemy aircraft	P.P.
			2 O.Rs Wounded	P.P.
			YPRES	
MONTREAL	17		In Brigade Reserve. Relieved by 27th Australian Infantry Regt and	P.P.
			arrived at MONTREAL CAMP.	P.P.
GODEWAERS- VELDE	18		Marched from MONTREAL CAMP to GODEWAERSVELDE Bn.H.Q. Estaminet de la Forge	P.P.
	19		At GODEWAERSVELDE	P.P.
	20		Do	P.P.

Army Form C. 2118.

WAR DIARY
or
INTELLIGENCE SUMMARY.
(Erase heading not required.)

Instructions regarding War Diaries and Intelligence Summaries are contained in F. S. Regs., Part II. and the Staff Manual respectively. Title pages will be prepared in manuscript.

Place	Date	Hour	Summary of Events and Information	Remarks and references to Appendices
GODEWAERSVELDE	21		Left GODEWAERSVELDE by train and arrived at VANDELICOURT	C/D.
VANDELICOURT	22		At VANDELICOURT	C/D.
	23		Do	C/D.
	24		Do	C/D.
	25		Left VANDELICOURT and marched to AUBREY CAMP in DIVISIONAL RESERVE. 13th Corps 1st Army. In Divisional Reserve	C/D.
AUBREY CAMP	26		Do	C/D.
	27		Do Working Party Found	C/D.
	28		Do Do	C/D.
	29		Do Do	C/D.
	30		Do Brigade Service at 10.30 a.m	C/D.

WM 31

War Diary
of
Hqrs. 7th Canadian Infantry Bde.
for
month of
OCTOBER 1917.

Confidential

Army Form C. 2118.

WAR DIARY

or

INTELLIGENCE SUMMARY.

for Month of October 1917.

(Erase heading not required.)

Instructions regarding War Diaries and Intelligence Summaries are contained in F. S. Regs., Part II. and the Staff Manual respectively. Title pages will be prepared in manuscript.

Place	Date	Hour	Summary of Events and Information	Remarks and references to Appendices
AUBREY CAMP	1		In Divisional Reserve	
"	2		do. Battalion inspected by Major-General and D.S.O. presented to Lt.Col. D.B. Garry, and Military Medals to Sgt Murphy, Sgt Hatt, Cpl Tasthill and Pte Mackenzie	
NEWAL TRENCH	3		Battalion moved into line and relieved 15th London Regt. Situation Quiet.	
"	4		In line – Situation Quiet	
"	5		do.	
"	6		do.	
"	7		do.	
"	8		do.	
"	9		do.	
"	10		do.	
ROUNDHAY CAMP	11		Relieved by 20th Lon. Regt. & moved to ROUNDHAY CAMP in Bde Reserve	
"	12		On Brigade Reserve	
"	13		do.	
"	14		do.	

Army Form C. 2118.

WAR DIARY
or
INTELLIGENCE SUMMARY.
(Erase heading not required.)

Instructions regarding War Diaries and Intelligence Summaries are contained in F. S. Regs., Part II. and the Staff Manual respectively. Title pages will be prepared in manuscript.

Place	Date	Hour	Summary of Events and Information	Remarks and references to Appendices
ROUNDHAY CAMP.	15.		In Brigade Reserve	
"	16.		do.	
"	17.		do.	
AURREY CAMP	18		Relieved by 21st Lon Regt and moved into Divl. Reserve at AURREY CAMP.	
"	19		In Divisional Reserve.	
"	20		do.	
"	21		Bar to M.M. presented by Major Murphy to Sgt Locker	
"	22		do. Working Parties under R.E. Officers for improvement of Camp	
"	23		do.	
"	24		do.	
"	25		do. Lord Mayor of London Inspected the Battalion	
SUPPORT	26		Relieved 4th Lon Regt & moved into Bde Support in RED LINE. Situation Quiet.	
"	27		In Brigade Support - quiet	
"	28		do	
"	29		do	
IN LINE.	30		Relieved 19th Lon Regt and moved into Line (Left sector front) Situation quiet.	

Army Form C. 2118.

WAR DIARY
or
INTELLIGENCE SUMMARY.
(Erase heading not required.)

Instructions regarding War Diaries and Intelligence Summaries are contained in F. S. Regs., Part II, and the Staff Manual respectively. Title pages will be prepared in manuscript.

Place	Date	Hour	Summary of Events and Information	Remarks and references to Appendices
In line	31		In line – quiet.	

W.H. Murphy
Major Commdg
1/8th Battn London Regt
1st London Irish Rifles

MHM694

November 1917. 1/8 London Regt. WO 32

WAR DIARY
or
INTELLIGENCE SUMMARY.
(Erase heading not required.)

Army Form C. 2118.

Place	Date	Hour	Summary of Events and Information	Remarks and references to Appendices
In line	1		In line Left section Quiet Casualties 1 OR Accidentally Killed	
"	2		"	
"	3		— do discharged on duty	
"	4		— " Raid carried out by 2nd & Right Brigade	Bombardment gave to right of 53rd Rd Lt 3rd Bn — very satisfactory
"	5		"	
"	6		"	
"	7		"	
"	8		Relieved by 19th and moved into SUPPORT POSITION – RED LINE – Raid by 31st Bgd on left	
SUPPORT	9		In support — Supplying working parties.	
"	10		"	
"	11		"	
MAROEUIL	12		Relieved by 6th Bn and moved into Corps Reserve in MAROEUIL Area	
"	13		Laboche Reserve — Cleaning up a/c and 12 hours by night – and 12 hours by night	Battn in Embusc at 2 hours notice by day 3pm and 12 hours by night cancs 21/11/17 @ 3pm
"	14		— training	
"	15		" do	
"	16		" do	2gen E.C. Inspection

Army Form C. 2118.

WAR DIARY
or
INTELLIGENCE SUMMARY.
(Erase heading not required.)

Instructions regarding War Diaries and Intelligence
Summaries are contained in F. S. Regs., Part II.
and the Staff Manual respectively. Title pages
will be prepared in manuscript.

Place	Date	Hour	Summary of Events and Information	Remarks and references to Appendices
MAROEUIL	17		Lectures Reserve & Training	
do	18		do	
do	19		do men provided by Lt Col Berry 1/5 Rfm reinforcement	
do	20		[Route march]	
do	20		2 Coy to Reserve - Bathing Etc.	
Y Huts	21		Bath in 'Y' Huts L.2.C. detail for W/100,000. Moved to be	
			attached to move to Infantry at short notice	
do	22		at 'Y' Huts.	
			Proceeded by march route to FOSSEUX	
FOSSEUX	23		" " " ACHIET LE PETIT	
ACHIET LE PETIT	24		" " " and Busses to ROCQUIGNY	
ROCQUIGNY	25			
do	26		at ROCQUIGNY	
HINDENBURG SUPPORT	27		Proceeded by march route and Busses to HINDENBURG SUPPORT. Transport	
			remained at LEBUCHERIE	
BARTON WOOD	28		Hindenburg Support - moved into Barton Wood - Heavy shelling & casualties	
do	29		Barton Wood. Heavy shelling and casualties	
do	30		do do	

Lt-Col Comdg
18th Bn. LONDON REGT
(LONDON IRISH RIFLES)

Vol 33

14/41

War Diary
1st Bn. Gordon Regt.

DECEMBER 1917

WAR DIARY or INTELLIGENCE SUMMARY

Army Form C. 2118.

1/18TH BN. LONDON REGT., 1ST LONDON IRISH RIFLES.

For month of December 1917

(Erase heading not required.)

Place	Date	Hour	Summary of Events and Information	Remarks and references to Appendices
BOURLON WOOD	1		In the line – Intense shelling – casualties heavy	
HINDENBURG SUPPORT	2		do - Relieved by 21st Bn. LONDON Regt and moved into HINDENBURG SUPPORT	
do	3		In HINDENBURG SUPPORT – Situation NORMAL	
do	4		do	
ROYAULCOURT	5		do – Relieved by 21st Bn. LONDON Regt. and moved into Divisional Reserve at ROYAULCOURT.	
do	6		In Divisional Reserve – enemy aircraft active	
do	7		do – village shelled by H.V. Gun	
do	8		do – Major C. BERESFORD (attd from 14th Bn) assumed Command	
do	9		do	
do	10		do – enemy aircraft activity. – The Battalion, at one hours notice came under orders of 141st LONDON Regt. and moved to HAVRINCOURT WOOD – Bn.Hd. remained at transport Lines	
HINDENBURG SUPPORT	11		Company moved into line – Situation NORMAL	
do	12		In line – Situation NORMAL	

Army Form C. 2118.

WAR DIARY
or
INTELLIGENCE SUMMARY.
(Erase heading not required.)

Place	Date	Hour	Summary of Events and Information	Remarks and references to Appendices
HINDENBURG SUPPORT	13		In the line - situation NORMAL.	A/
do	14		do do	
BERTINCOURT	15		do do - Relieved by 8th Bn. LONDON Regt and	
			moved into Divisional Reserve - outside BERTINCOURT.	
BOUZINCOURT AREA	16		Moved by Motor Route and train to Heavy Battery Camp in BOUZINCOURT Area.	
do	17		In Army Reserve - cleaning up.	
do	18		Moved into billets in BOUZINCOURT Village.	
do	19		In Army Reserve - training	
do	20		do	
do	21		do - Major Murphy M.C. assumed Command	
do	22		do	
do	23		do Church Parade	
do	24		do training and practicing Tactical Scheme.	
do	25		Christmas Day	
do	26		In Army Reserve - training	

Army Form C. 2118.

WAR DIARY
or
INTELLIGENCE SUMMARY.

(Erase heading not required.)

Instructions regarding War Diaries and Intelligence Summaries are contained in F. S. Regs., Part II. and the Staff Manual respectively. Title pages will be prepared in manuscript.

Place	Date	Hour	Summary of Events and Information	Remarks and references to Appendices
BOUZINCOURT area	27		In Army Reserve - training	
do	28		do	
do	29		do Battalion at 3 hours notice to move.	
do	30		do Practicing tactical Scheme.	
do	31		do Church Parade	
			training	

W.F. Murphy
Major. Comdg.
18th Bn. LONDON REGT.
(LONDON IRISH RIFLES).

WAR DIARY for month of January 1918.

Army Form C. 2118.

of

INTELLIGENCE SUMMARY.

(Erase heading not required.)

Instructions regarding War Diaries and Intelligence Summaries are contained in F.S. Regs., Part II. and the Staff Manual respectively. Title pages will be prepared in manuscript.

Vol 34

Place	Date	Hour	Summary of Events and Information	Remarks and references to Appendices
BOUZINCOURT	1		In Army Reserve - training	
-do-	2		-do-	
-do-	3		-do-	Tactical Scheme
-do-	4		-do-	
BERTINCOURT	5		Left BOUZINCOURT by tactical train and moved to BERTINCOURT	
In line	6		Moved into line. Relieved 7th East Yorks Regt in SUPPORT near FLESQUIRES.	
-do-	7		In line - quiet. Barton relieved 10th Yorks	
-do-	8		-do-	
-do-	9		-do-	
-do-	10		-do-	Heavy hostile shelling from 8.15 pm to 9.15 pm
In Reserve	11		-do-	Relieved by 19th Bn LONDON Regt and moved into Reserve
-do-	12		In Reserve	
-do-	13		-do-	
-do-	14		-do-	
In line	15		Relieved 19th Bn LONDON REGT in line - quiet	
			In line - quiet	

Army Form C. 2118.

WAR DIARY
or
INTELLIGENCE SUMMARY.
(Erase heading not required.)

Instructions regarding War Diaries and Intelligence Summaries are contained in F.S. Regs., Part II. and the Staff Manual respectively. Title pages will be prepared in manuscript.

continued

Place	Date	Hour	Summary of Events and Information	Remarks and references to Appendices
In line	17		In line - quiet	
BERTINCOURT	18		-do- Relieved by 23rd Bn LONDON Regt. and moved into Divisional Reserve at BERTINCOURT.	
-do-	19		In Divisional Reserve	
-do-	20		-do-	
-do-	21		-do-	
-do-	22		-do-	
-do-	23		-do- Divisional Commander's Inspection	
In line	24		-do- Relieved 8th Bn LONDON Regt. in Centre Section, FLESQUIERES	
-do-	25		RIGHT - quiet	
-do-	26		In line - quiet	
-do-	27		-do-	
In Reserve	28		-do- Relieved by 17th Bn LONDON REGT and moved in RESERVE	
-do-	29		In Brigade Reserve - working parties	
-do-	30		-do-	
-do-	31		-do-	

1/18th Bn London Regt.

SECRET
Copy No ___

1.

Operation Orders.
FRIEND.
28 - 1 - 18.

1. **RELIEF.** The Bn. will be relieved by FENCE on the night of 28/29th inst commencing at 4. 0 pm.
   Companies will be relieved in the following order

   HQ. Coy by HQ. Coy. FENCE.
   D.   "   "   C   "   "
   B.   "   "   A   "   "
   C.   "   "   B   "   "
   A.   "   "   D   "   "

2. **GUIDES.** 1 Guide per Platoon and 1 per Company H.Q. will report to Bn. HQ. at 5.30 p.m. and will proceed under Sergt. MORTIMER to HQ. FENCE. They will be shewn the billets to be occupied by their platoons and will guide relieving platoons in and their own platoon out.
   O.C. D Company will relieve Anti-Aircraft Battery supplied by FENCE at 5.30 p.m.
   (Separate Orders have been issued him).

2

Trenches and billets must be left in a clean and sanitary condition and usual certificate forwarded after relief.

3/ <u>STORES</u>. Companies will hand over as far as possible the stores received from EAR; and any surplus petrol cans etc will be taken out.

Careful check will be made on stores handed over and lists and copies of receipts will be rendered to H.Q. immediately after relief.

Works and wiring maps will be completed to date by front Companies and handed over, copies being brought out.

Gum boots will be handed over in good condition - any wet boots will be returned by Companies <u>early</u> today to Brigade Gumboot store and a receipt for same obtained and rendered to Bn H.Q. with stores receipts.

4. <u>COOKS</u>. One cook per Company should be sent early to ensure that fires at cookhouses taken

3

...over are continued and preparation made for next meal.

5. **HQrs.** After relief Bn HQ. will be at L.25.a.6.3. and Company HQ. as under.
 A & B - at - L.25.b.55.58.
 C & D - at - L.25 central.

6. **REPORTS.** The completion of reliefs will be wired to Bn HQ. as under.
 D — "DECIDED".
 B — "BEAUTIFUL".
 C — "COMPLETED".
 A — "ARRANGED".

7. **ACKNOWLEDGE.**

Chas. Hardy
Lieut. & Adjt.

Copy No 1 - file
 "   " 2 - C.O.
 "   " 3 - O.C. A Coy.
 "   " 4 - " B "
 "   " 5 - " C "
 "   " 6 - " D "

WAR DIARY or INTELLIGENCE SUMMARY

for February 1918. Army Form C. 2118.

(Erase heading not required.)

1/18TH BATTN. LONDON REGT. 1ST LONDON IRISH RIFLES
3 MAR. 1918

Place	Date	Hour	Summary of Events and Information	Remarks and references to Appendices
In Reserve	1		In Brigade Reserve - Relieved 20th Bn. and moved into line Right Sub-Sector	
FLESQUIERES RIGHT				
In line	2		In line – Quiet	
"	3		do.	
"	4		do.	
"	5		do.	
"	6		do. Hostile shelling round Bn. HQ.	
"	7		do.	
"	8		Relieved by 24th London Regt. + moved into Div Reserve at BERTINCOURT	
BERTINCOURT	9		In Divisional Reserve.	
"	10		do.	
"	11		do.	
"	12		do.	
"	13		do.	
SCREW TRENCH	14		Relieved 21st Bn. London Regt. in Screw Trench. FLESQUIERES SECTOR	
"	15		In line – Quiet.	

Army Form C. 2118.

WAR DIARY
or
INTELLIGENCE SUMMARY.

February 1918 (Cont'd)

(Erase heading not required.)

Place	Date	Hour	Summary of Events and Information	Remarks and references to Appendices
SCREW TRENCH.	16		In line - Quiet. NORMAL.	
"	17		do.	
"	18		do.	
"	19		do. Relieved 19 Left Trench Coy.	
"	20		do.	
"	21		do.	
"	22		do.	
"	23		do. Relieved by 2nd R.M.L.I. and moved into Cortha Reserve.	
VALLULART CAMP	24		Cortha Reserve - Cleaning up.	
"	25		do. - Training	
"	26		do. " do.	
"	27		do. " do.	
"	28		do. " do.	

Operation Orders No 8   SECRET
            by   COPY No 8
Lt-Col. W. W. Hughes D.S.O., M.C.
Commanding 1/17th London Regt.

                                In the field
Ref. Map MOEUVRES 1/20000.   13th Feby 1918

1. RELIEF.
The Battn. will be relieved by "S" Battn. Ldn. Rgt. tomorrow night 14th inst. and will proceed to BERTINCOURT entraining at BW 66 – K 32.b.2.4. Further details re trains will be notified later.
Coys. will be relieved by corresponding Coys of "S" Battn.
Order of Relief :- C, B, A, H.Q, D.

2. GUIDES.
Lt. H.J. CHAPPLE M.C. with 5 scouts will reconnoitre during the morning route to K 32.b.2.4 and will meet incoming Battn. at cross roads K 32.b.75.80 at 6.15 pm. and guide them to K 24.b.7.3. Scouts will remain there to guide Coys. out. Company guides as arranged between Coy. Comdrs. will be at K 24.b.7.3 by 7 pm. They will be provided with chits stating for whom they are guides.

3. TRANSPORT.
Mess cart, 1 Limber for Cooks gear & water carts will be at RED CHATEAU at 7p.
2 R.E. Limbers will be at K 24.b.95.10 at

FLESQUIÈRES – RIBECOURT Rd. by 7.30 p.m. where they will be loaded under the superintendence of Sgt. Swettenham.

3. All water tins surplus to Trench Stores, officers mess gear, and cooks utensils will be dumped at RED CHATEAU by 6.30 p.m.

4. TRENCH STORES

Lists of Trench Stores to be handed over will be rendered to Battn. Orderly Room by 4 p.m. 14th inst. Receipts for stores will be rendered to Battn. Orderly Room by 10 a.m. 15th inst. Separate receipts will be obtained for Gum-Boots, Biscuits and Documents.

5. TECHNICAL STORES.

Coy. Comdrs. will be held responsible that all Technical Stores & L.G. Magazines are all carried out. Technical Stores will be returned to R.S.M. by 10 a.m. 15th inst.

6. A.A. BATTERY.

An officer to be detailed later will proceed to BERTINCOURT to take over A.A. Battery from 5'. Battn. before 12 noon 14th inst.

7. SANITATION

All dugouts and latrines will be left in a clean and sanitary condition, and certificates to the effect that this has been done will be handed in at Battn. Orderly Room by 4 p.m. 14th inst.

8. CODE WORD FOR RELIEF COMPLETE
"BOMBS"

A.B.W. Brown

Issued through signals to:-
1. CO 2. Adjt. 3. A Coy. 4. B Coy. 5. C Coy.
6. D Coy 7. RSM 8. 19" Bn. 9. Q.M. 10. File

47th Division.
141st Infantry Brigade.

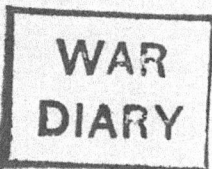

1/18th BATTALION

LONDON REGIMENT

MARCH 1918

Secret

1/18th London Regiment

WAR DIARY March 1918
or
INTELLIGENCE SUMMARY
(Erase heading not required.)

Army Form C. 2118.

Place	Date	Hour	Summary of Events and Information	Remarks and references to Appendices
Vallulart Camp	1		In Corps Reserve – Training – Field firing	
	2		Do	
	3		Do Church Parades	
	4		Do Training	
	5		Do – Test move received 6.45am & cancelled 7.10 am	
	6		Do	
	7		Do Battn Working Party – Tactical Scheme Lt Col G.H. Neely MC resumed Command	
	8		Do Training	
	9		Do Battn Working Party	
	10		Do Church Parades	
	11		Do Brigade Tactical Exercise	
	12		Do Training	
	13		Do Battn Working Party	
	14		Do Divisional Tactical Scheme	
	15		Do Training – Boxing Tournament	
	16		Do " – Gymkhana	

Army Form C. 2118.

WAR DIARY
or
INTELLIGENCE SUMMARY.
(Erase heading not required.)

Instructions regarding War Diaries and Intelligence Summaries are contained in F. S. Regs., Part II. and the Staff Manual respectively. Title pages will be prepared in manuscript.

Place	Date	Hour	Summary of Events and Information	Remarks and references to Appendices
Vallulark Camp	17		St. Patricks Day – Church Parade – Ceremonial & Inspection by Brigadier	
	18		In Corps Reserve – Training – Bathing – Gas Chamber	
	19		Do – Training – Bathing – Reconnoitring Line	
	20		Do – Moved into Line & relieved 17th Bn R.F. (2nd Bde) 2nd South Staffs (?) (2nd Res Bn) in Right Sector LA VACQUERIE SECTOR	
Line	21		Enemy attacked & captured Gulfoot Line – heavy casualties	
	22		Counter attacked & took up position on Highland Ridge	
	23		Do near Rocquigny	
	24		Do near High Wood	
	25		Do & joined Depot near Bullecourt	
	26		Moved from Bullecourt to Vaulchelles	
	27		" Vaulchelles to Vertecourt	
	28		At Vertecourt & moved up into Venles	
	29		In Reserve at Venles	
	30		Do	
	31		Do	

Lt Col Hugh Smith, Head
Aug. 18 1st London Regt.

141st Brigade.
47th Division.

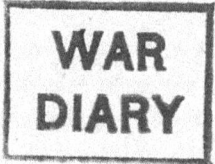

1/18th BATTALION

THE LONDON REGIMENT.

APRIL 1918

Army Form C. 2118.

WAR DIARY for month of April 1918.

INTELLIGENCE SUMMARY.

(Erase heading not required.)

1/6 London Regt.

Instructions regarding War Diaries and Intelligence Summaries are contained in F. S. Regs., Part II. and the Staff Manual respectively. Title pages will be prepared in manuscript.

Place	Date	Hour	Summary of Events and Information	Remarks and references to Appendices
SENLIS	1		In Divisional Reserve	
- do -	2		- do -	
- do -	3		- do -	
BOUZINCOURT	4		Moved to BOUZINCOURT under orders of 140th Infantry Bde	
- do -	5		In Brigade Reserve	P.F. Reserve Issued 17/4/18?
- do -	6		- do -	
SENLIS	7		Relieved by 21st Bn. and moved to SENLIS	
ACHEUX	8		Moved from SENLIS to ACHEUX. Left Supporting Division	
- do -	9		Left Supporting Division	
- do -	10		- do -	
MIRVAUX	11		- do - Moved by march Route to MIRVAUX	
DOMART	12		MIRVAUX moved by march Route to DOMART	
DOMVAST	13		DOMART moved by march Route to DOMVAST	
- do -	14		In Army Reserve at DOMVAST. Battalion Cleaning up.	
- do -	15		- do -	
- do -	16		- do - Training	

Army Form C. 2118.

WAR DIARY (contd)
INTELLIGENCE SUMMARY.
(Erase heading not required.)

Instructions regarding War Diaries and Intelligence Summaries are contained in F. S. Regs., Part II. and the Staff Manual respectively. Title pages will be prepared in manuscript.

Place	Date	Hour	Summary of Events and Information	Remarks and references to Appendices
DOM/AST	17		On Army Reserve	
- do -	18		- do -	
- do -	19		- do -	
- do -	20		- do - Divisional Commander inspected the Bn at training	
- do -	21		- do - Church Parade. Divisional Sports in afternoon	A.F.B.name[?] ford 7/1/17
- do -	22		- do - Divisional Commander inspected the Bn at training	
- do -	23		- do - Training	
- do -	24		- do - - do -	
- do -	25		- do - - do -	
- do -	26		- do - - do -	
- do -	27		- do - - do -	
- do -	28		- do - Brigade Church Parade	
- do -	29		- do - Training	
CARDONNETTE	30		- do - Moved to CARDONNETTE by lorries	

Lt. Col. Comdg.
1/8th Bn. London Regt.

CONFIDENTIAL

War Diary

18th Bn. London Regt.
(1st LONDON IRISH RIFLES)

for

MAY — 1918

Army Form C. 2118.

WAR DIARY for May 1918
or
INTELLIGENCE SUMMARY.
(Erase heading not required.)

Instructions regarding War Diaries and Intelligence Summaries are contained in F. S. Regs., Part II. and the Staff Manual respectively. Title pages will be prepared in manuscript.

WO 38

Place	Date	Hour	Summary of Events and Information	Remarks and references to Appendices
GORDONNETTE	1		In Corps Reserve Cuttipation Corps	
WARLOY	2		moved by route march to Divisional Reserve at WARLOY	
- do -	3		In Divisional Reserve	
- do -	4		- do -	
- do -	5		- do -	
- do -	6		- do -	
- do -	7		- do -	
- do -	8		- do -	
- do -	9		- do -	
In line	10		Relieved 2nd Bn LONDON Regt in left Subsector of by left Sub Sor	
- do -	11		In the line - Quiet	
- do -	12		- do -	
- do -	13		- do -	
- do -	14		- do -	
- do -	15		- do -	
Corps Reserve	16		- do - Relieved by 4/10th LONDON Regt and moved into Corps Reserve at C Sub	

Army Form C. 2118.

WAR DIARY
or
INTELLIGENCE SUMMARY.
(Erase heading not required.)

Instructions regarding War Diaries and Intelligence Summaries are contained in F. S. Regs., Part II. and the Staff Manual respectively. Title pages will be prepared in manuscript.

Place	Date	Hour	Summary of Events and Information	Remarks and references to Appendices
C 26 b	17		In Corps Reserve - Training	
- do -	18		- do -	
- do -	19		- do -	
- do -	20		- do -	
- do -	21		- do -	
- do -	22		- do -	
Subsect	23		- do - Relieved the 8th Royal Fus. & moved into Subsect LAVEVILLE Sect.	
- do -	24		In Subsect position - quiet	
- do -	25		- do -	
- do -	26		- do -	
- do -	27		- do -	
- do -	28		- do -	
- do -	29		- do - Relieved 10th Bn in Left Subsection of Left Sector	
In Line	30		In the Line - quiet	
- do -	31			

AF/20

1/8th Bn [signature]
For Lt Col Comdg
1/8th Bn [unit]

To all Companies

After Order.

Company Commanders will see that every man understands what he is to do under the various circumstances. They must immediately study the Defence Scheme and attached map with the Platoon Officer and Sergeants. The Platoon Officers will then go thoroughly into it with their Sections. It is of vital importance that every Section understands what is expected of it.

Ammunition and rifles must be closely inspected. Water bottles kept filled, as no time would be available to fill if ordered out. Iron Rations must be intact, — any man deficient should be brought before the Commanding Officer.

Bombs to be carried by bombers. All men able to throw a live bomb should carry two if possible.

8.5.'18.

To all Companies

After Order

Company Commanders will see that every man understands what he is to do under the various circumstances. They must immediately study the Defence Scheme and attached map with the Platoon Officer and Sergeants. The Platoon Officers will then go thoroughly into it with their Sections. It is of vital importance that every section understands what is expected of it.

Ammunition and rifles must be closely inspected, water bottles kept filled as no time would be available to fill if ordered out. Iron Rations must be intact — any man deficient should be brought before the Commanding Officer.

Bombs to be carried by bombers. All men able to throw a live bomb should carry two if possible.

8.5.1918.

DEFENCE SCHEME
18TH BN LONDON REGT

Reference Sheets 57d 62d 1/40000 & attached map

1. DISTRIBUTION OF TROOPS

The Divisional front is divided into two sectors each held by one Brigade in depth, two Battalions in front line one in support.

The Reserve Brigade will be disposed at WARLEY and 4th Royal Welsh Fusiliers about V.23. Central.

2. ACTION IN CASE OF ATTACK

The front line will be main line of resistance.

(a) FRONT BRIGADES

Should the enemy capture any part of front line, an immediate counter-attack will be made by Battalion Reserve.

Plans for immediate counter-attack and for counter-attacks by Support Battalions will be thought out beforehand to prevent delay in launching them.

(b) RESERVE BRIGADE

The Reserve Brigade with 2 Sections of M.G. Coy will move to assembly positions as follows:-

18th London	V.
19th London	C.
20th London & Section M.G.	V. 30 d.
141st T.M.B.	

3. ROLE OF RESERVE BRIGADE

(a) The Reserve Brigade will be prepared to move a Battalion forward to occupy the position vacated by either Support Battalions of Brigade in front line if either or both are moved forward for Counter-attack.

(b) To Counter-attack any part of Divisional front on orders from Divisional Headquarters.

(c) To occupy trench system
D.6.b.9.0 to W.13.c.1.0.

In the event of (a) para 3, the
19TH LONDONS will support 140TH Brigade
18TH LONDONS   "   "   142ND Brigade

A Liaison Officer will be sent from Battalion to report to Headquarters of Brigade it is supporting immediately warning of enemy attack is received.

In the event of (b) para. 3
The 19TH will attack on the right, the 18TH on the left with 20TH in support.
Reserve Brigade Headquarters will move to HENENCOURT CHATEAU.

In the event of (c) of para 3.
The Trench system will be divided into three and occupied by the three Battalions
18TH on Left
19TH in Centre
20TH on Right

4. TANKS

(a) One Coy of 4 tanks will act in Divisional area in case of enemy advance but independently of infantry

(x) "A" Coy No 2 Tank Battalion Mark V tanks (6 males 3 females) located at WARLOY will cooperate in any counter attack made by Reserve Brigade, or will move forward independantly to operate against hostile tanks.

W W Hughes
for Lt & A/Adjt
18th London Regt

Issued to
Copy No 1 S.O.
      2   "A"
      3   "B"
      4   "C"
      5   "D"
      6   T.O.
      7   Bde
      8   File

18th Lon Regt

Reference attached Defence Scheme.

The Brigade Commander considers that detailed instructions should have been given to Company Commanders as regards the action required or role to be played by them in any of the four possible eventualities — incly the move to the assembly area, and the formation to be adopted.

[signature]
Capt
Brigade Major
141 Inf Bde.

9.5.18

DEFENCE SCHEME
18TH BN LONDON REGT

Reference Sheets 57D 62D 1/40000 & attached Map

1. DISTRIBUTION OF TROOPS

The Divisional front is divided into two Sectors, each held by one Brigade in depth, two Battalions in front line, one in Support.

The Reserve Brigade will be disposed at WARLOY and 4TH Royal Welsh Fusiliers about V.23. Central.

2. ACTION IN CASE OF ATTACK

The front line will be main line of resistance.

(a) FRONT BRIGADES.

Should the enemy capture any part of front line, an immediate counter-attack will be made by Battalion Reserves

Plans for immediate counter-attacks and for counter-attacks by Support Battalions will be thought out before hand to prevent delay in launching them

(b) RESERVE BRIGADE

The Reserve Brigade with 2 Sections of M.G. Coy will move to assembly positions as follows:-

18TH LONDONS	V.25.c
19TH LONDONS	C.6.b
20TH LONDONS 2 Sections M.G. 141st T.M.B	V.30.d

3. ROLL OF RESERVE BRIGADE

(a) The Reserve Brigade will be prepared to move a Battalion forward to occupy the position vacated by either Support Battalions of Brigades in front line if either or both are moved forward for Counter-attack.

(b) To Counter-attack any part of Divisional front on orders from Divisional Headquarters

(c) To occupy trench system
D.6.b.9.0 to W.13.c.1.0.

In the event of (a) para 3. the
19TH LONDONS will support 140TH Brigade
18TH LONDONS " " 142ND Brigade.

A Liaison Officer will be sent from Battalion to report to Headquarters of Brigade it is supporting immediately warning of enemy attack is received.

In the event of (b) para. 3
The 19TH will attack on the right, the 18TH on the left with 20TH in Support.

Reserve Brigade Headquarters will move to HENENCOURT CHATEAU.

In the event of (c) of para 3.
The Trench system will be divided into three and occupied by the three Battalions
18TH on Left
19TH in Centre
20TH on Right

4. TANKS

(a) One Coy of Whippets will act in Divisional Area in case of enemy advance but independently of infantry

(b) "A" Coy No 2 Tank Battalion Mark V tanks (6 males 3 females) located at WARLOY will cooperate in any counter attack made by Reserve Brigade, or will move forward independantly to operate against hostile tanks.

W.D.Hughes Maj.
for Lt & A/Adjt
18th London Regt

Issued to

Copy No 1   C.O.
2   "A"
3   "B"
4   "C"
5   "D"
6   T.O.
7   Bde
8   File

SECRET.   Copy. No. 1.

1/18 Battn. THE LONDON REGIMENT.
   OPERATION ORDER   No 246
Ref/map Sheet 62.D.   28 May 1918

1. The 18th BATTALION will relieve the 19th.
   BATTALION in the LEFT SECTION on the night
   of 29th/30th May 1918.

2. Companies of the 18th BATTALION will relieve
   corresponding Companies of the 19th BATTALION.

3. Disposition of Companies will be as follows:-
   "A" Company RIGHT FRONT, "C" Company
   CENTRE FRONT, "B" Company LEFT FRONT
   and "D" Company in SUPPORT.

4. Order of Relief "D" "A" "B" "C" + H.Q.

5. Guides will be met on the track 100 yds
   NORTH of 19th Battalion H.Q. at 10 p.m.
   — 1 per platoon.

6. Advance parties of 1 Officer per Company
   and 4 C.S. majors will report to the
   19th Battn. H.Q. by 2 p.m. and will
   reconnoitre and take over Trench
   Stores etc.

7. All Trench Stores including all tools will be handed over, and receipts taken will be forwarded to Bn. H.Q. by 9 am. the 30th inst.

8. The 19th Battn. will take over from "A" Company the shift of ~~1~~ 1 NCO & 10 men at 4 p.m. and the shift of 2 men at 9 p.m. D Company will relieve the shift of 14 men at 8 pm. at the 19th Battn. H.Q.

9. Relief complete will be reported by code word "CHUNK"

10. ACKNOWLEDGE.

Issued at 10.45 am
29.5.18

P F Keane
Lieut & Adjt.

SECRET   1/19th Battn. The London Regiment   COPY NO 8

OPERATION ORDER NO 182

Refce. Sheet 62d.   28th May 1918

1. 19th Battalion will be relieved by the 18th Battalion in the Left Sector tomorrow night the 29th/30th May.

2. <u>Dispositions</u> Coys. of 18th Battn. will relieve corresponding Coys of the 19th Battn.

3. <u>Order of Relief</u>. "D" "A" "B" "C" H.Q.

4. <u>Guides</u> 1 per Platoon will meet relieving Coys of the 18th Battn. on the track 100 yds North of Battalion H.Q. at 10 p.m. and will report to 2/Lieut J.B. WHITE at 9.45pm. at Bn. H.Q. Platoon Guides will reconnoitre Overland route from Coy. positions to Bn. H.Q. tonight.

5. Advance parties of 18th Battn. will arrive at Coy. H.Q. during the afternoon to take over Trench Stores.
All S.O.S. Grenades, Aero Flares, Aeroplane Photos, Disposition Maps, Particulars of work in progress, and Washing tubs will be handed over. Receipts to be forwarded to Bn. H.Q. by 9am 30th inst.

6. On relief Coys will move to positions vacated by 18th Battn. as follows:-

    'A' Coy. in SQUARE TRENCH.
    'B'   "   HILL ROW.
    'C'   "   DARLING RESERVE.
    'D'   "   DARLING RESERVE.

Advance parties from each Coy. consisting of 1 Off. 1 N.C.O. + 1 man will proceed to their new positions

"A" Form
MESSAGES AND SIGNALS.

Army Form C 2121
(in pads of 100).

No of Message............

Prefix.........Code............m	Words	Charge	This message is on a/c of:	Recd. at........m
Office of Origin and Service Instructions	Sent			Date.............
....	At ....m.		...............Service	From.............
....	To..............			By.............
....	By.............		(Signature of Franking Officer)	

TO {

| Sender's Number | Day of Month | In reply to Number | **AAA** |

From		
Place		
Time		

The above may be forwarded as now corrected. **(Z)**

.... Censor | Signature of Addressee or person authorised to telegraph in his name

* This line should be erased if not required

(7700.) Wt. W492/M1647 110,000 Pads. 5/17 C & R Ltd. (E 1187) and take over all Stores.

O.C., Coys will make their own arrangements for guides to Support positions.

7. Transport Officer will send Rations and Water to Coy. Dumps tomorrow night and the Officer or N.C.O. of the advance parties will meet the Limbers on their respective Dumps and unload.

A.M. will arrange to send up cooked Rations tomorrow night pending the construction of Coy. Cookhouses.

1 Water Cart will be sent to Support Batt. H.Q. tomorrow night with H.Q. Rations.

8. After Relief 'D' Coy. will move to DARLING RESERVE and then proceed to SHRINE TRENCH for work. 18th Battn. will take over from D Coys Shift on the New Battalion H.Q. at 8 p.m.

9. Relief Complete will be reported by 'Priority' Wire – CODE-WORDS J.C.P. 182 received.

10. Acknowledge.

Issued at 7.15 p.m. to:-

1. Commanding Officer.
2. "A" Coy.
3. 'B' "
4. 'C' "
5. 'D' "
6. SIGS. OFR.
7. T.O. Q.M.
8. O.C. 18th London Regt.
9. War Diary
10. Spare.

(Sgd) J. Sheppard
Capt. Adjt.

"A" Form
MESSAGES AND SIGNALS.

Army Form C 2121
(in pads of 100).

No of Message............

Prefix........Code........m	Words	Charge	This message is on a/c of	Recd. at........m
Office of Origin and Service Instructions	Sent		................Service	Date............
....	At ....m.			From............
....	To...............			
....	By...............		(Signature of Franking Officer.)	By ....

TO {

Sender's Number	Day of Month	In reply to Number	**AAA**

*

From
Place
Time

The above may be forwarded as now corrected. **(Z)**

....
Censor — Signature of Addressee or person authorised to telegraph in his name

* This line should be erased if not required

(7700.) Wt. W492/M1647 110,000 Pads. 5/17 C & R Ltd. (E 1187.)

Operation Order L.I.R. 242
by Lt. Col. A. C. Thompson D.S.O. Commdg
18th Bn LONDON REGT.

---

1. **Move** — The Battalion will relieve the 23rd Bn. London Regt. in the Front Line on night 9/10th inst.
   A Coy will relieve A Coy in Support
   B   "   "   "   B   "   " Reserve
   C   "   "   "   C   "   " Right Front
   D   "   "   "   D   "   " Left Front

   The Battn will parade at 8 pm in the Rue du Bas Baillon. Head of Battalion at D Coys HQ. **Dress** Fighting Order. Greatcoats rolled inside waterproof sheet & carried on belts. Waterbottles filled. Battalion will move by Platoons at 200 yards distance.

2. **Guides** — Guides (1 per Coy) & Bn HQ will meet Companies at point V.22.c.8.8. at 9 pm. Platoon Guides at Bn HQ.

3. **Lewis Guns** — Lewis Guns Mess Gear will be carried on Companies Limbers and will move with their Coys.

4. **Billets** — Billets must be left in a clean & sanitary condition & Company Commanders will render to the Adjutant before they move off a certificate to this effect.

5. **Socks** — All men will carry at least 2 pair of Socks

6. **Trench Stores** — Coy Cmdrs will render to Adjt by 8 am tomorrow morning all details of Trench Stores, Maps, Defence Schemes, etc taken over with copies of receipts for same.

7. **Relief complete** — Coys will wire relief complete by Code Word "FANNY"

Issued at
1 60
2 Adjt
3 A
4 B
5 C
6 D
7 HQ
   TOS

"C" FORM.
MESSAGES AND SIGNALS.

Army Form C. 2123.
(In books of 100.)
No. of Message..............

Prefix SP Code FPK Words 17	Received. From Bde By ~~Harpeth~~ At ...m.	Sent, or sent out. To ...m. By	Office Stamp. Goda 29/5
Charges to Collect /			
Service Instructions ruhi Karl M...			

Handed in at ..... Bde ..... Office 6 .m. Received 6.13 .m.

TO Goda

*Sender's Number.	Day of Month.	In reply to Number.	AAA
BM590	29/5	—	

refce BM459 of to-days APPLE aaa added Bde concerned

FROM ...
PLACE & TIME ..... 6 pm.

*This line should be erased if not required.
(E1213).

18th London Regt.	"B" Coy. M.G. Bn.
19th London Regt.	518th Fld Coy. R.E.
20th London Regt.	4th R.W.F.
141st T. M. Bty.	Left Group Arty$\frac{1}{2}$

---

1. Reference B.M.S. 459 of 29th May, Zero hour will be 2 a.m. on the first night that wind is favourable.

2. Cancel para 5 and substitute the following:-

    "Code words will be used as follows:-

    MARJORY   - Operation WILL take place to-night.
    CUTHBERT - Operation WILL NOT take place to-night.
    DANIEL   - Operation completed."

3. Acknowledge

B.M.S. 477.

2nd June 1918.

Captain,
Brigade Major.
141st Infantry Brigade.

```
18th Lon.Regt.      "B" Coy.M.G.Bn.              S E C R E T.
19th Lon.Regt.      518th Fld.Coy.R.E.           47th Div. G.90/1/9.
20th Lon.Regt.      4th R.W.F.
141st T.M.Bty.      Left Group Arty.
```

1. "D" Special Company R.E., now have projectors installed at E.7.d.0.6.

2. These will be fired at early dawn on the 30th May if wind is favourable; otherwise on first favourable day. Zero hour will be notified later.

3. Targets will be the wooded bank running from E.8.b.0.5. to E.2.d.6.0. and bank running from E.8.b.4.0. to E.8.b.9.2.

4. This will necessitate :-

    (a) All troops being withdrawn from the RED triangle shown on attached tracing. Ø

    (b) All troops within the BLUE triangle shown on the attached tracing wearing their box respirators from Zero - 5 minutes till Zero + 10 minutes.

    Bursts of artillery and machine gun fire will be directed on to the targets at Zero.

5. Code words will be used as follows:-
   CHARLES   - operation WILL take place tonight.
   APPLE   - operation WILL NOT take place tonight.
   FORTRESS - operation completed.

6. ACKNOWLEDGE.

B.M.S.459.
29th May 1918.

Captain,
Brigade Major,
141st Infantry Brigade.

Ø Issued to Battns., T.M.Bty. and 518th Fld.Coy.R.E.

"A" Form.
MESSAGES AND SIGNALS.

Army Form C.2121
(in pads of 100).

TO 18th 19th 20th Lon. Regt. 141 TM Bty
"B" Coy M.G.Bn, 518 Fld Coy RE, 4th Bn R.W.7
Left Group Arty

Sender's Number.	Day of Month.	In reply to Number.	AAA
*BM.606	30/5		

Refce BM.459 of 29th inst Projectors will now be fired at 1.30 am on night 30/31st May if wind is favourable aaa a similar discharge will be taking place on the 58th Div front on Quarry at W.27.b.8.8 at the same hour aaa acknowledge

Ack

From V U H 1

Capt BM

War Diary

1/18th Bn London Regt

June 18

Confidential

Army Form C. 2118.

Vol 39

WAR DIARY for June 1918

INTELLIGENCE SUMMARY.

(Erase heading not required.)

Instructions regarding War Diaries and Intelligence Summaries are contained in F. S. Regs., Part II. and the Staff Manual respectively. Title pages will be prepared in manuscript.

Place	Date	Hour	Summary of Events and Information	Remarks and references to Appendices
In line	June 1st		Ref. to SENLIS 1/20,000. The Battalion was holding the front line system of the LAVIEVILLE Sector extending from E.1.b.90.60 on the right to E.2.a.4.0 on the left with the 5th Batn LONDON REGT on the right flank and the 8th Batn LONDON REGT. on the left flank and the 19th Batn LONDON REGT. in Support. The disposition was as follows :- "A" company on the right, "C" company in the centre, "B" company on the left and "D" company in Support. The day was fairly quiet but the enemy kept up a rather desultory fire on our front line. Casualties 3 other ranks wounded. Sgt. C.S. HARDY, Pioneer Sgt. was mortally wounded thro' a gun shot wound. A.T. MACKENZIE Batt. was killed by a P.G. Company. The Battalion had during the tour at the line on June 1st kept under the impression of a hostile attack of the great importance. The 18th Hussars were sent up and in the line. No disturbance had taken place during the tour. No Infantry patrols were sent out, and 4 VERY and POINEER trenches, on the West side of trench and the enemy trench. The enemy kept a slack bombardment with thus artillery on their trench about 2.30 am. but no Infantry attack followed. Battalion relieved 4 am. on	

2353 Wt. W5344/1454 700,000 5/15 D.D.&L. A.D.S.S.Forms/C 2118.

WAR DIARY
INTELLIGENCE SUMMARY.

Army Form C. 2118.

(Erase heading not required.)

Instructions regarding War Diaries and Intelligence Summaries are contained in F. S. Regs., Part II. and the Staff Manual respectively. Title pages will be prepared in manuscript.

Place	Date	Hour	Summary of Events and Information	Remarks and references to Appendices
In the trenches	1.7		had continued throughout the morning and afternoon. Casualties 2/Lt CURWEN killed and 1 other rank wounded. 2/Lt [?] returned from the Gas School and was sent up to assist "C" Company. 2/Lt [?] was wounded and admitted to hospital sick. 2/Lt [?] [?] LONDON REGT. relieved the 30th Batn. LONDON REGT. on our right. The Battalion was relieved by [?] 4th [?] for June 3rd. The Lieutenant Commander and his [?] arrived at 9.30 a.m. and proceeded to go round our system of trenches. The enemy had [?] throughout the day. Casualties nil.	
In the trenches	3.5		The Battalion was relieved the [?] as for June 1st. Two tanks and a machine gun were placed in EDITH TRENCH in order to take the [?] the work [?] and in YANKS TRENCH and the new support trench. The enemy was quite throughout the day. All heavy trench mortars came into action at [?]. Casualties nil.	
	6.6		The Battalion was relieved in [?] as for June 5th with the distribution of the Companies [?] changed. "A" Company on the right and "D" [?] South of the ALBERT–AMIENS [?]	

WAR DIARY or INTELLIGENCE SUMMARY

Army Form C. 2118.

Place	Date	Hour	Summary of Events and Information	Remarks and references to Appendices
			and "B" Company on the left. The two platoons of "C" Company were withdrawn from the front line into the new support trench. The remaining two platoons of "B" Company H.Q. trench in PIONEER TRENCH between the support platoon of A's "B" Companies. "D" Company remained in DIRTY TRENCH while two Lewis Gun positions of four guns each was established in the new Pidion Trench and at its junction with DIGGER AVENUE, and in a small trench at E.4.a.60.70. to fire on F.S.O.S. lines. Work was continued on YARRA TRENCH and on the life site in YARRA and PIONEER TRENCH, the digging of the new support trench was continued. Wiring was carried out by A & B companies and a new trench from "B" Company Sap spent-looked to a French in the bank at E.2.a.4.0. Forty men were detailed at our battl. during the day. Hostile artillery was very slight, very little movement being observed in the back area. A German patrol captured two men who were in position of BUSH-POST at E.2.C.35.15. Casualties 2.OR missing. The Battalion dead holding the line as for June 6th. work was continued on the new fire slope in YARRA and PIONEER TRENCHES and on the new	
On line	7/6			

WAR DIARY
or
INTELLIGENCE SUMMARY.
(Erase heading not required.)

Army Form C. 2118.

Place	Date	Hour	Summary of Events and Information	Remarks and references to Appendices

There was practically no hostile activity beyond a little whizzbang fire. A patrol from "B" Company whilst out on our front captured one prisoner. The 19th Bn LONDON REGT made a raid in the night, they failed to penetrate into the German trenches or to secure identification. Gas projectors were fired into the enemy lines at 2.30 am. This produced no retaliation whatsoever. About 110 mm were barked during the day. Casualties nil.

June 8th. No particulars relating to this line is for June 4th. Shook was continued on the full sides on YARRA and PIONEER TRENCHES and on the rear support trench.

The TRENCH REEKS (?) joined the 4/R QUEENS. 18th Division on our L/c. L.O.I.P. (?) talked (?) heavy refire during the night. Large numbers of Gas shells were burst on our ground and fires were lit, reaching its maximum about 2.30 am. The bombardment signal more intensely

WAR DIARY or INTELLIGENCE SUMMARY

Army Form C. 2118.

Place	Date	Hour	Summary of Events and Information	Remarks and references to Appendices
In line	9th		a few miles South, and it turned out to be their preliminary bombardment for their attack between MONTDIDIER and NOYON in the morning of the 9th. Casualties 1 O.R. killed 1 O.R. wounded. The Battalion holding the line as before. Quiet 8k. There was practically no activity on our front, but the bombardment continued steadily until arming on our right. The 5th Bath. LONDON REGT. relieved us in the line, the relief being complete about 2 a.m. On completion the Battalion moved back into bivouac at C.21.b. Casualties 1 O.R. wounded.	
Bivouac at C.21.b	10th	9. a.m.	The Battalion had reported all present in bivouac at C.21.b. at 9 a.m. Bathing was done in the afternoon. Company at 2.30 p.m. The Battalion moved forward at C.21.b. The Companies were at the disposal of Company Commanders for cleaning up, re-organisation and training.	
do.	11th			
Bivouac	12th		Battalion in bivouac at C.21.b. Conferences at the disposal of Company Commanders for training. The Divisional	

WAR DIARY or INTELLIGENCE SUMMARY

Army Form C. 2118.

Place	Date	Hour	Summary of Events and Information	Remarks and references to Appendices
Anneville	June 13		Jollies gave a concert at 5.30 pm the band of the 83rd Australian Battalion opened the show with several splendid selections of music. The following officers joined the Battalion from the Auckland Kings: 2/Lt R.K. Slosman, 2/Lt G.A. Fea, 2/Lt A. Ruffett, 2/Lt J.G. Taylor, 2/Lt J.R. Boyke, 2/Lt A. Duff, together with 68 other ranks. The Battalion on arrival at C.21 b Operation Orders was received to relieve the 30th Battn. LONDON REGT in the LANIÉVILLE LINE. Major to W. Hughes D.S.O. M.C. and Capt. V.I.G. Cults went up in the morning to reconnoitre, attend representation of the Companies and HQ went up in the afternoon. The Battalion moved off at 8.30 pm and the relief was reported complete at 11.30 pm. The disposition of the Companies is as follows :- LANIÉVILLE LINE three Companies. "A" Company on the right from D.11.b.10.25 to D.10.d.60.15. "B" Company from D.10.d.60.15 to D.11.a.30.15. "D" Company from D.11.a.30.15 to D.6.d.10.50. "C" Company in SUPPORT at D.16.c.5.4. H.Q. Anneville Station. S.A.A. Reserve at D.9.b.45.60. the 9th Battn. ROYAL WELSH FUSILIERS forming the LANIÉVILLE LINE on our right. Tactically the Battalion is at the disposal of the G.O.C. 113th Brigade. C.S.M. Kempf left for England to take up a commission.	

Army Form C. 2118.

WAR DIARY
or
INTELLIGENCE SUMMARY.
(Erase heading not required.)

Place	Date	Hour	Summary of Events and Information	Remarks and references to Appendices
	14th		The Battalion holding the LANIEVILLE LINE. The companies were finding 40 men each to work in dug-outs on the construction of Machine Gun dug-outs. The remainder were trained in Musketry and Lewis Gun. "C" Company Lewis Gun were fired on the range. R.S.M. J.D. Bickmann M.M. left for England to take up a Commission. Father HURLEY visited the Battalion for the first time for many months whilst in the line.	
	15th		The Battalion holding the LANIEVILLE LINE. Forty men per Company being engaged on building Machine Guns dug-outs, the remainder were employed on making a "bun" of 3" on the parapet and 6" on the parados, this being now considered priority work. The Lewis Gunners of "A" & "B" Companies carried out firing on the range, together with the snipers. The Brigade Transport Competition took place at 9.30 a.m. Lt. RICKS. M.O.R.C. U.S.A. proceeded to England on 14 days leave, Capt. SEWAR R.A.M.C. taking his place. Casualties nil.	
	16th		The Battalion holding the LANIEVILLE LINE. Ten men per Company were engaged on building Machine Gun dug-outs, the remainder on clearing the	

WAR DIARY
or
INTELLIGENCE SUMMARY.
(Erase heading not required.)

Army Form 2118.

Place	Date	Hour	Summary of Events and Information	Remarks and references to Appendices
			Line " on the parapet and parados. The latter work was countermanded by telephone about 10 p.m. and the men were ordered to build additional fire steps as the result of the Corps Commander's visit to a portion of the line during the afternoon. Good work was accomplished on the fire steps. The R. C's attended Divine Service at BAISIEUX. The Officers of the 6th Battn LONDON REGT. 58th Division came up to reconnoitre the line. The Battalion took up 1,800 francs for the Divisional Horse Sweepstake. The result of the transport competition issued as follows 20th Battalion, 19th Battalion, 18th Battalion. About 11.30 pm a Brigade message was received to send down our wiring party to proceed to the rear billeting area on the early morning of the 14th. 2nd Lieut. L.G. DOMINY took over charge of the party. Another message was received at 1.15 am to send down our surplus stores and Lewis Guns. The lorries arrived for same about 3 a.m. Casualties 3 other ranks wounded.	
	14/-		The Battalion holding the LANIEVILLE LINE. Operation Orders were received	

Army Form 2118.

WAR DIARY
or
INTELLIGENCE SUMMARY.
(Erase heading not required.)

Place	Date	Hour	Summary of Events and Information	Remarks and references to Appendices
			that the relief by the 6th Battn LONDON REGT. 58th Division would take place that night, and on completion of relief the Battalion would entrain to PICQUIGNY. The advance parties of the 6th Battn. arrived at 3.30 p.m. The relief was reported complete at 11.50 p.m. On completion of relief the Battalion moved to BOIS RUPERT, had breakfast, and entrained at 4 a.m. to PICQUIGNY (Ref AMIENS Sheet) arrived thus about 7.30 a.m. Casualties nil	
18th			(Ref. AMIENS Sheet) The Battalion in billets at PICQUIGNY. All troops fairly well billeted. The following officers joined from Divisional train. 2/Lieut E Drummond A Coy, 2/Lieut R.R. Stevens C Coy., Lieut A.O. Steele B Coy. and 2/Lieut A.L. Doust A. Coy. from hospital having previously served with the Battalion. 184 other ranks joined the Battalion.	
19th			The Battalion in billets at PICQUIGNY. The companies were at the disposal of the Company Commanders for Re-organisation and cleaning of arms and equipment. The Commanding Officer and the Adjutant attended a Brigade conference at 10 a.m. re training.	
20th			The Battalion in billets at PICQUIGNY. The Battalion paraded for training	

WAR DIARY
INTELLIGENCE SUMMARY.
(Erase heading not required.)

Army Form C. 2118.

Instructions regarding War Diaries and Intelligence Summaries are contained in F. S. Regs., Part II. and the Staff Manual respectively. Title pages will be prepared in manuscript.

Place	Date	Hour	Summary of Events and Information	Remarks and references to Appendices
	21st		at 9 a.m. and were inspected by the Colonel after which training was carried on under the supervision of the Company Commanders. Lt V.C. Carson and 2/Lt. G.A.R. Harcourt rejoined the Battalion from the Divisional Camp. Capt. C.S. Gorley and Capt. C.R. Vincent M.C. were sent to Field Ambulance. Capt. A. Mackenzie-Smith rejoined the Battalion. The Battalion in billets at PICQUIGNY. The Battalion paraded at 9 am and continued training under the Company Commanders until 12.30 pm and in the afternoon from 2 pm to 4 pm. The Divisional follies gave a performance at 5.30 pm.	
	22nd		The Battalion in billets at PICQUIGNY training carried out under the supervision of the Company Commanders.	
	23rd		The Battalion in billets at PICQUIGNY. The Brigade held a Church Parade. The Divisional General was present and presented ribbons to various N.C.Os. and men after the Service. The Colonel and the Adjutant went to reconnoitre the front of the XXXI French Corps. The Battalion in billets at PICQUIGNY, and paraded for training under	
	24th			

Army Form C. 2118.

WAR DIARY
INTELLIGENCE SUMMARY.
(Erase heading not required.)

Instructions regarding War Diaries and Intelligence Summaries are contained in F. S. Regs., Part II. and the Staff Manual respectively. Title pages will be prepared in manuscript.

Place	Date	Hour	Summary of Events and Information	Remarks and references to Appendices
	25th		The Commanding Officers at 9 a.m. Capt G.S.A Straefe rejoined the Battalion.	
			The Battalion in billets at PICQUIGNY and paraded for training at 9 a.m under the Company Commander. Lt General BUTLER the Corps Commander visited the men during their training. Major L.A. Hafield D.S.O. M.C. and Capt E.M. Ellis M.C. went to reconnoitre the XXXI Hants Corps front.	
	26th		The Battalion in billets at PICQUIGNY, and paraded for Company training at 9 a.m. The trials of the new Petroineur two pass off at 5.30 pm. Instructions to the Divisional trials Carried out. Lieut. J.R Roney joined the Battalion and 2/Lieut. J.D Butler went on a Course.	
	27th		The Battalion in billets at PICQUIGNY training under the Company Commander. The Commanding Officers went to interview the Army Commander. A Sergeants Gala was held at 5.30 pm, on the return the billets were loud. The "SHAMROCKS" the Battalion Concert Party entertained the men at 6.30 pm.	
	28th		The Battalion in billets at PICQUIGNY Company training was carried out.	

WAR DIARY
or
INTELLIGENCE SUMMARY.

(Erase heading not required.)

Army Form C. 2118.

Place	Date	Hour	Summary of Events and Information	Remarks and references to Appendices
	29		The Battalion football team played the remainder of the Battalion at football during the afternoon, the remainder won 2 - 1. The Shamrocks gave a concert in the evening.	
			The Battalion is billets at PICQUIGNY. Company training was carried out. Several men were sent to the Field Ambulance with P.U.O. Several hundred the health of the troops had been much better than other units in the Brigade. Lieut. F.J. Burberry rejoined the Battalion. A meeting of all Officers, N.C.Os. and Sergeants was held at 3 p.m. to nominate the representatives of the Sports Committee and the Canteen Committee. The following were elected to be members of the Sports Committee.	
			President Major A.H. Hatfield D.S.O. M.C.	
			Father Hurley	
			1/Lt. A.L. Jones	
			1/Lt. A. Mackenzie (Sports Officer)	
			Revd. 2/Lt. G. Poole	
			2/Lt. A.G. Donnelly	

Army Form C. 2118.

WAR DIARY
or
INTELLIGENCE SUMMARY.
(Erase heading not required.)

Instructions regarding War Diaries and Intelligence Summaries are contained in F. S. Regs., Part II. and the Staff Manual respectively. Title pages will be prepared in manuscript.

Place	Date	Hour	Summary of Events and Information	Remarks and references to Appendices
	30th		C.S.M. Dobson S.	
			C.Q.M.S. Loxley K. (Secretary)	
			A/Sergt. Allen R.A.	
			Transport Sergt. Ditchman G.	
			L.Q.M.S. Thorne A.E.	
			Major A.H. Huffer D.S.O. M.C.	
			Capt. Em. Ellis M.C.	
			The following to represent the Canteen Committee.	
			The Battalion in billets at PICQUIGNY. The Brigade Commander took the Commanding Officer and Adjutant on their tactical exercise at 5.30 p.m. Lieut. O.J. Dearne rejoined the Battalion from a course. 2/Lieut. L.A. Moss joined the Battalion.	

AC Chapman Lt Col Comdg
18th Bn. LONDON REGT.
(LONDON IRISH RIFLES).

SECRET   Copy No. 1

1/18th Bn. THE LONDON REGT.
OPERATION ORDER No. 247.

Ref. Maps 62.D. 1/40,000   9th June 1918

1. The Battalion will be relieved by the 24th Bn. in the LEFT Section LEFT Sub-Sector tonight 9/10th June. On relief the Bn. will move into Divisional Reserve in C.15.d.

2. Relief will be as follows :-
   A Coy. 18th relieved by C Coy 24th as RIGHT FRONT Coy.
   B "   "   "   " B   "   "   " LEFT FRONT Coy.
   C "   "   "   " D   "   "   " SUPPORT Coy.
   D "   "   "   " A   "   "   " RESERVE Coy.

3. Four guides per Company, two for H.Q., two for Lewis Gun Battys. to be at BN.H.Q at 7.30 p.m. These will guide the incoming Companies from Brigade H.Q.

4. The Q.M, with 4 C.Q.M.S. will arrange for the billeting of Companies and BN H.Q. Coys. will take over from their opposite ones ie A from A etc.
   The Q.M. will arrange for guides to meet Companies at C.29.a.7.8.

II

5. All petrol tins to be returned to Bn. H.Q. by 5 p.m. **prompt**. Any full cans remaining will be used to fill water bottles of men in the line and then sent down.

6. All trench stores, secret maps, defence schemes, work in practice, and permanent working parties with R.Es, will be carefully handed over to incoming Company Commanders. The necessary receipts to be obtained and forwarded to Bn. Orderly Room by 2 pm 10th inst.

7. The T.O. will arrange for the following limbers :-
One limber for Company Officers' trench kits and cooking utensils, and A. B & C. Coy cooking utensils to be at the end of DIRTY TRENCH as soon after dark as possible.
One limber to collect H.Q. and Coy's cooking utensils and 18 improvised pack hot food containers from Bn HQ.
Two limbers to be at Bn HQ for Lewis Guns from 11 pm onwards.
Mess Cart for H.Q. Officers' mess kit, trench kit, and Aid Post stores
Horses for Commanding Officer, Sec-in-Command, Adjt, MO and Company Comdrs to be on main ALBERT - AMIENS Road

III

about D.16.b.9.1" from 11.30 pm onwards

8. Route on completion of relief :—
main ALBERT - AMIENS Road as far
as FRANVILLERS, thence to C.29.a.y.8.
where guides will be met.

9. Completion of relief will be reported
to Bn HQ. by the code word "THANKS"

10. ACKNOWLEDGE.

F.H. Carless Capt & Adjt
1/18th Bn. LONDON REGT.

9th June 1918
Issued at 1 p.m.

WAR DIARY or INTELLIGENCE SUMMARY

Army Form C. 2118.

1/18TH BATTN. LONDON REGT., 1ST LONDON IRISH RIFLES
11 JUL 1918

Vol 40

Place	Date	Hour	Summary of Events and Information	Remarks and references to Appendices
Ref. Amiens 62.000 PICQUIGNY	1918 July 1		The Battalion in billets at PICQUIGNY. Parade 9am. The Battalion took part in the Brigade Tactical Exercise, forming the Advance Guard to the Brigade moving on the FERRIERS - PICQUIGNY road advancing towards ABBEVILLE. The Battalion being completion at the following weights took place in the Afternoon commencing at 3 p.m. 10.7. 9. 8. 7 stone.	
	2		2/Lt W.C.D. CURTIN went on a Musketry Course. The Battalion at PICQUIGNY and took part as the Advance Guard to the Brigade in the Brigade Tactical Scheme of the 1st January. An outpost line in position W of PICQUIGNY. A rather summary and unsatisfactory match was held in the afternoon at 2.30 p.m.	
	3		Lt TOTTON M.C. rejoined the Battalion. The Battalion in billets at Picquigny. Paraded at 9 am and marched to the Assembly position in the Bois de NEUVILLE preparing to making an attack on the ridge of trenches on the hill by TENTFOL FARM. The position should (-) grid and the main assault well in excess of about	

Army Form C. 2118.

WAR DIARY
or
INTELLIGENCE SUMMARY.
(Erase heading not required.)

Place	Date	Hour	Summary of Events and Information	Remarks and references to Appendices
			the final objective. Major General George and the Brigade Commander were present at the attack.	
			The Divisional Summing Galore were held in the afternoon at PICQUIGNY.	
	4		The Battalion was Billets at PICQUIGNY. Assembled in the Rue de NEUILLY for the attack on the following day. The advance being made by lines of sections making the fullest use of ground in order to assemble on the jumping off line. Then advance to every up the slopes for the final assault by TINQI then and to every up the slopes for the final assault on enemy. The attack throughout was extremely well carried out.	
	5		The Battn. in Billets at PICQUIGNY. Paraded at 9 a.m under the Battn. in Billets at PICQUIGNY. Paraded at 9 a.m under the Commanding Officer. Company training was afterwards carried out.	
	6		The Battn. assembled at known and proceeded to witness a demonstration of STOKES eneral Gorla's Battery A.G.L. L.G. J Sub. M.G. detailed to the Brigade H.Q.	

Army Form C. 2118.

WAR DIARY
or
INTELLIGENCE SUMMARY.
(Erase heading not required.)

Instructions regarding War Diaries and Intelligence Summaries are contained in F. S. Regs., Part II. and the Staff Manual respectively. Title pages will be prepared in manuscript.

Place	Date	Hour	Summary of Events and Information	Remarks and references to Appendices
	7		The Battn at PICQUIGNY and paraded for Divine Service at 11 am. M. Gnl R.W.R. Luey K.C.B. spoke a few words on our removal of the Battn from the Bois. A.B. Bishop of Amiens addressed the men in the Church later.	
	8		The Battn in billets at PICQUIGNY Paraded at 9 am and made an attack on the Bois de NEUILLY moving in the Wake of the smoke and advancing towards BERNOL-FERON at a rate faster than required to capture the ground. The attack was covered by smoke and the entrance was assaulted by the leading Coys when the Wire and trenches there had been overcome.	
	9		The Battn in billets at PICQUIGNY. The Coys were taken over Aam and tested on Company turnout by Lieut Col G.W. Allen attached Battn as Visitor at 9 am in place of Major R.P.H. Wood D.S.O on the Gnral Listing Picked the 15th Bn London Regt in the afternoon and lost 2-0.	
	10		The Battn in billets at PICQUIGNY. Paraded for company drill at 9 am	

WAR DIARY
or
INTELLIGENCE SUMMARY.

(Erase heading not required.)

Army Form C. 2118.

Place	Date	Hour	Summary of Events and Information	Remarks and references to Appendices
			sends Major A.L. Hughes R.E. V.C. and continued with Coopers Sap ap	
			H. Col. Hughes R.E. the adjutant and four company Commanders went	
			up to reconnoitre the trenches with a view of taking over the line	
			4/U R.W.K. being an operation order to relieve the 7/th R.W. Kents to	
			12th Division on the night also of Durward front covered at	
			Sent of Winter	
		11.30 pm	Previous 6 11.30 pm and reached WARLOY at 2.45 pm when he was	SENLIS Special Sheet. 1/20,000
			ready for the Battalion. C.O. was required to take command of the	
			Battalion the C.O.C. approved of proceeding to X Redoubt	
			V.D.C.8.6 camp 1/2000. Relief was completed by 11.15 pm	
			... Runners were lying at V.30.15.90 - V.30 ...	
			Royal Fusilier No 41 ... N.Y.L. Scale 1/20 6.6 ... 7 lab.	
			... Hudson ... V.29.7.9 ... K.O.S.B. ... hot known ...	
			... ... V.29.0.6.6 V.30.d.2.5	
			V.29.c.3.1. "B" Coy. in ... trenches MINT ... 29.4.6.7 V.30.c.0.0. -	
			D.H. in NAILSE ST TRENCH V.30.9.6.5 "C" Coy in CRAFTY CORSE V.29.9.38	
			V.29.2. 40.90. B 44 V.29.2. 90. 40 ... Barricades hd.	

WAR DIARY
or
INTELLIGENCE SUMMARY.

(Erase heading not required.)

Army Form C. 2118.

Instructions regarding War Diaries and Intelligence Summaries are contained in F. S. Regs., Part II. and the Staff Manual respectively. Title pages will be prepared in manuscript.

Place	Date	Hour	Summary of Events and Information	Remarks and references to Appendices
	12		The Battalion shelled — dispositions as for 11 July 1918. 9th Brigade shelled the Battn in the morning. Work was carried on in making the enemy attitude. During the day the Battn were at work on improving Trenches — WARRE & WALLACE — MURRAY — WARRE 30.	
	13		WARRES. Work on improving old allied & Battalion support defences continued. Work away from allied & Battalion defences on the neighbourhood of YONGA & ALBERT-AMIENS Road when 11 – 12 during 12. Work was done by WARR & on MURRAY SPRING POINT. WALLACE and MORROW lock. From WALLACE support line making a 3' keen lock between to Hedley. Hedges was completed. 2 large huts were were formed by R.A. batteries h.t.	
	14		Inspection as yesterday. The enemy artillery a little more active — a little harassing shelling all over the neighbourhood more particularly in ALBERT — POUCHY Road. Enemy aeros shewed to believe the 19th = O.R. Lewis night in the light sector the O.O. & 2nd Lieut. Making him wounded the line. Work was done on deepening	

Army Form C. 2118.

WAR DIARY
or
INTELLIGENCE SUMMARY.
(Erase heading not required.)

Instructions regarding War Diaries and Intelligence Summaries are contained in F. S. Regs., Part II. and the Staff Manual respectively. Title pages will be prepared in manuscript.

Place	Date	Hour	Summary of Events and Information	Remarks and references to Appendices
			and known as BENJAMIN STREET. 33 ORs from 6/13 & D. W. from K. & O.Y.L.I. 200 yards trench was watched by the night was going out making arcs difficult. Work on our trenches was also done. Lieut A.N.B. Thompson went on special leave. Lieut HW Scott was sent for to replace him in B. Coy. Casualties nil.	
	15		The Batta. was for yesterday, today and tomorrow, being in Operation Orders the Batta. relieved the 19th Bn. London Regt. on the right sub-sector. Disposition as follows: "D" Coy to take over of "A" on the front line system D. Coys two platoons on left front sub BRISBANE TRENCH, "B" & "C" Coys two platoons on right sub MELBOURNE TRENCH - Two two platoons in RIDGE TRENCH. The relief was carried out with a minimum of casualties. During day enemy artillery was active all along the front. They replied in a feeble way to our 18p followed by N.B. Coy. barrage which was from YC 30.2.40.85 to as along 100 yds with D.B. after several minutes S. from VC.30.2.40.85 to a distance of affair several minutes long. After 30 min the barrage of [illegible]	

Army Form C. 2118.

WAR DIARY
or
INTELLIGENCE SUMMARY.

(Erase heading not required.)

Instructions regarding War Diaries and Intelligence Summaries are contained in F. S. Regs., Part II. and the Staff Manual respectively. Title pages will be prepared in manuscript.

Place	Date	Hour	Summary of Events and Information	Remarks and references to Appendices
	17		Patrols shelling our line	
			The enemy shelling our reserve line unusual for	
			this hour. Heavy MILLS TRENCH shelled by enemy during	
			the early hours of night. A patrol went out 11.30 p.m.	
			2/Lt MICHAEL and FCH of No 11 platoon of "C" Coy	
			entered the GER trench and — Rees VINCENT	
			returned from leave. Officers off.	
			Casualties –	
	18			
			HENENCOURT CHATEAU at 3.30 pm	

WAR DIARY
or
INTELLIGENCE SUMMARY.
(Erase heading not required.)

Army Form C. 2118.

Instructions regarding War Diaries and Intelligence Summaries are contained in F. S. Regs., Part II, and the Staff Manual respectively. Title pages will be prepared in manuscript.

Place	Date	Hour	Summary of Events and Information	Remarks and references to Appendices
			Lieut Vincent P.L. took out a patrol of "A" Coy to attack of Becker occupied bank of E.S.R.S. as three posts had been seen there in morning — no enemy was seen. Patrol was out 10 pm — 2 am. There were some good sniping during night. Lieut BURNAY M.C. regained from Brigade Training Camp & took command of "D" Coy. Lieut R. MACKENZIE-SMITH M.C. and Lt. Brig. Luig back. Lt. R.S.P.F. H. NEOL. — now went on Paris leave. Canadian Rail.	
	19		The Battn. was for yesterday. The Brigadier went round in the morning and called at H.Qrs. Artillery barrage was ordered for evening "B" Coy & two D.L.W. the front line and "C" relieved "D" in Brigade Support. There were a lot of aeroplanes up. "D" Coy patrol went out — saw a searchlight signal to the STEVELLS — confirm of H.Q.R. near our front line trench and opened at 8 p.m. On 2nd Lieut VINCENT and 1 O.R. officer and 9	

Army Form C. 2118.

WAR DIARY
or
INTELLIGENCE SUMMARY.

(Erase heading not required.)

Instructions regarding War Diaries and Intelligence
Summaries are contained in F. S. Regs., Part II.
and the Staff Manual respectively. Title pages
will be prepared in manuscript.

Place	Date	Hour	Summary of Events and Information	Remarks and references to Appendices
			platoon of "A" by went out at 10 p.m. and tho' the shells and searched the Boche line - they stuck to get a Boche in which they were not successful. Work was done on our C.T. from BRISBANE SUPPORT to MELBOURNE TRENCH - wiring was done in front line to enable white men also to better Browbies	
	20		The Battn as was on yesterday. The 2nd Bn RA - 131 U.S.A. Regt reported the 2 platoons of 1st & 2nd Batts at night. Buses & Britain & 1st 6th C.T. from our MALIN TRENCH to LANGEMCOURT CHATEAU at 10.30 am to support the firing line & the KAMIL SCARPE. our DHQ also HQ did. A Patrol went out 10.30 p.m. 2/Lieut TAYLOR & 1 Pilkon of "C" Coy to visit Bosch Trenches they went through stables but did not succeed in reaching Boche Sunken Rd. returned at 2.30 am.	
	21		The Batty returned to support fire on our C.T. from ... to Boche ...	

10

WAR DIARY
or
INTELLIGENCE SUMMARY.
(Erase heading not required.)

Army Form C. 2118.

Instructions regarding War Diaries and Intelligence Summaries are contained in F. S. Regs., Part II. and the Staff Manual respectively. Title pages will be prepared in manuscript.

Place	Date	Hour	Summary of Events and Information	Remarks and references to Appendices
	22		was confirmed by Lupor Shelters in front line. There was a little shelling on the valley on MILLER COURT – ALBERT ROAD during the night. Casualties Nil. The Battn as for yesterday – The 3rd Battn U.S.A. 131 Regt relieved the platoons of 2nd Bn. Major ALLEN & Lt. STROTZ m H.Q. The Bn's several scouts like sent kinty the day with the Bn's Scout – a patrol went out at 10.30pm to get in touch with the enemy, the Hof king to obtain an identification – they gutter touch and had 3 casualties wounded & returned at 3am. Lieut "SCHMIDT" of 2nd Battn 131 U.S.R. Regt went with patrol which was under Lieut VINCENT MC the patrol had all felt air identification. Some Hun 3 OR's known to be missing. The Battn in line as yesterday.	
	23		London Regt came on line to relieve and went away at night. A patrol of Opr Sea & Lt Michael & 4 OH picked up A boy started at 11.15 pm. they object was to recon Bridge Corner and got in about 4 h wires all ... Bn. He knew what they	

WAR DIARY
or
INTELLIGENCE SUMMARY.
(Erase heading not required.)

Army Form C. 2118.

Place	Date	Hour	Summary of Events and Information	Remarks and references to Appendices

wounded last night about 150 yds from the German trench - shot thro' the leg and unable to move. On approaching bombs were met with rifle and machine gun fire, bombs also being thrown. The bigger men threw them so too well and they abandoned the attack. A raid by an sgt of the 22nd London during the latter part of the night was more successful as prisoners were brought in.

2.52.0/64.9.5. Wagon was killed by a shell and several wounded. A good - returned will & several bombers at 11 to wait to attack German line in LONSONNE. Counted I buried in Italian Dump.

The Rath. Weather was dull & quiet during day, preparing for a like shower in afternoon battery. Relay was supplied with guides on the emery points. At 1.30pm Smoke of the X Co's & B V22 ESS. The attack was completely hidden but the Bn did not succeed in its entire. It appears they were met by one bombs and rifle fire which had been brought up on the enemy also came on & took possession of Fort V.C.A. platoons also came

12

WAR DIARY
or
INTELLIGENCE SUMMARY.
(Erase heading not required.)

Army Form C. 2118.

Instructions regarding War Diaries and Intelligence Summaries are contained in F. S. Regs., Part II. and the Staff Manual respectively. Title pages will be prepared in manuscript.

Place	Date	Hour	Summary of Events and Information	Remarks and references to Appendices
	25		out and embarked at HENENCOURT CHATEAU. Lt. S. J. Hoole was slightly wounded during the relief. Casualties 1 Offr. Wounded	
			The Battalion in Billets at WARLOY – Little rather bad weather was reported the men cleaning up getting rifles etc ... making latrines. The Commg Officer attended a conference cleaning up ammunition ... at Brigade at 6 p.m. He arrived at Offrs mess at 9 p.m. and discussed the work in the line and general description of the Bath taken by Officers & men and general ... said it would be a log to show the Brigadier Comdr an about nothing during the morning. The Brigadier called during the morning. 10 Platoons and detachs from MOLLIENS at BUS regained ... during the marching and the following Officers 2/Lt Sheridon to command B Coy 2/Lt Ruffett C " D " " D Coy forced the town	

Army Form C.2118.

WAR DIARY
or
INTELLIGENCE SUMMARY.
(Erase heading not required.)

Instructions regarding War Diaries and Intelligence Summaries are contained in F.S. Regs., Part II. and the Staff Manual respectively. Title pages will be prepared in manuscript.

Place	Date	Hour	Summary of Events and Information	Remarks and references to Appendices
	26		Assumed command of Camp details. The Canteen was open in WARLOY & took £200 pes.	
			Baths in WARLOY - Engaged in cleaning up - a working party of B. Coy & 3 Platoons were in front of HENENCOURT left at 4.30pm returned 12.30pm. 3 Platoons going to line marched to MOLLIENS au BOIS leaving here at 5.30pm under 2/Lt TAYLOR. 2/Lts HENRY & MANN went with these platoons. Major HUGHES M.C. remains in command of LONDON IRISH there. The Brigadier General called at Bn H.Q.	
	27		Baths at WARLOY. Capt Lt M Ellis M.C. and officers from all Coys and n.c.o.'s reconnoitred AULI LAVIEVILLE LINE in view of which Battn acting on Brigade Orders the Battn relieved the 20th in COURT SUPPORT & JACOB'S SUPPORT and CAVALRY TRENCH. Left WARLOY at 8.30pm and was in situ at V.22.c.8.8. at 9.45pm. The companies were disposed as follows:
A Coy HQ V.22.7.5.5
B " V.22.a.8.9
C " V.22.a.8.1 & 8.3
D " V.22.c.2.2 - C.5.4
HQ Sunken Road V.22.c.3.4 - C.4.8.	
			Capt Alcock left for leave @ ED. 2/Lt Burney M.C. remained at WARLOY personnel to go on leave to ENGLAND on	
	28th			

Army Form C. 2118.

WAR DIARY
or
INTELLIGENCE SUMMARY.
(Erase heading not required.)

Instructions regarding War Diaries and Intelligence Summaries are contained in F. S. Regs, Part II. and the Staff Manual respectively. Title pages will be prepared in manuscript.

Place	Date	Hour	Summary of Events and Information	Remarks and references to Appendices
	28		The Batt'n in support in Reid position. The trenches very wet after the heavy rain – work was done on reconstructing bivouacs. There was enemy shelling on left all the morning and some shells on Bn HQ and there were some casualties amongst R.E. and Working parties. Working parties were provided in 8 hour shifts by all Companies for deep dug-out work. The Bugows called during the morning with ta Bde Int. Offr. During the night the enemy shelled the Valley on two occasions with Gas & H.E. Casualties 1 killed and 2 wounded. Lieut Fentott of the Australian C.E. was attached to us for instruction in patrols and raids.	
	29		The C.O., Adjt & Coy Commdrs went forward to reconnoitre the sector to which we go tomorrow night. Working parties were found for R.E. on deep dugouts. Lieut Lintott instructing platoons of A. by on patrol and raid work. The new C.F. Padre Fall HODEE was brought up by Padre TAYLOR & held a service at 6pm. MKR was carried on on enforcing discipline. The 15g sent a party of R.E. to do similar work. Col SEAGROVE DSO called with reference to taking over from us tomorrow night. The Boche Arty fairly active all round the neighbourhood and sending up night lights in the SERVUS VALLEY.	
	30		Batt'n as for yesterday, work continued on shelters and dugouts in trenches and went. Relief upon Canadian Entire the Battalion moved up to the line the nature the 44th Battalion in the night Advance of Bn Hd held at the front front. 15 Guides were met at X Rds V24.C.2.3	X Rds V24.C.2.3

WAR DIARY
or
INTELLIGENCE SUMMARY.

(Erase heading not required.)

Army Form C. 2118

Place	Date	Hour	Summary of Events and Information	Remarks and references to Appendices
	31		at 9.30 pm. The relief was complete by 1 am. Roumatin Wil "A" Coy sent out a patrol at night. Battn in Right Sub. Section of left sector of Divl front. Reconnoitering parties of 3/131 U.S.A. Regt. for relief tomorrow night. Left MANOR remains with us till relief. — Work on cleaning up refuse on trenches and rubbish continued. "A" Coy sent out a fighting patrol which got into touch with Bosche in Quarry and had 1 killed and 2 wounded. The man killed could not be brought in owing to fire of the enemy. The burial parties in during the morning. The Bosche active with French mortars on front line during the day. Operation orders issued for the relief tomorrow night when we go out to CONDY	

E. N. Ellis Capt.
for O.C London Irish Rifles

141st Bde.
47th Div.

18th BATTALION,

LONDON REGIMENT,

AUGUST 1918.

War Diary
of
18th London Regt. (1st Lon Irish Rifles)
for
August. 1918.

Confidential

"A" Form
MESSAGES AND SIGNALS.

Army Form C. 2121
(In pads of 100.)

No. of Message............

Prefix........Code........m.	Words	Charge.	This message is on a/c of :	Recd. at......m.
Office of Origin and Service Instructions	Sent		..................Service.	Date............
....	At ....m.			From ....
....	To			
....	By		(Signature of "Franking Officer")	By..................

TO—

| Sender's Number. | Day of Month. | In reply to Number. | A A A |

From
Place
Time

The above may be forwarded as now corrected. (Z) ....

....
Censor.   Signature of Addressor or person authorised to telegraph in his name

* This line should be erased if not required.

Order No. 1625. Wt. W3253/   P 511. 27/2. H. & K., Ltd. (E. 2634).

Army Form C. 2118.

WAR DIARY FOR AUGUST 1918.
INTELLIGENCE SUMMARY.
(Erase heading not required.)

147
VOL 41

Instructions regarding War Diaries and Intelligence Summaries are contained in F. S. Regs., Part II. and the Staff Manual respectively. Title pages will be prepared in manuscript.

Place	Date 1918	Hour	Summary of Events and Information	Remarks and references to Appendices
Rive	August 1		Batts in Right Sub-sector of Coll Sector of Right front. American Officer arrived to take over in view of relief in the evening. The Brigadier-General called in the morning. Relief on the orders of the 131st Bath. 131 Regt. U.S.A. were not completed till HENENCOURT CHATEAU and relieved also on our Sector just before the relief the 131st Regt. on our left made a raid on the Sector Left of the HAIRPIN which advised a further advance of retaliation which delayed the relief somewhat. R. Col. men out plied anything & casualty. The C.O., I.O., Coy Comdr. & 10 men per Coy. O.S. Mo. and No.1's of L.Gs. remained in for 24 hours with the American troops. The Battn. marched back to CONTAY with half at WARLOY per Bus. Coy. "C" arrived at CONTAY at 7 a.m. Casualties NIL.	
CONTAY	2		9 a.m. Reveille. Coys. cleaning up in afternoon. The C.O. & other officers & new returned on supervising the O.C. were indeed back to the line to discharge a patrol in front of our Brigade front. It was thought that the Boche were relieving or meant to by this area. He went front 9 4 H.Q. of 31st Battn. 131 U.S.A. per lorry. Leaving line at 8 p.m. with LIEUT. VINCENT, M.C. Orders were received at 12 noon from Brigade to be ready to move at 1 hours notice.	
	3		Bath at CONTAY. Morning spent in cleaning up. Orders received from Brigade that 19th cleaning up and no to be ready to move immediately. Orders received that the Boche had left origin all along the front of our Division. Bath were in at MARGARET THEATRE in the CHARIKOCK park & performance was received with much applause. Bath moved at 5 p.m. arriving in WARLOY at 7.15 p.m. Back Bill being the relief being: - CARSON. WALLABY. MURRAY. WAREGO. Billet in BOUZINCOURT - MILLENCOURT ROAD no before the relief were MAJOR HUGHES D.S.O., M.C. left over command of the	
		7.15 a.m.		

Army Form C. 2118.

WAR DIARY for August, 1918.

INTELLIGENCE SUMMARY.
(Erase heading not required.)

Instructions regarding War Diaries and Intelligence Summaries are contained in F. S. Regs., Part II. and the Staff Manual respectively. Title pages will be prepared in manuscript.

Place	Date	Hour	Summary of Events and Information	Remarks and references to Appendices
In Support			20th Battn. 2/Lt RONEY, "C" Coy, went down sick. Lt-Col. NEELY, M.C. also sick attached to the Australians. Capt. E.M. ELLIS, M.C. temporarily in command of Battn. Several men were left behind sick under 2/Lt MARTIN who were also sick. Patrols reached the bank of the ANCRE in ALBERT under direction of Lt-Col. NEELY, M.C. Casualties NIL.	
	4		20th Battn. no ops yesterday. The General called in the morning and said that we should be taking over the new front line tomorrow night. A reconnoitring party for AUSTRALIA STREET — 2 officers + 50 men from "C" + "D" Coys. 2/Lt STEVENS in charge. 2/Lt SNELL went down sick. Lt-Col. NEELY, M.C. called in mid-day. Took to Brigade HQ. 2/Lt TAYLOR + HILL informed the Battn. from Brigade training camp. Transfd. to "C" Coy. Latter to "B" Coy. 2/Lt MARTIN rejoined from WARLOY. Lieut VINCENT, M.C. went down to WARLOY in the a.m. to LE TOUQUET for 10 days rest. Casualties NIL.	
	5		20th Battn. no ops yesterday. Relief in operation. Orders to relieve the 3rd Battn. 131 U.S.A. Regt. The C.O. reconnoitred the front in the morning + met Lieut KERNAN who they accompanied thus over positions — "C" + "B" Coys. in the old Boche line and "A" + "D" Coys as CAREY, WARD, SWAN — Batt OR Boundary CAREY South Battn. North Battn. AUSTRALIA. Coys moved off at 9 p.m. The relief was complete by 12.45, which was quick, as all were very dark + pouring with rain, + the formed a succesfl. Two patrols of "B" Coy — 1 under 2/Lt MACKENZIE + 1 under 2/Lt VERNON — 1 Serjeant + 15 ORs each + 1 Lt. went into ALBERT as far as the ANCRE when the enemy were quiet. No further information collected without casualties. Battn. HQ. MELBOURNE RIGHT Rd.Stn H.R. — "A" Coy, CAREY Toh in W.26.a, WARD + SWAN in W.26.b — "D" Coy, CAREY in W 20. C + d. & SWAN in 20.d. — "B" Coy in Boche W.21.d. 2.5. and onwards to MILLEN COURT — ALBERT ROAD. — "C" Coy	

Army Form C. 2118.

WAR DIARY for August, 1918.

INTELLIGENCE SUMMARY.
(Erase heading not required.)

Instructions regarding War Diaries and Intelligence Summaries are contained in F. S. Regs., Part II. and the Staff Manual respectively. Title pages will be prepared in manuscript.

Place	Date	Hour	Summary of Events and Information	Remarks and references to Appendices
In line			On Recche & front line from W 22 C.1.3. southwards to MILLENCOURT ROAD. 2/Lt MARTIN at N.Q. as Intell. Officer. Casualties NIL.	
	6		The Battn. on the 6th inst. and 7th. On Adjutant's arrival the front of "D" Coy moved forward and to support this Coy the left platoon of "O" Coy moved forward to N. of QUARRY at W.27. & of front touch with the 2nd W. York. 17 6th B. to the M railway and headquarters at W.22.d.7.4. Whilst at 17 6th B. 2/Lt NEELY M.C. 2/Lt Macchenzie & a patrol of 12 O.R. approached Lt. Col. NEELY M.C. 2/Lt Macchenzie & a patrol of 12 O.R. arrived at. at W.9.C.1.3. where near ALBERT + were fired on from the cathedral. 2/Lt Macchenzie was wounded in the arm of which he died. 2/Lt N.E.E.LY M.C. & 3 OR got his body away. Warning received this that a hostile force at W.45.c.9.3., a fight ensuing in the course of which 2/Lt Keene & his men ("D") to attack if + on hearing which will send my own line about 9.45 p.m. and during the operation. The boy left own line about 9.45 p.m. MILLENCOURT-ALBERT ROAD. B.P.Coluct. 8 Platoon front - MILLENCOURT-ALBERT ROAD. 2.P.Coluct.19 BAZINCOURT-ALBERT ROAD. Lts.Baxter under Lieut KEANE proceeded across Albert-Alhencourt road towards its objective, followed about 100 yds. by 2/Lt HALL M.C. + remainder who met 2 accomplices Lt Col. NEELY M.C.+ 2/Lt ELLIS, M.C. & party of 12 2/Lt Baxter American corner between the trio + his platoon Coy ELLIS, M.C. & party of 12 2/Lt Baxters 2/Lt. + rifle fire, 2/Lts HALL with Capt ELLIS + remained 2/Lt HALL with a + contacted with the Am. HOLD 1 OR + wounded several and rifle fire, Avid. KEANE front line 2/Lt HALL 1 OR + wounded several went to withdraw owing to support became 2/Lt HALL had 3 wounded. All Canalties were carried back 2/Lt NICHOLL and his platoon encountered an enemy - 2/LtBAXTER and his men encountered a M.G. fire from the vicinity and this men encountered a M.G. fire from the vicinity at W.2.5. & 9.3. from which his men hadowning to which he had M.G. fire from the cathedral and owing to which he had to withdraw. - 2/Lt Casualties 2 Capt B.N.ELLIS M.C.	

Army Form C. 2118.

WAR DIARY for August, 1918.
INTELLIGENCE SUMMARY.
(Erase heading not required.)

Place	Date	Hour	Summary of Events and Information	Remarks and references to Appendices
In line.	7.		killed) 2/Lt R.W.E. HALL and J.D.R. BAXTER wounded; 2 O.Rs. killed, 7 wounded, 1 missing.	
			Battn. in same position. A very quiet day. 'C' Coy. pushed out posts towards Railway embankment to connect up with the 19th Bn. A.I.F. Regt. 2/Lt MACKENZIE with a patrol reached ALBERT to try & find Bosch by the enemy but found that a patrol of some 40 or 50 were picked up a certain amount of equipment dropped by the retreating men. No hostile harassing into ALBERT during the night and no enemy being encountered with gas. 2/Lt BROOKES joined the Bath. for duty and was posted to "D" Coy.	
	8		A quiet morning. Battn. disposed as for yesterday. At 8 p.m. ALBERT was heavily bombarded with H.E., shrapnel & gas shell. M.G. & L.G.s continued on the operation. Enemy put our fire into ALBERT almost immediately. All Bosches 5.50 and our patrols about into ALBERT almost immediately. All Brooks had cleared out except two Officers whose heads which fired on our patrols by 5.95. The 2/Lt Stoll[?] proved a very bad obstacle to a patrol during Barrage. At 2/Lt STOLL[?] three casualties added to others our 2nd 6" and 60 patrol were stopping short by old German line and B.	
	9		This Bn. practised & continued during "Stand to" with additional shells to the lighter fires. The remainder of the day was quiet. The Bn. 11 Division carried and an attack which was partially successful, but were forced to [...] appeared to be most successful. Major Hughes joined the Batth. II (Capt Col) A.G. KEANE relieved to Cadre command of Batth. Battn. 2/Lt SLAVEN(?) (Capt. R.) 2/Lt MARTIN received an L.G. gun transfer course. The L. Sergeants of Bath. pieceded on such relieved another L.P. Colours in this line. 2/Lt. TEA proceeded to Junior of Camp. 2/Lts. Humming[?] & [...] joined from Camp.	

Army Form C. 2118.

WAR DIARY for August 1918.

INTELLIGENCE SUMMARY.
(Erase heading not required.)

Instructions regarding War Diaries and Intelligence Summaries are contained in F. S. Regs., Part II. and the Staff Manual respectively. Title pages will be prepared in manuscript.

Place	Date	Hour	Summary of Events and Information	Remarks and references to Appendices
In Line	10		A/Col. NEELY M.C. selected as one of officers to be presented to H.M. THE KING & H.M. Q/H. MICHAEL & escorted by H.M. THE KING & H.M. Q/H. MICHAEL one platoon pas and ALBERT only a few enemy aircraft active and street not noisy. Bn was disposed as for yesterday. Very quiet day with practically no shelling. A/Col NEELY left the line in the afternoon. Arrangements for relief of the Battn started at 4 p.m. In accordance with order to b/s on the right also started at night relief completed to the part of ALBERT west of the river developing well to the part of ALBERT to the E. of MEAULTE. The 13th Bn. relieved in the line by the 8 B Bn. NORTHANTS Brigade. 18th Division. Relief complete. Bn comp. left on of relief at 12 am moved into BRIDLY in WARLOY.	
WARLOY	11		2/L Batt. at BIVIVS at WARLOY Batta. arrived F.M.O. at 11.45 and marched to BOIS DE MAL. Accommodation had to be improvised as their H.Q. & Officers arranged orders arrival of H.Q. staff there were 3 billets. 56th Division train E.4 passed through during night only to relieve 56th Division train E.4 passed through during night are to be shipped on close [illegible]	
BOIS DE MAL	12		2/L. Batta. accommodated in BOIS DE MAL. On morning spent in improving camp into Bn. teams and 1st Battle supplied Regiment was procured to Battn. Division on the 2/L C.O. and to talk with army Nos. 10 Column S/15, C.R. M.S. & Platoon of Division formed and assembled to at 6 p.m. and night the aid of a Division termed from the Divisional Y.M.C.A. some 2000 attended amongst whom were the Brigadier commander, who praised for were through to relieve Beaconfil Bn C - 58 Bn Bole. Passing aerial activity not very great	

WAR DIARY for August 1918.

INTELLIGENCE SUMMARY.

Army Form C. 2118.

Instructions regarding War Diaries and Intelligence Summaries are contained in F.S. Regs., Part II. and the Staff Manual respectively. Title pages will be prepared in manuscript.

(Erase heading not required.)

Place	Date	Hour	Summary of Events and Information	Remarks and references to Appendices
	13		Battn in bivouacs in BOIS DE MAI. Battn moved by route march from BOIS DE MAI to bivouacs in J.19 (Sheet 62 D N.E.). Route QUERRIEU — LAHOUSSOYE — FRANVILLERS — HEILLY. The whole Battn arrived in new area at about 5.30 p.m. only one train load having fallen out en route to accommodate 2 ft trainload in full number of stragglers, shells and trench mortar ammn. O.C. Coys. Transport Limbers + O.M. Stores at BONNAY. During the night a light front deluge of rain + about 1000 yds from Battn H.Q. had an enemy aeroplane in flight on 3 Germans being killed while one escaped in trenches.	
	14		Battn in bivouacs - shelters + dug-outs in J.19. The men between nine ANCRE + afternoon to work placed with clean clothes, being employed in clearing up the ground each evening. Aircraft dropped bombs in vicinity of bivouacs — no casualties. 40 casualties.	
	15		Battn in bivouacs etc. at J.13. Battn turned at 9.15 a.m. orders received at 11 a.m. for which operation of defensive of any possible advance due if may speed in rest.	
	16		Battn ordered no. for 125th Battn carried out attack on the high ground HEILLY from the RAILWAY S of HEILLY to the 84.583 BEARD WOODS. Buried in Bn afternoon word of the one into of into the now ANCRE. He was later lost of the period left. Information the actual was repealed at 6 p.m.	
	17		Battn on rest etc. Battn turned at 9.15 a.m. during which M. General Sir A.J. GODLEY K.C.B., K.C.M.G. 10th Corps. Commanded, arrived in a car and held our former inspection of the Battn. He was very pleased	

Army Form C. 2118.

WAR DIARY for August 1918.

INTELLIGENCE SUMMARY.
(Erase heading not required.)

Instructions regarding War Diaries and Intelligence Summaries are contained in F. S. Regs., Part II. and the Staff Manual respectively. Title pages will be prepared in manuscript.

Place	Date	Hour	Summary of Events and Information	Remarks and references to Appendices
	15		indeed and particularly admired the flashes and green cuffs of the Rifles. After the Inspection Coys spent nearly two hours at Coy. Commdrs. for General Remainder of day spent in rest.	
			Sunday. Bath. Church Parade at 10.30 a.m. The Brigadier was present and the Battn in deployed part. The afternoon was devoted to cricket, a match with the 1/5 Essex Rgt. between Batn. Oficers and Transport Station, the latter winning by 9 runs.	
	19		Batn. marched Incesand & service on car's ground as per 16th inst. The SHAMROCKS gave an open-air Concert which was highly appreciated by the Troops. Operation orders received for Batn. to move forward & relieve 17th London Regt.	
IN SUPPORT	20		Coys carried out Tactical Scheme in the morning and prepared for move up to the line. Battn moved forward in accordance with O.O.3 and relieved the 17th London Regt in support in area W.G.7 TAILLES WOOD.	
	21		Rain returned to be last night. Enemy artillery occasional shell around 47th Bn. in line. Much of 12 to 10.00 in our left and an occasional 4.7 from Batn. in section with 12th Bn. The 14th Inf. Bde attacking on the 47 fronts knocked 19 hundreds on left, 20th hundreds on right, 14 London Irish Rifles in support. The Brigade moved forward to the assembly position at the ...	xxx
	22		moved at 4.45 am 22nd inst. Battn. H.Q. were formed at K.11.d.8.7. The advance by Coys was quite successful by 7 a.m. R.R. Btn Rgts. about K.11.d.8.7. The advance by Coys was quite successful and Very respect about five hundred prisoners, who, some after a stubborn defence and were ... of the attack. Casualties during the day 1 officer & 11 MACKENZIE and about 25 O.Rs. Killed and wounded.	

Army Form C. 2118.

WAR DIARY for August 1918.

INTELLIGENCE SUMMARY.

(Erase heading not required.)

Instructions regarding War Diaries and Intelligence Summaries are contained in F.S. Regs., Part II. and the Staff Manual respectively. Title pages will be prepared in manuscript.

Place	Date	Hour	Summary of Events and Information	Remarks and references to Appendices
			The Batt. moved forward to the attack at ZERO, 4.30 a.m. following 500 yds. in rear of the leading Battn. The enemy put down a very heavy Bar. and H E barrage on the Old British line at ZERO and for two hours following. The Battn. progressed favourably and the objective (marked in blue on Map A) was attained by 7 a.m. The following Batt. Coy. Officers were wounded. Lieut. C. R. C. VINCENT "A" Coy. - all the Batt. Coy Commanders and all their platoons moved forward took command, and led them to their objective and remained there. Batt. H.Q. moved forward with	
		7 a.m.	147th Inf Bde. at 5.25 a.m. and 106 of the Brigade Platoons badly needed ammunition supplied by two 3 Platoons of "B" Coy. Bell had moved through the same. Officer in "D" Coy. at one time 3 officers (including Batt. Comdr.) and 102 O.Rs. On completion of this the platoons were split up and formed a gap which had been left between 142 Bde. and	
		4 p.m.	147 Bde. At 4 p.m. the enemy heavily shelled the 142 Inf. Bde. and thin ettachment drove them back. Some considerable numbers straggled through the H.Q. and were closely formed by them. This was was established by Batt. from his C.O. to the support platoons of W. of BROWN LINE. These party in BROWN LINE, 142 Inf. Bde. and 17th Battn. front line, then pushed up and held BROWN LINE as far as FORKED TREE.	
	6.30 p.m		Enemy broke in HAPPY VALLEY, BROWN LINE of our attachment held. In touch with 13 R. Brig. also on right of FORKED TREE.	
	9 p.m.		Conference of C.Os. of Brigade. C.Os. L.I.R. and 17th Hundred reconnoitred and found unoccupied. Line E of BRAY-MEAULTE ROAD and our line running S. of some from PEAR TREE.	
22/23	mid.night		Right of 17th Battn. 140 full Bde. formed Bn. pickets. L.I.R. withdrawn to new position in support. 15th Battn. Right. L.I.R. withdrawn to new position in support.	
23	10.45 a.m.		Right of 17th Battn. was much under heavy attack across L.I.R. and to their rear, two platoons right + centre L.I.R. dug furiously. 19th Coy. had however just been ordered to push up.	

Army Form C. 2118.

WAR DIARY for August 1918.

INTELLIGENCE SUMMARY.

(Erase heading not required.)

Place	Date	Hour	Summary of Events and Information	Remarks and references to Appendices
	24		A circus establishing M.G. and rifle posts at BRAY-MÉAULTE ROAD. Lieut. VINCENT and rifle platoon of "D" coy, who were forward of the BRAY-MÉAULTE ROAD, with portion of 19th Bn. in reserve in the day, then withdrew W of main road. Enemy artillery was however very active all through the day on line of sunken road, being the avenue of approach were received that the 14th Inf. Bde. was to make good the line of the sunken road to enable the 140 Inf. Bde. to form up for their attack on the GREEN LINE. This operation was carried out by 50 O.Rs. per coy. at 10 p.m. and was entirely successful (resulting in the each capture of 2 officers and 65 O.Rs. and 7 M.G's.) The Battn. remained on this line and bivouacked.	
	25		The M.O. left Bn. passed through the Bde. to attack the GREEN LINE at 1 a.m. but it rapidly becoming apparent there was heavy shell-fire carried losses for it & the two Bdes. to withdraw. These men were however collected by the 11th K. and helpers formed to their original position. The enemy heavy artillery fire continued not allowing the Battn. to consolidate with any complete their positions on the BROWN LINE all day. At 9.30 p.m. Bn. was relieved by the 11th Essex of the GREEN LINE at S. Valerys Quarries and from there marched to heights E of M.G. to hold up road between Battn. and clearing to heights E of the railway E of BRAY-MÉAULTE ROAD (from F.27.b.2.9 – F.20.d.15 (62 D N.E.) The 14th Inf. Bde. after this was attached to G.O.C. 58th Div. to [...] 24 hrs. then relieved to the command of G.O.C. 47th Div. which bn. became known as Green Reserve Battn. It was at 4 a.m. on 26th that the return fmt. It of the Battn. took effect. During the [...] the Bn. enabled captured equipment and conveyed it to L.G. [...] [...] of rifle ammn. joined the Battn. in its march to Canada G.A. [...] (G.R.C.) at HAPPY VALLEY. Casualties from August 23rd to date: 5 officers wounded 7, being Lieut. Col. G.H. NEELY, M.C. (on duty), 2/Lt. A.F. MACKENZIE, 2/Lt. LA MANN	

Army Form C. 2118.

WAR DIARY for August 1918.

INTELLIGENCE SUMMARY.
(Erase heading not required.)

Instructions regarding War Diaries and Intelligence Summaries are contained in F.S. Regs., Part II. and the Staff Manual respectively. Title pages will be prepared in manuscript.

Place	Date	Hour	Summary of Events and Information	Remarks and references to Appendices
	26		2/LT. E. MICHAEL, D.O.M., 2/LT. R.D. VERNON, LIEUT. O.R.C. VINCENT, M.C., 2/LT A.H. FARRANT (gassed). O.R.s killed + wounded 204. The A.D.C. Division and the Brigade Commander visited the Batt. during the day and congratulated the Commanding Officer on the success of the Batt. during its previous days fighting.	
	27		Batt. in some position. Slight shelling principally in direction of the COPSE. All A.G.s captured from enemy were cleaned from damaged dumps and sent down to Brigade. Total: 63 light and heavy M.G.s and 6 T.M.s. Also a few anti-tank Rifles. The C.O. inspected two dumps the morning & the number up of the day being spent in resting up, and refitting etc. Reinforcements and tailors. The Batt. received light Coy's in the afternoon to the SOMME at BRAY to see the 2nd Entrs. attack of the platoon from MOLLIEN - AU-BOIS rejoined the Batty. and about 135 man R.O. Coy + H.Q. were sent back to the Junction to B. Battalion 2/Lts. HILL, SIMPSON & HAMMOND joined the Batt. LIEUT MACDONALD reported to the Transport Lines.	
	28		LT KEANE rejoined the Batt. and relieved the Adjutant Capt. T.F.G. CARLESS. C.O. and staff proceeded to the Transport Lines at MERICOURT L'ABBÉ, calling Rds HQ on the way. The Arrow + a systematic emptying out of all over was carried out, and a part of 140 man was successfully sent up to join the Batt. The C.O. returned to the Batt. along to p.m. The A/M returning for the night. Capt. OVRLING and 2/LT MARTIN rejoined the Battalion and A.C.L. RICKS and PAGES (gassed).	
FAVIERE WOOD	29		The Batt. moved from the GREEN LINE to FAVIERE WOOD in the evening stopping at CARNOY in the way for tea. Rations were suddenly received on the morning for the transport lines by motor to a position ½ mile N. of MANE 72 move to dal F at 3 p.m. at 1.30 p.m. a draft of 200 O.R. arrived. They were roughly paraded to Coys 50 to each Coy. a source from the 12/11th Suffolks taking charge of each Coy's draft.	

WAR DIARY for August 1918.

INTELLIGENCE SUMMARY.

Place	Date	Hour	Summary of Events and Information	Remarks and references to Appendices
	30		Lieut MACDONALD taking charge of the whole. Having had the aer/p/ followed the transport which had already moved to MARIETZ. The aeroplane riding on ahead found out locations of Batts. and moved forward in the evening via MARICOURT with the relieve to join up again. a quiet night was spent in an Artillery HQ in the wood.	
	31		At 6.50 am orders were received for a move at once, as the 47th Div. were to move forward through the 12th Div. the 142 Inf. Bde forming the advanced guard the 141 Inf. Bde being in support. the Batt. moved forward as an advance guard to a position N.E. of MAUREPAS, Batt. HQ and A Coy in the wood with C & D Coys forming the advance. B and D Coy took up a position in the MAUREPAS RAVINE the Batt. was accommodated about 8.45 a.m. at 11am orders were received for 141 Inf. Bde to move forward towards HOSPITAL FARM to the objective detailed third between 142 Inf. Bde. and 58th Div. The Bde moved about 2 p.m. 20 pdrs. iv. 20th Batt. in front, 19th Batt. in Reserve. The Batts. moved in artillery formation, "C" Coy on Right, "A" Coy on Left, "B" in Support, through LE FORREST and took up a position at 4.10 p.m. S.W. of HOSPITAL FARM with "A" Coy in HOSPITAL FARM. 20th Batth. came under fire from 5. G/s finishing with shells stopped from the direction of ARDENLU WOOD. as this came down the slopes of MAUREPAS ridge to LE FORREST. it was found however necessary on account of the rifle and m/g fire from a small town in a wood at the Left of the line is mainly opposed by the left of the 58th Div. Riumour Batt. 58th Div. at 6.30 p.m. orders were received for the Batt. to advance up to the 142 Inf. Bde. in a position S. of ARDENLU WOOD and in rear of the 142 Inf. Bde. Heavy enemy Shelling caused shortly after, and nine other ranks were casualties in the way. 142 Inf. Bde on the Left had 58 Div. attacked with the 142 Inf. Bde on the Left and 58th Div on the Right the objective being the HALLU-RANCOURT-BOUCHAVESNES ROAD. 20/21st LI Bn to be left B Bn to form a defensive flank N. 19 Inf. Batth in support. 21st Bn 20th Bn Right Batth. ZERO – 1 hour in a line running E.N. and	

Army Form C. 2118.

WAR DIARY for August 1918.

INTELLIGENCE SUMMARY.

(Erase heading not required.)

Instructions regarding War Diaries and Intelligence Summaries are contained in F. S. Regs., Part II. and the Staff Manual respectively. Title pages will be prepared in manuscript.

Place	Date	Hour	Summary of Events and Information	Remarks and references to Appendices
NEEDLE WOOD			S. about 200 yds W. of HOSPITAL FARM. "A" Coy on Right with "B" Coy in left Support, "B" Coy Right Support. A gap of about 1000 yds had been purposely left 142 Bde. and 141 Bde. this gap was supposed to be covered by M.G. fire but this the M.Gs. failed to do. The Batn. gained their objective but lost heavily in doing so, 60% of the casualties however being caused by our own barrage which was very short.	
		11 a.m	The enemy shells who were very heavy all the morning put at 11. a.m. the enemy were seen to be attacking hard a stand through was stopped in front, executed an effecting a lodgment in the gap between the 142 Inf. Bde. and our left. A Company of the 19th Battn. led by Lt. T.I. JONES. M.M. and O.S. Coy counter-attacked successfully drove out the enemy and captured 25 prisoners. Heavy shell & M.G. fire continued all day and caused heavy casualties.	
		5 p.m	At 5 p.m. posts had been established on the RANCOURT–BOUCHAVESNE'S ROAD, but owing to RANCOURT still being in possession of the 142 Bde. and in spite of attempts and enquiries on the left of the Battn. and counter-attacked by the 19th Battn. London Regt., no M.G. fire continued to push in all it attempts and enquiries on the left of the Battn. were relieved during the night by the 19th Battn. London Regt. and withdrew to NEEDLE WOOD (5 companies.	

Approved Lt.Colonel
O.C.
London Irish Rifles

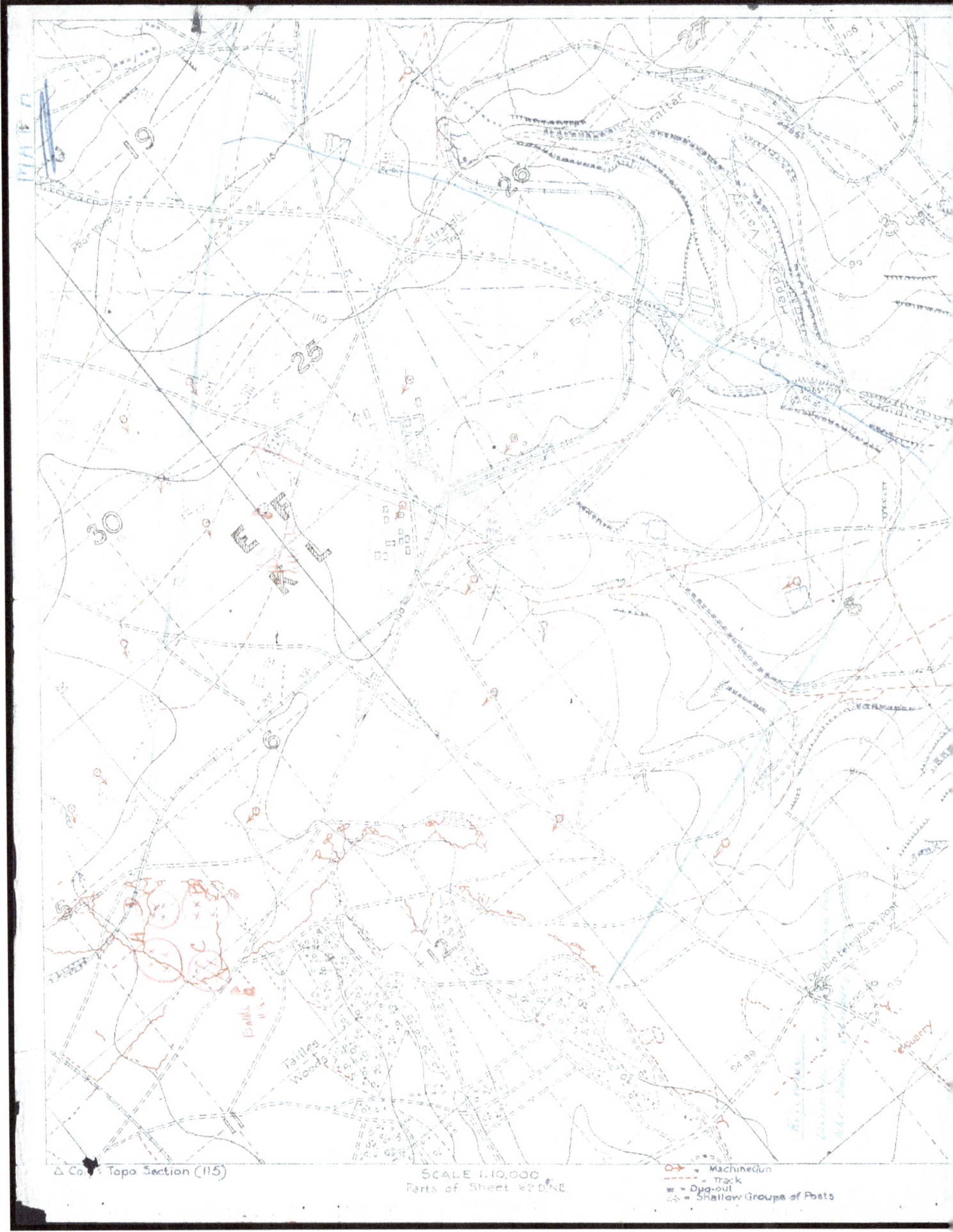

ø insert Map ref. or mark on map.

1. I am at ø _____
2. I am at ø _____ and am consolidating.
3. I am at ø _____ and have consolidated.
4. Am held up by M.G. at ø _____
5. I need :-
    Ammunition.
    Bombs.
    Rifle Grenades.
    Water.
    Very Lights.
    Rations.

6. Counter attack forming up at ø _____
7. I am in touch with _____ on Right at ø _____
                                                      Left _____
8. I am not in touch on Right
                        Left ø _____
9. Am being shelled from ø _____
10. I estimate my present strength at _____ Rifles.
11. Hostile (Battery   )
           (Machine gun) active at ø _____
           (Trench Mortar)

Time   Name.
Date   Rank.
Hqrs. at.   Platoon.
                        Company
                        Battalion.

1. In the event of capture, a soldier must give his name and rank, if so required. Any soldier who gives any further information than this is betraying his country and his comrades.

2. All documents should be taken from Officers and N.C.O. prisoners, but not from private soldiers.

3. All captured documents will be forwarded without delay to Brigade H.Q.

4. No personal property is to be taken from prisoners.

Army Form C. 2118.

Instructions regarding War Diaries and Intelligence Summaries are contained in F.S. Regs., Part II. and the Staff Manual respectively. Title pages will be prepared in manuscript.

WAR DIARY for month of September 1918.

or

INTELLIGENCE SUMMARY.

(Erase heading not required.)

118th Bn.

Place	Date	Hour	Summary of Events and Information	Remarks and references to Appendices
	1		On the morning of the 1st the Battalion attacked in support to the 19th & 20th Battalion and reached its objective 600 yards short of ST PIERRE VAAST - MOISLAINS WOODS. That night we were ordered to relieve the 6th Service Rifles who held the left of the Divisional front. This did so with a draft of 200 recruits who came up that night.	
	2		On the morning of the 2nd we took advantage of an attack proceeding on our right to mop up a pocket that had been left by the 21st Battalion in AMAZON and AMULET Trenches. During this operation we captured 2 Officers and 65 other ranks and drove a party of about the same strength into the 142 Bde front where they surrendered. On the night of the 2nd we were relieved by Companies of the Machine Gunners and marched back to HOSPITAL FARM.	
	3		At HOSPITAL FARM. Resting, and refreshing.	
	4		At HOSPITAL FARM. Resting, and refreshing. On the evening of the 4th we moved forward to HIT CUT just east of the BOUCHAVESNES - RANCOURT Road	
	5		On the morning of the 5th the Battalion advanced behind the 19th & 20th Bns. across the CANEL DU NORD just north of MOISLAINS under heavy shell fire and advanced between the QUARRY west of PERONNE - NURLU Road. The leading Battalions were held up 600 yds short of their objective when we joined them. The attack was returned at 7 pm. The 19th & 20th Bns. and the left half of the 19th Bn. failed to attack but objective was the QUARRY. At it I was impossible to get into the QUARRY unless the enemy was driven from the main road, two substantial and made good. Two companies were pushed through the 19th & 20th Bns. that captured and consolidated the line of the main Road & 18th remained two companies north up the QUARRY.	
	6		On the morning of the 6th the 19th & 20th Bns. were ordered to capture the line of trenched 800 yds east of the PERONNE - NURLU Road by 8 AM. Redoubled to Brigade HQ. that they had done so, whereupon the London Scot. were to receive order to push through them, capture the village of LIERAMONT and establish a line running North and South 600 yds East of LIERAMONT. The 12th. Division on the left and the 41st Division on the	

WAR DIARY
INTELLIGENCE SUMMARY

Army Form C. 2118.

(Erase heading not required.)

Instructions regarding War Diaries and Intelligence Summaries are contained in F. S. Regs., Part II. and the Staff Manual respectively. Title pages will be prepared in manuscript.

Place	Date	Hour	Summary of Events and Information	Remarks and references to Appendices
	7.		Right were to conform to the Advance of the 49th Division. At 8:10 AM the 19th & 20th Bns and still held on the PERONNE - NURLU Road by some marked Gunned. A patrol of the London Scots advanced on the right flank of the 19th Bn across the road. About half the remnant formed and captured the remainder, and the advance was then resumed by the 19th & 20th Bns. The London Scots following immediately behind pushed through them and advanced on LIERAMONT. The 7th & Division on the Right did not move forward from EPINETTE WOOD till 11.30 AM. and the 12th Division on the Left debouched from the village of NURLU at 1.47 pm. We captured the village of LIERAMONT and reached our objective 600 yds East of the village at 1.12 pm. The Battalion was relieved from this position the Same night by units of the 58th Division. On completion of relief the Bn. moved back to huts East of MOISLAINS. Bn. was met by cookers etc.	
	8.		Battalion arrived in huts about 5.30 AM. Orders received to prepare to entrain W. of MOISLAINS at 7 AM. The Battalion had breakfasts, obtained their packs, which had been brought to the huts by Transport in the early morning and moved off to the embarking point at about 8 AM. After waiting for about an hour the Battalion & 2 too men under the Senior for whom busses had not been provided, embussed and proceeded to CORBIE, which was reached about 4 pm. Billets' good.	
			At CORBIE. Morning spent in refitting and bathing. At 6 pm a Concert was given by the "SHAMROCKS" in the Convent Hall of the ANZAC CORPS. This Concert was undoubtedly the best the Troupe has given to date, and the audience was over 400, very largely Australian.	
	9.		At CORBIE. Orders received to entrain at 10 AM - did not do so until 3 pm. Learned CORBIE for CALONNE - RIQUART at about 4.30 pm CALONNE was reached about 6 AM to march Battalion marched from CALONNE to billets in RAIMBERT. Billets clean and comfortable, but very scattered. Remainder of day spent in refitting.	
	10.		At RAIMBERT. Remainder at disposal of Company Commanders for refitting and cleaning up	
	11.			

Army Form C. 2118.

WAR DIARY
-or-
INTELLIGENCE SUMMARY.
(Erase heading not required.)

Instructions regarding War Diaries and Intelligence Summaries are contained in F. S. Regs., Part II. and the Staff Manual respectively. Title pages will be prepared in manuscript.

Place	Date	Hour	Summary of Events and Information	Remarks and references to Appendices
RAIMBERT	12		At RAIMBERT. Bn Parade at 11.0 am on the Main Road outside Bn HQ from where the Battalion marched to TERFAY CHATEAU Grounds for drill and relieved by the Commanding Officer. Battalion Dinner at 7.30 pm in the evening at Bn HQ at which the Brigadier and his staff were guests of the Battalion. The following officers joined the Battalion during the evening, and were posted to companies as follows :- Lieut F.L. HAINES "B" Coy, 2/Lt C.H. GIPP "B" Coy, 2/Lt Y.S. SANDERSON "C" Coy, 2/Lt G.H. PICTON "D" Coy. The Battalion Band and Runners changed again from "SHORTS" into Trousers owing to the cold weather.	
RAIMBERT	13		Battalion Parade 9.15 am. marched to Chateau Grounds, where Battalion Drill and Company Training was carried out. A concert was given in the evening by the "SHAMROCKS" to which 150 of the inhabitants of RAIMBERT were admitted free. The Stars Band not good enough to be noticed by the village children. The following officers joined the Battalion and were posted to companies as follows :- 2/Lt G TANNATT "A" Coy, 2/Lt F GARSIDE "A" Coy, 2/Lt R.G APPERY MM. "B" Coy, 2/Lt A.T. HARWOOD "C" Coy, 2/Lt F.N. KING "C" Coy, 2/Lt S.A. COVERDALE "A" Coy, 4/Lt L.T. DEWSON "D" Coy.	
RAIMBERT	14		Battalion Parade 9.15 am - had to be washed out owing to the bad weather. Company carried out indoor training, especially Lewis Gun classes. Lieut R. SHERIDAN joined the Battalion from hospital and reported to "B" Company.	
RAIMBERT	15		Battalion Guarded at Divine Service at 11.30 am. Rev Mr Wills officiated. On completion of Service the Battalion formed up in line on the road for inspection by the XIII Corps Commander. Lt Gen Sir H.K. Morland, K.C.B, K.C.M.G, A.S.O. On completion of which the Battalion marched past in Column of Route. A men's Smoking Concert was held in the evening in a large marquee.	
RAIMBERT	16		Battalion Parade at 9 AM marched to TERFAY Chateau Grounds for Bn drill after which Commanding Commanding had Company training. At 6 pm the "SHAMROCKS" gave a Concert in the School on completion of which the Bn Wills went to Brigade H.Q. to play for a dinner to which the Brigadier and Guards Commanding Officer	

Army Form C. 2118.

WAR DIARY
or
INTELLIGENCE SUMMARY.
(Erase heading not required.)

Instructions regarding War Diaries and Intelligence Summaries are contained in F. S. Regs., Part II. and the Staff Manual respectively. Title pages will be prepared in manuscript.

Place	Date	Hour	Summary of Events and Information	Remarks and references to Appendices
RAIMBERT	17		The Battalion paraded to the ranges at B.6.d (Sheet 44 B) for the whole day. Cookers and dinners were taken out and dinner had out on the range. In the evening the Orchestra went to play at Divnn at Divisional H.Q.	
RAIMBERT	18		Parties allotted to the Bn. for the whole morning; whilst not training the "SHAMROCKS" went to Lewis Gunnery were continued by Companies. The training of CAUCHY-a-la-TOUR to give a concert to the Machine Gun Battalion. (Showed 45 fts)	
RAIMBERT	19		Battalion Parade 9.15 A.M. after which companies at own continued training. Sports under Platoon Commanders for the whole morning. Parade finished at 12 noon owing to the Battalion Sports in the afternoon. Held at 3 p.m. in TERFAY Chateau Grounds. The afternoon was most successful all the open events won by the Battalion. Whilst the Commanding Officer won the Officer Bending, also the Jumping. Lieuts A & B Capt Sir Charles Yeilwick XIII Corps A.D. being 2nd in Class A. On conclusion of the Sports the Corps Commander very kindly presented the prizes	
RAIMBERT	20		A very wind day on which very little intra company could be done. Lewis Gun classes were continued in billets.	
RAIMBERT	21		Battalion paraded 9.15 A.M. and marched to TERFAY Chateau Grounds where training was carried out	
RAIMBERT	22		Battalion attended Divine Service in the concert Hall. The following Officers joined the Bn. and were posted to Companies as follows: – Lieut J.P. ASHBRIDGE "A" Coy. 2/Lt. E.P. JOHNSON "A" Coy 2/Lt. A.R. SMITH "B" Coy. 2/Lt. K.R. SHREWSBURY "C" Coy. 2/Lt. J.K. O'DONOGHUE "A" Coy.	
RAIMBERT	23		Battalion paraded at 9.15 a.m. and marched to TERFAY Chateau Grounds for training. "A" Company on the ranges. 2/Lieut A.T. EAGGER joined the Bn. and posted to "B" Coy.	
RAIMBERT	24		Battalion Paraded at 9.15 A.M. and marched to TERFAY Chateau Grounds. Company training carried out. The shallott drink used being the platoon. "A" Company on the ranges.	

Army Form C. 2118.

WAR DIARY
INTELLIGENCE SUMMARY.
(Erase heading not required.)

Instructions regarding War Diaries and Intelligence Summaries are contained in F. S. Regs., Part II. and the Staff Manual respectively. Title pages will be prepared in manuscript.

Place	Date	Hour	Summary of Events and Information	Remarks and references to Appendices
RAIMBERT	25		Battalion paraded at 9.15AM Battalion Training carried out at FERFAY Chateau Ground.	
RAIMBERT	26		The same as for previous day.	
RAIMBERT	27		Left RAIMBERT at 9 AM and proceeded by march route to PIERREMONT via PERNES and TANGRY Pickets sent out and scouted.	
PIERREMONT	28		Raining hard. Battalion employed on cleaning up.	
PIERREMONT	29		Battalion paraded for Divine Service at which the Major General and Brigadier were present. Training order received re move northward.	
PIERREMONT	30		A very wet day. The Battalion paraded early in the morning but had to return to billets owing to heavy rainfall. Company carried on in billets with small arms drill, Lewis Gun instruction and interior economy.	

Gaffney Lt Col.

War Diary.
of.
1/18th London Regt. (1st London Irish Rifles).
for
October 1918.

Confidential

"A" Form
MESSAGES AND SIGNALS.

Army Form C. 2121
(in pads of 100).

No of Message............

Prefix ......Code......m	Words	Charge	This message is on a/c of :	Recd. at........m.
Place of Origin and Service Instructions				Date............
....	Sent At ....m.		.................Service	From............
....	To............		....	By............
....	By		(Signature of Franking Officer)	

TO {

| Sender's Number | Day of Month | In reply to Number | **AAA** |

From
Place
Time

The above may be forwarded as now corrected.   **(Z)**

.... Censor   Signature of Addressor or person authorised to telegraph in his name

* This line should be erased if not required

(7700.) Wt. W492/M1647 110,000 Pads. 5/17 C & R Ltd. (E 1187.)

Army Form C. 2118.

WAR DIARY for month of October 1918.
INTELLIGENCE SUMMARY.
(Erase heading not required.)

Instructions regarding War Diaries and Intelligence Summaries are contained in F. S. Regs., Part II. and the Staff Manual respectively. Title pages will be prepared in manuscript.

Place	Date	Hour	Summary of Events and Information	Remarks and references to Appendices
PIERREMONT.	1		Moved by march route to ST POL. Entrained at ST POL Station for MERVILLE, and moved by march route to bivouac in field near ESTAIRES. Arrived in billets about 1 A.M. 2nd inst.	
ESTAIRES AREA	2		Left ESTAIRES AREA by march route about 14.30 to relieve a Brigade of the 59th Division in front of HARLECH CASTLE. Information received that the enemy had withdrawn.	
	3		Orders received @ 04/10 ordering the Battalion to move at 0700 to gain touch with the enemy. The Battalion moved forward in artillery formation to South of FROMELLES. Hostile machine Gun fire and snipers very active from the Right. 2/Lieut. J.K. O'DONOGHUE (wounded) and approx. 30 other ranks casualties.	
	4		Advance resumed at 0500. The 143rd Infantry Brigade passed through the 141st Infantry Brigade. The Battalion still slipped and proceeded due East in support to the 19th & 20th Battalions who were subsequently held up near the Railway north of RADINGHEM.	
	5		The Battalion was relieved by the 1/15th London Regt. and moved to O.Y.a in Divisional Reserve. The day was spent in cleaning up etc.	
	6		Battalion in Divisional Reserve. Day spent in cleaning up, refitting of clothing and boots by the Tailors & Shoemakers respectively. The armourer inspected Lewis Guns and rifles.	
	7		The Battalion as for yesterday. Warning Order received to be prepared to relieve 143 Infantry Brigade on night of 8th/9th.	
	8		The Battalion as for yesterday. The Battalion bathed in towns. The warning order received yesterday cancelled, and warning order received to be prepared to relieve 140th Infantry Brigade on night 9/10th.	

Army Form C. 2118.

WAR DIARY
—or—
INTELLIGENCE SUMMARY.
(Erase heading not required.)

Instructions regarding War Diaries and Intelligence Summaries are contained in F. S. Regs., Part II. and the Staff Manual respectively. Title pages will be prepared in manuscript.

Place	Date	Hour	Summary of Events and Information	Remarks and references to Appendices
	9		The Battalion as for yesterday. After dark Battalion moved up and relieved 21st Lon London Rfls. in the Left Subsector. Divisional Front.	7/Lt Lt R.S. Berry proceeded on leave.
	10.		The Battalion in the line. Enemy very quiet all day with the exception of a ½ hour strafe during the afternoon of all calibre - including yellow X Gas. "A" Company relieved "C" Company in front line who moved back as Reserve Company	
	11.		The Battalion in line as for yesterday. Hostile Artillery very quiet.	
	12.		The Battalion in line as for yesterday. Situation quiet. Very wet day. "E" Company relieved "A" Company in front line.	
	13.		Battalion in line as for yesterday. Situation very quiet. Warning Orders received of relief by 54th Division, and that the enemy were withdrawing that night (Information from prisoners) and that all Guns had been with- drawn East of Lille with the exception a few guns to cover his retirement.	
	14.		Battalion in line as for yesterday. At 7.15. A.M. London Rfls. on our Right raided the enemy's lines at 05.00. Message received from Brigade that a German Burial Parsah had been tapped ordering withdrawal on the front last night.	
	15.		Battalion in line as for yesterday. Embankment clear of the enemy. the Battalion was ordered to reassemble round RADINGHEM and dispatch into Divisional Reserve This relief was afterwards cancelled for 1st Bn. 7/K[?]. . D. S.T.M[?]/H/H/ TELLEY wheeled for duty from Base and posted to D Company	

Army Form C. 2118.

WAR DIARY
or
INTELLIGENCE SUMMARY.
(Erase heading not required.)

Instructions regarding War Diaries and Intelligence Summaries are contained in F. S. Regs., Part II. and the Staff Manual respectively. Title pages will be prepared in manuscript.

Place	Date	Hour	Summary of Events and Information	Remarks and references to Appendices
	16		The Battalion in line as for yesterday. Battalion H.Q. was taken over by 172nd Infantry Brigade and Battalion kitchens at 12.00 hours to new FROMELLES where Bn. entrained at 1500 hrs for ESTAIRES arriving there about 17.00 hrs. Billets very good.	
	17		Battalion in billets in ESTAIRES. Entrained at LA GORGUE and returned supply train to AIRE Station and moved by march route to billets at LAMBRES. Billets good. Division came under direct orders of Fifth Army.	
	18		At LAMBRES. Cleaned up and scrubbing of equipment.	
	19		The Battalion in billets at LAMBRES. The Battalion paraded at 10.15 on the main road and marched to field just outside the village for inspection by the Commanding Officer. Lt. J. Clement reported from Base for duty and posted to A Company.	
	20		The Battalion in billets as for yesterday. An "as strong as possible" Brigade Church Parade was to have taken place during the morning, but owing to bad weather, this was cancelled. The Divisional Commander intended holding it in a hangar at the disused aerodrome at C1c X d at which about 50 per Battalion were present. 10 O.R. of this Battalion were decorated.	
	21		The Battalion in billets as for yesterday. The Battalion paraded at 09.15 on the main road LAMBRES - duct Y.M.O. Battalion training was carried out.	

Army Form C. 2118.

WAR DIARY
or
INTELLIGENCE SUMMARY.
(Erase heading not required.)

Place	Date	Hour	Summary of Events and Information	Remarks and references to Appendices
	22.		The Battalion in billets as for yesterday. The Battalion paraded at 09.15 - dress T.M.O. - and proceeded to the training ground in the neighbourhood of the Aerodrome at C.I.E. & d. Battalion training was carried out. Lt. G.A. Burren reported from Base for duty and posted to "D" Company.	
	23.		The Battalion in billets as for yesterday. The Battalion paraded at 09.15 on Main Road - dress T.M.O. - "A", "C" & "D" Companies proceeded to the Training Ground in the neighbourhood of the Aerodrome, and carried out training. "B" Company proceeded to the Range at N.10.d.60.00 for firing practice. The 142nd Infantry Brigade carried out a Tactical Scheme in the ST. VENANT AREA. One Officer from each Company attended. A football match was played between the XI Corps School LINGHEM and the Battalion Team. Result Corps Schools 1 Battalion NIL. The Officers held a dinner in the School Room in lieu of the Battalion Celebration Room at 19.45. The Battalion Orchestra played selections during the dinner and various members of the "SHAMROCKS" entertained afterwards. Notification had received that the following Decorations were awarded.	

D.S.O.   Lt. Col. G.H. NEELY. M.C.
Bar to M.C.   Capt. C.F. BURNAN. M.C.
M.C.   Capt. T.F.G. CARLESS.
M.C.   5/Lt. C.H. GIBBON.
M.C.   Capt. C.A. FEA.
M.C.   7/Lt. F.E. TAYLOR.
M.C.   5/Lt. G.H.R. STANCOURT.
M.C.   Capt. G.F.H. WRAIGHT.

D.C.M.   590048 C.S.M. TILRY. J.
D.C.M.   590414 C.S.M. FULLER. R.

WAR DIARY
INTELLIGENCE SUMMARY

Army Form C. 2118.

Place	Date	Hour	Summary of Events and Information	Remarks and references to Appendices
	24.		The Battalion in billets as for yesterday. The Battalion carried out a Tactical Exercise in the FONTES - LAMBRES Area commencing at 09.30. (Ref. map. 36 A) Disposition "B" Company FRONT - "C" Company RIGHT and "D" LEFT IMMEDIATE SUPPORT - "A" Company RESERVE. INTENTION. The Enemy had been driven out of his positions FONTES - LAMBRES. Information received that the enemy had been reinforced and was holding X Road at N.34.d. - road junction N.34.a.8.6 - N.34.a.0.9 - N.27.b.9.9 - N.21.central WITTERNESSE inclusive. Hostile MGs located at N.28.d.1.4 & N.28.a.central. Hostile battered action from direction of RELY and LONGHEM. Prisoners captured stated that he had been told by officer that a further withdrawal to LIGNY-LES-AIRE - ESTREE BLANCHE line was expected. They were to retire if heavily attacked. The XI Corps will continue the offensive at 10.00 hrs 25th Oct. 19th Div. RIGHT. 47th Div. CENTRE 57th Div LEFT. The 47th Div is to attack with 140 Inf.Bde on RIGHT, 141 Inf.Bde on LEFT and 142 Inf Bde in SUPPORT. Inter-Brigade Boundary June N16.cent. - N.36.cent. 141 Bde will attack with 19th LONDONS on RIGHT, 1st L.I.R on LEFT. 20th LONDONS in SUPPORT. 1st Objective June N.28.d.25. - N.27.b.5.3. - M in LINGHEM - N.20 central 2nd Objective Road N.34.a.2.8 - N.27.c.2.9. - N.20. d.2.0. One 18 pdr Section and one M.G. Section will be attached to each of attacking Battalions, also 2 Vms. The final Objective to be captured and consolidated. Patrols being pushed out to maintain contact with the enemy. Capt H A. STAPLES M.C. returned from Xth Corps School to duty and posted to "B" Company	
	25		The Battalion in billets as for yesterday. The Battalion paraded on the main Road LAMBRES at 09.15 - drill T.H.O. "A" "B" & "D" Companies proceeded to the Training Ground in the neighbourhood of the Aerodrome for Battalion training. "C" Company proceeded to the Range for Lewis & practice. Orders were received during the afternoon for move to forward Area. Transport moved off to ESTAIRES Area. Battalion specially detailed provided ahead to LOMMES.	

Army Form C. 2118.

WAR DIARY
— or —
INTELLIGENCE SUMMARY.
(Erase heading not required.)

Instructions regarding War Diaries and Intelligence Summaries are contained in F. S. Regs., Part II. and the Staff Manual respectively. Title pages will be prepared in manuscript.

Place	Date	Hour	Summary of Events and Information	Remarks and references to Appendices
	26		The Battalion in billets as for yesterday. Left LAMBRES and moved to BERGUETTE Station thence by train to PERENCHIES and hence by march route to LOMME. Billets good, empty houses. Battalion cleaned equipment and got all ready for march through LILLE.	
	27		The Battalion in billets at LOMME. Cleaned up.	
	28		(Sunday) The Battalion left billets at LOMME and moved by march route through the town of LILLE in the following order. Band, H.Q., A, C & D Companies. 2 cookers of limbered transport, 1 small cart. "B" Company provided a Cordon round the GRANDE PLACE. The Battalion marched "At Attention" from PORTE DE CANTELEU until after crossing the GRANDE PLACE. A 10 minutes halt was called before reaching the GRANDE PLACE in order to allow time for the Army Commander to present his Standard to the Mayor of LILLE. The remainder of the Transport moved from LOMME to new billets in the FAUBOURG DE FIVES Area. The Battalion on completion of march through LILLE proceeded to this Area. Billets very good — all officered and men of the men in beds.	
	29		Battalion in billets in the FAUBOURG DE FIVES Area. Warning Order received to be prepared to move forward on the 30th inst. Combined at the disposal of Company Commanders for training.	
	30		The Battalion in billets as for yesterday. Moved by march route to WILLEMS. Billets good but scattered.	
	31		The Battalion in billets at WILLEMS. Moved by march route to billets in TEMPLEUVE. Billets good.	

W. Hughes Major

Comdg 1/18 th Bn. LONDON REGT.
(LONDON IRISH RIFLES).

War Diary
of
1/18th Battn. London Regt.
for
November 1918

Confidential

Prefix......Code...............m.	Words	Charge		This message is on a/c of		Recd...........to.
Office of Origin and Service Instructions.	Sent					Date.................
....	At.............m.			.... Service.		From.................
....	To............					
....	By............			Signature of "Franking Officer."		By.................

TO {

Sender's Number.	Day of Month.	In reply to Number.	**A A A**
*			

From				
Place				
Time				

The above may be forwarded as now corrected.   **(Z)**

.... *Censor.*   Signature of Addressor or person authorised to telegraph in h's name

* This line should be erased if not required.

Wt. W492/M1647 100,000 pads. 4/17. W. & Co., Ltd. (E. 1187.)

Army Form C. 2118.

WAR DIARY

or

INTELLIGENCE SUMMARY.

(Erase heading not required.)

for Month of November 1918.

Place	Date	Hour	Summary of Events and Information	Remarks and references to Appendices
At TEMPLEUVE	1.		Companies paraded at 09.15 and carried out training under Company Commanders until 12.30. As it was All Saints' Day a special church parade for Roman Catholics was arranged to enable them to attend Mass at the Parish Church TEMPLEUVE at 09.00. The C.O. rode over to HOUILLY during the morning to reconnoitre the positions occupied by the 19th Bn. LONDON Regt. in support. Company commanders also did so in the afternoon. The undermentioned were awarded the M.M. for gallantry and devotion to duty in the field. 592993 Sergt. CHILTON. S. 592434 Sergt. CARROLL. R.	
At TEMPLEUVE	2.		Baths allotted to the Battalion until 13.00 hours. At 16.15 the Battalion moved off to relieve the 19th Bn. LONDON Regt. in support round HOUILLY. HQ, A, B, and D Companies billeted in HOUILLY itself, while C Company had two platoons in an fly found at RUMEZ and two at RAMEGNIES-A-CHIN. The German shelled heavily with A.E and Gas during the night, obtaining one direct hit on a barn occupied by A Company. Several Gas casualties were caused.	
At HOUILLY	3.		Intermittent shelling all day, chiefly with H.E. The Bn. was mainly occupied cleaning and improving billets, also digging all-trenches for shelter in case of heavy shelling. Lt. ASHBRIDGE and Sergt. CULLEN each took a patrol out across the ESCAUT CANAL and obtained valuable information. Both patrols were especially commended	

Army Form C. 2118.

WAR DIARY
or
INTELLIGENCE SUMMARY.
(Erase heading not required.)

Instructions regarding War Diaries and Intelligence Summaries are contained in F. S. Regs., Part II. and the Staff Manual respectively. Title pages will be prepared in manuscript.

Place	Date	Hour	Summary of Events and Information	Remarks and references to Appendices
At HOUILLY	4.		A bright, sunny day, enabling the Boche to watch us very closely from MONT. ST. AUBERT, so that all movement was restricted as much as possible. The C.O. and Company Commanders visited the front line Battalion (19th LONDONS) during the day, preparatory to relieving them at night. The relief was completed without disturbance by the enemy. Two patrols went out during the night but one failed to cross the ESCAUT CANAL owing to the bad condition of the bridge the patrols were to cross by.	
	5.		At PONT-A-CHIN. Dispositions were as follows. C Company on the left front, occupied a farm house E. of RAMEGNIES-A-CHIN, B Company in the trenches in PONT-A-CHIN and D Company on the Right a chateau on the S. side of the latter village. A Company in Reserve and Bn. H.Q. occupied parts of a large aeroplane repair shop situated S.W. of PONT-A-CHIN. The enemy kept up steady gun fire and intermittent trench mortar activity throughout the day. A daylight patrol of our C, consisting of 2 N.C.O's, L/Cpl BREESE. A.E and L/Cpl WOOLGAR. G.H., and 4 O'Ranks, crossed the canal about midday, took a German Post completely by surprise and captured the entire garrison of five Prussians.	
	6.		A very wet day. The Battalion was to have been relieved by the 22nd London Regt. but owing to the terrible state of the weather the relief was postponed 24 hrs. by special orders of the Major General	

Army Form C. 2118.

WAR DIARY
or
INTELLIGENCE SUMMARY.
(Erase heading not required.)

Instructions regarding War Diaries and Intelligence Summaries are contained in F. S. Regs., Part II. and the Staff Manual respectively. Title pages will be prepared in manuscript.

Place	Date	Hour	Summary of Events and Information	Remarks and references to Appendices
	7.		This was the last day which the Battalion spent in the line before the signing of the armistice. Three patrols were out at dawn to discover whether the boche who was expected to withdraw overnight, had actually retired, but his presence was soon discovered by rifle fire from his line. 2/Lt. T.D. BAXTER took a small party of men out during the morning to engage an enemy post which had been discovered. He was directing the fire of his men when he was struck by a bullet and killed on the spot. His body was discovered during the evening and taken back to WILLEMS. At 1900 the Battalion was relieved by the 22nd LONDON Regt. and marched by Companies via TEMPLEUVE to WILLEMS. Capt. H.A. LANE joined the Battalion, and was temporarily posted to A Company.	
	8.		The Battalion spent the morning cleaning up under the supervision of platoon Commanders. Companies were at the disposal of Company Commanders for training in Physical drill, bayonet fighting and tactical platoon exercises. 609858 Rfn MOORE. E.M awarded the Croix de Guerre.	
	9.			
	10.		At 0800 hours the Battalion with transport moved off from WILLEMS and marched via TEMPLEUVE and LE TRESNOY to LA TOMBE, arriving there at 1300 hrs, originally with the intention of following up the enemy who had withdrawn from the line of the ESCAUT. Owing to the absolving of the front, however, the whole Division was finished out by the units on either flank, so that it became unnecessary for us to proceed further. Billeting therefor was taken in hand at-	

Army Form C. 2118.

WAR DIARY
or
INTELLIGENCE SUMMARY.
(Erase heading not required.)

Instructions regarding War Diaries and Intelligence Summaries are contained in F.S. Regs., Part II. and the Staff Manual respectively. Title pages will be prepared in manuscript.

Place	Date	Hour	Summary of Events and Information	Remarks and references to Appendices
	11.		LA TOMBE at once and by 1600 the whole Battalion was quartered in the village.	
	12.		Early the following morning the Battalion marched into TOURNAI to relieve the 15th Bn. SUFFOLK Regt., and to take over the Piquetting of the town. There was some delay in getting the men into the billets, because the SUFFOLKS had received orders to stand by, but eventually they left the town, and enabled us to occupy our quarters. At TOURNAI. "B" Company provided all guards for piquetting the town, while the remainder of the Battalion devoted three hours of the morning to cleaning of arms, clothing and equipment, and interior economy. One hour close order drill completed the day's work.	
	13.		At TOURNAI. The piquetting of the town having been cancelled. Companies were at the disposal of Company Commanders during the morning for training, as follows:— Rapid marching, — Platoon Drill, — Company Drill, — Guard Mount, — Gas mask. "Shamrock" gave a concert at "B" Company's billets in the evening.	
	14.		At TOURNAI. The Battalion left TOURNAI at 0900 hours, and marched via LEUSE and LIGNE to HOUTAING, where it arrived at 1700 hours. All four Companies were billeted in rooms above the stables in the grounds of the Château LA KERLIÈRE.	
	15.		At HOUTAING the whole Battalion marched to LIGNE at 08.15 hrs and spent five hours cleaning up a portion of the damaged BRUSSELS - LILLE railway line.	

Army Form C. 2118.

WAR DIARY
or
INTELLIGENCE SUMMARY.
(Erase heading not required.)

Instructions regarding War Diaries and Intelligence
Summaries are contained in F. S. Regs., Part II.
and the Staff Manual respectively. Title pages
will be prepared in manuscript.

Place	Date	Hour	Summary of Events and Information	Remarks and references to Appendices
	16.		At HOUTAING. The Battalion again provided a working party to fill up mine craters and clear debris on the railway line running through LIGNE, from 0900 to 1400 hours.	
	17.		At HOUTAING. A further stretch of railway line running through LIGNE was cleared by the Battalion from 1000 to 1400 hrs, thus completing the three days work arranged for by the Division.	
	18.		At HOUTAING. The Battalion formed up at 08.40 and marched off to LA TOMBE via LIGNE, LEUSE and TOURNAI at 08.45, arriving at its destination at 17.30. A midday meal was served to the men during an hour's halt at BARRY. On arrival at LA TOMBE the Battalion was billeted at the college and adjoining buildings. Snow fell during the day and the state of the roads rendered marching extremely difficult. The C.O. left the Battalion to take temporary command of the Palisade.	
	19.		At LA TOMBE. After spending the night at LA TOMBE, the Battalion moved off again at 0900 hours and proceeded to march to PERONNE, by way of TOURNAI. Billeting in this village was extremely difficult owing to the lack of accommodation, and very few comfortable quarters were found either for officers or men.	
	20.		At PERONNE. Companies were at the disposal of Company Commanders all the morning for cleaning and adjusting equipment, and physical drill. The following Officers joined the Battalion – 2nd Lt H.C. TYSON, 2nd Lt. W. BURTON. M.M., 2nd Lt. H.C. STAGG, 2nd Lt. G.W. SMITH, 2nd Lt T.H. WARREN also rejoined.	
	21.		At PERONNE. Companies were again at the disposal of Company Commanders. A number of returns relating to demobilization and the Divisional Education Scheme were dealt with and during the afternoon two Companies bathed at the Baths at CYSOING.	

Army Form C. 2118.

WAR DIARY
or
INTELLIGENCE SUMMARY.
(Erase heading not required.)

Instructions regarding War Diaries and Intelligence Summaries are contained in F. S. Regs., Part II. and the Staff Manual respectively. Title pages will be prepared in manuscript.

Place	Date	Hour	Summary of Events and Information	Remarks and references to Appendices
	22		The remained two Companies and H.Q. halted during the morning while the rest of the Battalion carried on with Physical and close order drill by Companies. An N.C.O.'s Class paraded for instruction under the R.S.M. Lt Col. G.H.NEELY. D.S.O. M.C. and Capt. C.A.FEA. M.C. rejoined the Battalion.	
	23		The Battalion paraded on the Green at PERONNE at 09.30 for practice in ceremonial drill, during the course of which the Brigadier General came to see the Bn. At midday the Companies returned to billets for Educational Training. Subject - Dictation	
	24		At PERONNE. Divine Service for all C of E men on the Green at 10.00. R.C's attended a service at the Parish Church, and services for Non-Conformists were also arranged.	
	25		The Battalion paraded in drill order on the Green at 09.30 for Ceremonial Drill under the Commanding Officer. The last hour of the morning was devoted to Educational Training.	
	26		The Battalion again paraded for Ceremonial Drill in the morning, and completed the day's work with an hour's Educational Training.	
	27		The Battalion formed up on the new PERONNE - TEMPLEUVE Road in front of the Church at PERONNE, and proceeded by march route to HAUBOURDIN, at 08.30 together with the other Units of the Brigade. The route selected for the move led through SAINGHIN - MERCHIN - RONCHIN - LOOS, and marching was not easy owing to the fact that all the road were paved with cobble stones and still in a greasy state. The Battalion arrived at HAUBOURDIN at 14.00 and spent the night in a large school house in the RUE DE L'EGLISE.	

Army Form C. 2118.

WAR DIARY
or
INTELLIGENCE SUMMARY.
(Erase heading not required.)

Instructions regarding War Diaries and Intelligence Summaries are contained in F. S. Regs., Part II. and the Staff Manual respectively. Title pages will be prepared in manuscript.

Place	Date	Hour	Summary of Events and Information	Remarks and references to Appendices
	28.		A very hot day. The Battalion continued it's march, and at 08.00 moved off to BETHUNE via FOURNES - LA BASSEE and ANNEQUIN. After a long difficult march under bad conditions the Battalion arrived at BETHUNE shortly after 16.00, and put up for the night in MONTMORENCY BARRACKS.	
	29.		The Battalion set out on the third and final stage of it's march at 09.30 and moved to LIERES, going through CHOCQUES and LILLERS. This village offered neither comfort nor amusement to the men, in fact practically all the men billets in the place were almost unfit for human occupation.	
	30.		At LIERES. Companies were at the disposal of Company Commanders all the morning. The following Officers joined the Battalion. 2/Lt. H.A. MURRAY. 2/Lt. A.H. BLAZEY. 2/Lt. T.H. CRAWCOUR. 2/Lt. L.A. DAVIS.	

G Neely
Lt. Col. Comdg.
18th Bn. LONDON REGT.
(LONDON IRISH RIFLES).

War Diary
of
1/16 Bn London Regt
for
December 1918

"A" Form.
MESSAGES AND SIGNALS.

Army Form C. 2121.
(In pads of 100.)
No. of Message..........

Prefix...... Code...... m.	Words.	Charge.	This message is on a/c of:	Recd. at...... m.
Office of Origin and Service Instructions.	Sent			Date..........
....	At........m.		............Service.	
....	To......			From
....	By......		(Signature of "Franking Officer.")	By........

TO				

Sender's Number.	Day of Month.	In reply to Number.	AAA
*			

From
Place
Time

The above may be forwarded as now corrected.   **(Z)**

.... Censor. | Signature of Addressor or person authorised to telegraph in his name.

*This line, except **AAA**, should be erased if not required.
Wt. W 3253/P511. 500,000 Pads. 1/1s. B. & S. Ltd. **(E2389.)**

WAR DIARY for the Month of December 1918

INTELLIGENCE SUMMARY.

(Erase heading not required.)

Army Form C. 2118.

WO 45

Place	Date	Hour	Summary of Events and Information	Remarks and references to Appendices
At LIERES.	1.		Divine Service for all denominations. All C of E men paraded for service in the Convalescent YMCA hut at 11-15, and there was also a celebration of the Holy Communion at 12-15 in the school. Roman Catholics attended a service in the Parish Church. Lieut. Non-conformists and Presbyterians to fall in at the school. Capt. H. A. Stapples took over command of "C" Coy. in place of Capt. V. C. CANNAN, who was appointed Camp Commandant. Officer. The CO rode over to WESTRE-HEM with a small party in the morning to ascertain whether this village offered better accommodation for the Battalion than LIERES, but was finally decided not to move.	
At LIERES.	2.		Companies were out the disposal of Coy Commanders during the morning, and spent most of the time cleaning up in view of a possible move. Two officers reconnoitred LILLERS during the afternoon, to ascertain the possibilities of billeting the Battalion there. Lieut R. SHERIDAN rejoined the Battalion from Hospital, and 2/Lt. P. R. CAVILL joined from the base.	
At LIERES.	3.		Companies paraded under their Commanders during the early part of the morning, latter carried out some instructional training. All arrangements for the moving of the Battalion at LILLERS were completed	

Army Form C. 2118.

WAR DIARY
or
INTELLIGENCE SUMMARY.
(Erase heading not required.)

Instructions regarding War Diaries and Intelligence Summaries are contained in F. S. Regs., Part II. and the Staff Manual respectively. Title pages will be prepared in manuscript.

Place	Date	Hour	Summary of Events and Information	Remarks and references to Appendices
AT LIÈRES	4		Companies carried out close order drill in parts of the mornings. Training and finished the days work after an hours instruction in simple subjects.	
AT LIÈRES	5		The Battalion Paraded on the road opposite the square in VMC at 9.30 AM and was inspected by the C.O. The Drums & Orchestra rehearsed all the morning under the direction of Capt Y.C CANNAN. The usual instructional classes were held. In the afternoon a proportion of officers and men attended a Lecture at the ALL-CHANGE THEATRE in ALSACE-LORRAINE given by Mr. MASTERMAN SMITH. A football match was played between teams representing C and D coys.	
AT LIÈRES	6		Companies were at the disposal of Coy commanders until 11.15 AM. Educational classes from 11.30 – 1 p.m.	
AT LIÈRES	7		Company parade technical classes as usual during the morning. The Battalion were bathed in the course of the day at the baths in the neighbouring village of BEAUERY.	

WAR DIARY or INTELLIGENCE SUMMARY

Army Form C. 2118.

Place	Date	Hour	Summary of Events and Information	Remarks and references to Appendices
LIERES	8		The Battalion paraded at 11-15 am the road facing the garden in the centre of the village for Divine Service in the Canadian Y.M.C.A. tent. Roman Catholic, Non-Conformist and Presbyterian services were held in the School Room. The baths at BELLERY were at the disposal of the Battalion for all men who were unable to take on Saturday.	
	9		Company parades and instructional classes during the morning, and in the afternoon D Coy left the village in order to occupy the 3rd Army Instructional Camp at PERNES, which had been allotted to the Battalion.	
	10		The remainder of the Battalion left LIERES shortly after 10% and proceeded to march to PERNES via PERNAY. The weather was extremely unfavourable, as it was snowing steadily during most of the morning. The camp lines on the arrival were fairly prepared for the reception of the Battalion and no time was lost in getting all fixed.	

Army Form C. 2118.

WAR DIARY
or
INTELLIGENCE SUMMARY.
(Erase heading not required.)

Instructions regarding War Diaries and Intelligence Summaries are contained in F. S. Regs., Part II. and the Staff Manual respectively. Title pages will be prepared in manuscript.

Place	Date	Hour	Summary of Events and Information	Remarks and references to Appendices
In camp at PERNES	11		A wet rainy day. After a short Battalion parade on the football ground the boys returned to the camp and carried out some individual training in their huts. The Armourer Sergeant party paraded under Lieut. V. C. CANNAN.	
	12		Owing to the inclemency of the weather no Battalion parade was possible, so boys were obliged to remain under cover. The Gunnery instructors dispersed and succeeding classes were instructed in work through Lewis Gun and Hotchkiss and Commercial Methods. The Armourers performed in the camp theatre from 6-8 P. the performance including several new artists and amateurs.	
	13		Battalion parade having been rendered impossible by the state of the weather, boys again paraded indoors for physical and arms drill. Educational classes were held as usual. In the afternoon Mr FORBES ARBUST gave a very interesting lecture on "RUSKIN: RECONSTRUCTION" in the camp theatre. The Armourers performed at Divi H.Q. in the evening. At mid-day the Lieut-General accompanied by the Brigadier General visited the camp.	

Army Form C. 2118.

WAR DIARY
or
INTELLIGENCE SUMMARY.
(Erase heading not required.)

Instructions regarding War Diaries and Intelligence Summaries are contained in F. S. Regs., Part II. and the Staff Manual respectively. Title pages will be prepared in manuscript.

Place	Date	Hour	Summary of Events and Information	Remarks and references to Appendices
	14		Bad weather prevented Battalion Parade being carried out. Companies carried on in the Hats, Gymnasium etc. & Educational classes were held as usual.	
	15		The Battalion paraded at 10-20 A.M. for Divine Service in the Theatre. Roman Catholics Mass at PERNES CHURCH at 09-00. Non-Conformists and Presbyterians went to the Y.M.C.A. Hut near PERNES STATION for service at 11-00	
	16		Company parades were held under cover owing to bad weather. The Battalion were allotted baths at the "Brasserie" PERNES. Educational classes were held as usual. Arrangements for the freedom of honours of a Hos. St. was Team was made by Major - W.M. Hayles D.S.O. M.C. & a very interesting test carried out in the Theatre for practice.	
	17		Continuance of bad weather rendered Battalion parade impracticable. The usual programme for wet weather was therefore carried out. In the evening a combined stand from the 18th & 20th Battalions gave a recital in the Camp Theatre. The performance was very much appreciated, it consisted chiefly of selections from musical comedies and somewhat of a ball music.	
	18		A very stormy day with the usual Company entertainment provided. A lecture on RUSSIA was given by Mr. BRENNAN	

WAR DIARY
INTELLIGENCE SUMMARY
(Erase heading not required.)

Army Form C. 2118.

Place	Date	Hour	Summary of Events and Information	Remarks and references to Appendices
	19		Company parade & educational classes. In the evening a concert was given by Sgt. Harronato, to which the 19th & 20th Battalions were invited. A very successful show, most of the items being old favourites.	
	20		The Commanding Officer inspected the Battalion at 10-00 on the road leaving the theatre. A full marching order parade. Physical drill, arms drill & classes followed the inspection. In the afternoon, a football match (Bryant Trophy) which had been postponed for several days owing to bad weather, was played against the 21st Battalion. A good game, which we won 3-1, but I was amazed by the indifferent sportsmanship of some of the onlookers. Canteen accounts for the period Aug-Dec, were published this day, showing a balance of the sum of £48-15-11 & a balance on stock & money in hand of £39-15-4.	
	21		Company parades & classes in the morning. In the afternoon a football match was played against the 15th Battalion at FERFAY. The 15th won after an excellent game 3-0. A "Demobilization Office" was started today under the direction of Lieut. T.L. HAINES.	

Army Form C. 2118.

WAR DIARY
OF
INTELLIGENCE SUMMARY.
(Erase heading not required.)

Instructions regarding War Diaries and Intelligence Summaries are contained in F. S. Regs., Part II. and the Staff Manual respectively. Title pages will be prepared in manuscript.

Place	Date	Hour	Summary of Events and Information	Remarks and references to Appendices
	22		The Battalion paraded for Divine Service in the Theatre at 10-00 hrs. Roman Catholics Mass at PERNES CHURCH at 09-00 hrs. Non-Conformists at Y.M.C.A. hut at 11-00. The Guest Demobilisation forms (Z16) were received throughout the Battalion today. 2/Lt. GIPP proceeded on leave, being a party for demobilisation.	
	23		2/Lt. STANBURY proceeded on leave. Very wet & stormy, with a strong westerly gale. Companies marched at PERNES three fold. CAPT. LANE proceeded on leave. 2/Lt. PICTON returned from course.	
	24		Companies were placed at the disposal of Company Commanders. Educational parades as usual. The Brigadier-General and I.O.C. Division visited the troops in the morning & expressed to the Battalion their best wishes for a happy Christmas.	
	25		CHRISTMAS DAY. In the morning Church Parades for Roman Catholics & C.E.s were held. At 12-45 the men had a cold lunch, and at 15-00 hours a Christmas dinner was served in the Dining Hall and Theatre at which the Officers waited.	

Army Form C. 2118.

WAR DIARY
or
INTELLIGENCE SUMMARY.
(Erase heading not required.)

Instructions regarding War Diaries and Intelligence Summaries are contained in F. S. Regs., Part II. and the Staff Manual respectively. Title pages will be prepared in manuscript.

Place	Date	Hour	Summary of Events and Information	Remarks and references to Appendices
	25.		The menu was as follows:- Soup, Rissoles, Roast Beef, Roast Turkey & Roast Pork, Potatoes, Turnips & Onion Sauce, Christmas Pudding & Custard, Beer, Rum Punch. The Officers had a special dinner at 6-30, a very successful function, owing to the efforts of Capt V.C. CANNAN and the Mess Treasurer.	
	26.		BOXING DAY. This day was observed as a holiday & there were no parades. A football match had been arranged (Officers v Sergeants) had to be postponed on account of the state of the ground. At 6 p.m. the Sergeants held their Christmas Dinner, followed by a concert to which the Officers were invited. 2/Lt SANDERSON proceeded on leave.	
	27.		Companies were at the disposal of Company Commanders during the morning. Educational parades as usual. The continuance of frost & rather made all outdoor parades impossible.	
	28.		At 11-30 the Commanding Officer gave a lecture on "Demobilisation" Companies were again placed at the disposal of Company Commanders with special reference to the question of men re-enlisting in the Regt.	

Army Form C. 2118.

WAR DIARY
OR
INTELLIGENCE SUMMARY.
(Erase heading not required.)

Instructions regarding War Diaries and Intelligence Summaries are contained in F. S. Regs., Part II. and the Staff Manual respectively. Title pages will be prepared in manuscript.

Place	Date	Hour	Summary of Events and Information	Remarks and references to Appendices
Belhem Camp	29.		In the evening the "Shamrocks" gave a concert practically all the items were new. "The show" was very successful. A levy was placed at the disposal of the Battalion this day, and conveyed a party of 20 to LILLE. LT HAINES proceeded on leave.	
			The Battalion paraded at 09.50 for Divine Service in the Theatre. Roman Catholics at PERNS CHURCH. Non-conformists at the Y.M.C.A. Hut. 2/LT BLAZEY left the Battalion (to which he was attached) to rejoin the 1st Batt. Middlesex Regt.	
	30.		Companies were at the disposal of the Company Commanders during the morning. Educational classes as usual. In the evening a party of 20 Sisters from No. 12 Stationary Hospital, together with some Voluntary Aid Sisters from Lethem, came to the camp at the invitation of the Commanding Officer. After tea, a concert was given by the "Shamrocks" which was most successful. Supper was served at 7-30 & a most enjoyable evening spent	

Army Form C. 2118.

WAR DIARY
or
INTELLIGENCE SUMMARY.

(Erase heading not required.)

Instructions regarding War Diaries and Intelligence Summaries are contained in F. S. Regs., Part II. and the Staff Manual respectively. Title pages will be prepared in manuscript.

Place	Date	Hour	Summary of Events and Information	Remarks and references to Appendices
	31.		Companies were again placed at the disposal of Company Commanders during the morning. During the educational parade, Capt RICE-OXLEY an inspector from England visited the classes.	
			O.R.229	

W Cates Cptraut
Lt. Col. Comdg.
18 th Bn. LONDON REGT. (LONDON IRISH RIFLES).

War Diary
of
18 London Regt
for
Jan 1919

Confidential

"A" Form
MESSAGES AND SIGNALS.

Army Form C. 2121
(in pads of 100).

No. of Message....................

Prefix..........Code...........m.	Words	Charge	This message is on a/c of	Recd. at..........m.
Office of Origin and Service Instructions.	Sent			Date..................
....	At............M.	...............Service.	From ....
....	To............		
....	By............	(Signature of "Franking Officer.")	By............

TO {

Sender's Number.	Day of Month.	In reply to Number.	AAA

From
Place
Time

The above may be forwarded as now corrected. (Z)

Censor.   Signature of Addressor or person authorised to telegraph in his name
† This line should be erased if not required.

Wt. W492.. 1647 100,000 pads. 4/17. W. & Co., Ltd. (E. 1187.)

Army Form C. 2118.

Appx 46

WAR DIARY
or
INTELLIGENCE SUMMARY.
(Erase heading not required.)

Instructions regarding War Diaries and Intelligence Summaries are contained in F. S. Regs., Part II. and the Staff Manual respectively. Title pages will be prepared in manuscript.

Place	Date	Hour	Summary of Events and Information	Remarks and references to Appendices
PERNES	JAN 1		Companies paraded at 9.30 for inspection and at 10.00 the Commanding Officer gave a lecture to the Battalion officers on Esprit de Corps. This completed the parades for the day. 2/Lt CAVILL proceeded to England on special leave to morrow. 2/Lt PICTON went on ordinary leave.	
	2		Companies were placed at the disposal of Company Commanders during the morning. The usual educational lecture was held in the afternoon by Mr HETTS on the parade in the Theatre. In the evening a concert was arranged and the Stage by the concert party of the 19th Battalion was given in the Theatre. The Brigade Commander attended and was sent to the Brigade Commander congratulating him on being awarded the C.B. Capt. H.A. LANE was mentioned in despatches and awarded the OBE in the new years honours list.	
	3		Company and Educational parades were held as usual. At the invitation of the matron several officers went to No. 12 Stationary Hospital ST POL the evening and were entertained by the nursing staff.	
	4		Parades today were interfered by the morning shortly in order that as many men as possible could go	

WAR DIARY or INTELLIGENCE SUMMARY

Army Form C. 2118.

Place	Date	Hour	Summary of Events and Information	Remarks and references to Appendices
contd	4		to FLORINGHEM to see a match against the 17th Batt. At 1330 hrs practically every one available was paraded and headed by the band the battalion marched to FLORINGHEM. The 17th were beaten 4-0. In the evening the Brigadier General Major Lewis, Wilkinson, Lane-Fox, Duffin & Lieut Naylor dined with the Officers.	
	5		The battalion paraded at 9050 for Divine Service in the Theatre. The G.O.C. Division and the Brigadier General were present. Non-conformists & R.C.'s paraded for service at 1040 & 0850 respectively.	
	6		Company & Educational parades as usual. In the evening the SHAMROCKS played at Divisional HQrs. 2/Lt TANNATT proceeded on leave. Lt P.F. KEANE was awarded the M.C. in the new years honours list.	
	7		Company Educational parades as usual. 2/Lt KING proceeded on leave.	
	8		In the morning a drill competition was held consisting of 10 minutes P.T. 5 minutes handling	

Army Form C. 2118.

WAR DIARY
or
INTELLIGENCE SUMMARY.
(Erase heading not required.)

Place	Date	Hour	Summary of Events and Information	Remarks and references to Appendices
Enfild	8		2 arms & 5 minutes rapid drill by a section of 8 men under the section commander. The men were very keen. The competition was won by "D" Coy with 73 points. C Coy were second with 70 points. The Brigadier General Captain COWAN - DOUGLAS M.C and RSM TREZOWNA acted as judges. 2/Lt DEWSON proceeded on leave.	
	9		Company and Educational parades as usual. In the afternoon the Battalion played 2nd Bde hqrs in the 2nd round of the football competition winning 8-0	
	10		Companies were placed at the disposal of coy cmdrs Educational parades as usual Capt LANE returned from leave.	
	11		The battalion paraded at 9.30 in Musketry Order and marched to TANGRY aerodrome. Batt. drill was carried out for half an hour & the batt. then returned to camp arriving at 12.40. 2/Lt SANDERSON ret'd from leave. Demobilization having been speeded up, 2/Lt JONES was also 14 men were sent away. demobilized	

Army Form C. 2118.

WAR DIARY
or
INTELLIGENCE SUMMARY.
(Erase heading not required.)

Instructions regarding War Diaries and Intelligence Summaries are contained in F. S. Regs., Part II. and the Staff Manual respectively. Title pages will be prepared in manuscript.

Place	Date	Hour	Summary of Events and Information	Remarks and references to Appendices
	12		Divine service here held as usual. C.E's in the Neuke R.C's at PERNES in the Church & non-conformists in the Y.M.C.A huts. 15 men were demobilized 2/Lt EAGGER proceeded to England in charge of a party for a dispersal camp.	
	13		Baths were allotted to the Batt during the day. Company and educational parades as usual.	
	14		C. Coy went on the range. Other Coys carried out drill and training. In the afternoon a lecture was given by Mr BROAD on "Reconstruction" 2/Lt SEABY proceeded to England for demobilization.	
	15		Batt parade was ordered for this day but owing to bad weather it was cancelled. Coy and educational training was carried out. In the afternoon the battalion played the 19th in the final of the Bde. football competition winning 2-0	
	16		Coy and Educational parades in the morning. In the evening a concert was given by the SHAMROCKS	

Army Form C. 2118.

WAR DIARY
or
INTELLIGENCE SUMMARY.
(Erase heading not required.)

Place	Date	Hour	Summary of Events and Information	Remarks and references to Appendices
	17		boys again played at the disposal of Coy Cmdrs. Lt. J. P. ASHBRIDGE was demobilized and Lt. F. CLEMENT became education officer in his place.	
	18		Educational parades only were held in the morning. In the afternoon the Batt. marched to AUCHAEL where a match was played against the 22nd Batt. The 22nd won 2-0. After playing extra time 2/Lt ANDERSON was demobilized	
	19.		Church parades as usual. 2/Lt W BURTON was demobilized.	
	20		The Batt. paraded at 10.00 hours and proceeded to FLORINGHEM aerodrome where a Brigade ceremonial parade was held. Lieut. Gen. MILDREN C.B. CMG. D.S.O addressed the battalion and thanked them for the good work done during the last phase of the war. Lt R. SHERIDAN proceeded to England for demob.	
	21		Coys were at the disposal of Coy. Commanders during the morning. In the afternoon	

Army Form C. 2118.

WAR DIARY
or
INTELLIGENCE SUMMARY.
(Erase heading not required.)

Instructions regarding War Diaries and Intelligence Summaries are contained in F. S. Regs., Part II. and the Staff Manual respectively. Title pages will be prepared in manuscript.

Place	Date	Hour	Summary of Events and Information	Remarks and references to Appendices
Con t'd	21		A football match was played against the 1st Service Rifles result. CSR 4 L.I.R. 1 In the evening the Concert party of the 236th Bde RFA visited the camp and gave an excellent entertainment in the Theatre. Capt. W.R.B. BERRY proceeded to England for demobilization.	
	22		Companies at disposal of Coy. cmdrs during the morning. Educational classes as usual C & D were then amalgamated under the command of Capt. LANE O.B.E. 2/Lt STAGG returned from R.A.F course	
	23		Coy. and Educational parades as usual B Coy. were on the range during the morning	
	24		The batt. paraded at 1015 in full marching order for inspection by the Commanding Officer Educational classes were carried on from 1130. 2/Lt STAGG was demobilized.	
	25		Coy. and Educational parades as usual during the morning. 2/Lt DAVIES was demobilized 2/Lt KING returned from leave	

Army Form C. 2118.

WAR DIARY
or
INTELLIGENCE SUMMARY.
(Erase heading not required.)

Instructions regarding War Diaries and Intelligence Summaries are contained in F. S. Regs., Part II. and the Staff Manual respectively. Title pages will be prepared in manuscript.

Place	Date	Hour	Summary of Events and Information	Remarks and references to Appendices
	26		Church Parades for C of E, R.C. & Nonconformist 2/Lt SANDERSON demobilized.	
	27		Baths were allotted to the Battalion during the morning at PERNES. Physical training and education were carried out after bathing. Major W.W. Hughes D.S.O M.C. returned from leave. 2/Lt A.R. SMYTH proceeded on leave	
	28		Coys at disposal of Coy Commanders during the morning. Education at 1130. Up to this day 17 officers and over 300 men have been demobilized	
	29		Coys at disposal of Coy Cmdrs during the morning. In the evening the concert party of the Div'n Ammunition Column gave an entertainment in the theatre.	
	30		Coy parades for P.T and drill were held. Educational classes at 1130	
	31		Coy and Educational parades	

G.H. Neely? Lt/Col
LT. COL. COMDG.
LONDON IRISH RIFLES.

Army Form C. 2118.

WAR DIARY
or
INTELLIGENCE SUMMARY.

(Erase heading not required.)

For the month of February 1919.

Place	Date	Hour	Summary of Events and Information	Remarks and references to Appendices
Rouen	Feb 1st		Company & Education parades in the morning. The SHAMROCKS gave their final entertainment in the theatre. The party having finished the demobilization of sound members moved on to the demobilization of sound members	
	Feb 2nd		Church parades as usual. The Buyoniers attended a C.E. parade in the theatre at 11.00 hours. 2/Lt E.A. Leslie proceeded on leave	
	Feb 3rd		At 10.00 hours the Battalion paraded for the funeral of Pte BUSH of "C" Coy who died on Friday 31st January from heart failure. He was buried in the British Military Cemetery near PARNES. The 19th Battalion moved into the camp this day from PARNES.	
	Feb 4th		Companies at the disposal of company commanders. Baths were allotted to the Battalion at RAINDAY	RAIN DAY
	Feb 5th		Companies at disposal of company commanders. For several days the number of men of working parties at the town, the economy of their absence practically the whole available strength of the Battalion rendering educational parades impracticable.	

Sgd. G.A.M. WRIGHT M.C. Lieut.Col.
For Demobilization

Army Form C. 2118.

WAR DIARY
or
INTELLIGENCE SUMMARY.

(Erase heading not required.)

Instructions regarding War Diaries and Intelligence Summaries are contained in F. S. Regs., Part II. and the Staff Manual respectively. Title pages will be prepared in manuscript.

Place	Date	Hour	Summary of Events and Information	Remarks and references to Appendices
	Feb. 6th		Working parties for the camp resembling & civilians at FRANKS STATION met General during the morning Lt. J. H. WARREN proceeded to England for demobilization	
	Feb. 7th		Working parties as usual, remainder of companies at the disposal of Company Commanders for recreation	
	Feb. 8th			
	Feb. 9th		Working parties & education during the morning. A Brigade Church parade, C of E, unaccompanied was held in the camp theatre at 11 o.c. The F.G.C.M. Davies and the Brigadier-General, 151 Brigade attended. The service was conducted by the Rev. C.E.F. Hodge C.F. & the sermon preached by the Rev. C.A. THOMAS C.F.	
	Feb. 10th		Various working parties were provided during the morning & the remainder of the companies were placed at the disposal of Company Commanders for P.J. recreation Capt V.E. CONNAN proceeded on leave.	

Army Form C. 2118.

WAR DIARY
or
INTELLIGENCE SUMMARY.
(Erase heading not required.)

Instructions regarding War Diaries and Intelligence Summaries are contained in F. S. Regs., Part II. and the Staff Manual respectively. Title pages will be prepared in manuscript.

Place	Date	Hour	Summary of Events and Information	Remarks and references to Appendices
	Feb/	11th	Companies at the disposal of Company Commanders during the morning for company work. Afternoon the Companies at the disposal of Company Commanders.	
	"	12th	Bathe at FOSSEUX. RAIMBERT met at the disposal of the Battalion until 11.00 hours	
	"	13th	All available men were employed in working on the rifle-range at I.T. L.6. over PERNES STATION. Filling in trenches.	
	"	14th	The Battalion carried on with work at the Rifle Range. 3/4th FAGGER draw'd from here. A football match 10th v 19th was won 5–1	
	"	15th	Working Party as usual. Lt Col L.H.F. NEELY, D.S.O. M.C. proceeded to Paris. Major H.W. HUGHES, D.S.O. M.C. assumed command of the Battalion in the absence of the C.O.	
	"	16th	Church parades as usual. At about 04-45 a gas attack was opened by the Germans somewhere N. of the 19th Battalion. The mist was merely slight, though together practically the whole of the effects of the occupant of	

Army Form C. 2118.

WAR DIARY
or
INTELLIGENCE SUMMARY.
(Erase heading not required.)

Instructions regarding War Diaries and Intelligence Summaries are contained in F. S. Regs., Part II. and the Staff Manual respectively. Title pages will be prepared in manuscript.

Place	Date	Hour	Summary of Events and Information	Remarks and references to Appendices
W.F.W.E			Working parties as usual employed on range etc. at I.T.B+D	
	18th		Felling in trenches	
			Same as yesterday. Lieut TYSON proceeded on leave	
	19th		2/Lt KING took over education classes	
			Working parties as usual & educational classes	
			2/Lt A SMYTH returned from leave	
	20th		Baths for Coy - men at PERNES. Educational training afterwards	
	21st		Working parties & one at range I.T.B+D	
			Our afternoon we had a boxing contest in the theatre.	
			Fly weights - 10 - 3 min rds - C.S.M CHILTON & Rfn. ABRAHART	
			Bath Yrs & London Regt.	
			Feather weights - 6. 2 min rds - Rfn DAY v Rfn. JONES.	
			both Yrs & London Regt.	
			Coy. exhibition were very good. The fly weights completed full time	
			& JONES was winner.	
			Feather weights went 4 rounds & C.S.M CHILTON referred & ABRAHART	
			The theatre was full. The Brigadier attended	
			The weights anything authorised	

Army Form C. 2118.

WAR DIARY
or
INTELLIGENCE SUMMARY.
(Erase heading not required.)

Instructions regarding War Diaries and Intelligence Summaries are contained in F. S. Regs., Part II. and the Staff Manual respectively. Title pages will be prepared in manuscript.

Place	Date	Hour	Summary of Events and Information	Remarks and references to Appendices
	Feb. 22nd		Working parties as usual & education	
	23rd		Brigade Divine Service	
	24th		Working parties again. LT TYSON to have the rank of Captain.	
	25th		All fatigue continued with one. 2 LT KING proceeded on leave to AMIENS. Working parties & education as usual. Draft of 50 men & 2 officers LIEUT CLEMENTS returned from leave &	
	26th		Working parties as usual. took command of the Company	
	27th		Working parties as usual. Lt CRAWSHAW returned from hospital. CAPT. H. A. LANE O.B.E. acting Brigade Major. 2LT KING returned from leave.	
	28th		Working parties as usual. education. Lorries sent to SAILLY for reinforcements.	

M Laule Captain
LT. COL. COMDG.
LONDON IRISH RIFLES.

5/3/19

War Diary
of
18th London Regt.
for
March 1919

Confidential

MESSAGE FORM. Series No. of Message _____

In	Recd. At _____ By _____	Army Form C 2128
ALL v_____	Sent	(pads of 100).
Out _____ v_____	At _____ By _____	

PREAMBLE _____

M.M. Offices { Delivery _____ v
              { Origin _____

PREFIX _____ Words _____

TO _____
_____
_____

FROM
Place

Originator's Number	Day of Month	In reply to Number

TIME OF ORIGIN   TIME OF HANDING IN
                   (For Signal use only)

Originator's Signature
(Not Telegraphed)

4063. Wt. W5622/G1276. 937,500 pads(48). 10/18. S.O.,F.Rd.

Army Form C. 2118.

WAR DIARY
or
INTELLIGENCE SUMMARY.
(Erase heading not required.)

Vol 4

Instructions regarding War Diaries and Intelligence Summaries are contained in F. S. Regs., Part II. and the Staff Manual respectively. Title pages will be prepared in manuscript.

Place	Date	Hour	Summary of Events and Information	Remarks and references to Appendices
Forces	March 1st		Working parties as usual at Habl Kebar. PERKS Station	
	2nd		Nothing further as usual at Habl Kebar. PERKS Station	
			2nd Lieut SMITH proceeded to 159th R.F.A. for course	
			Capt CANAN returned from leave	
	3rd		Working parties as usual at Habl Kebar. PERKS Station	
	4th		Working parties as usual at Habli Kebar. PERKS Station	
			2Lt KARGER proceeded to XIth Corps Arment Magazine Camp BARKIN to do duty	
			there. 2Lt G. SMITH proceeded on leave to ENGLAND.	
	5th		Working parties as usual	
			Generals Court Martial convened here.	
			Lieut LEWIS to VMS for operation, also one evacuated to similar	
			Working parties as usual at Habl Kebar PERKS Station	
			Capt TYSON returned from leave	

Army Form C. 2118.

WAR DIARY
INTELLIGENCE SUMMARY.
(Erase heading not required.)

Place	Date	Hour	Summary of Events and Information	Remarks and references to Appendices
Pernes	March 1st		Squads were inspected for Shifting kowaer. Shifting Ranges & Range.	
			Marching party to the Lines	
		5th	Lt. Col. F. A. Marks D.A.A.C. returned from leave	
	7th		25 O.R.s. returned from Leave found near BRUAY.	
			Working parties & Guards at Field Rifles & Range.	
	9th		Bayonet Drill Course	
	10th		12.45 afternoon working party at Inventry.	
	11th		50 N.C.Os. reported and 4 reverting knowledgeation	
	11th		Working parties as usual	
			21 O.R.s. proceeded to BARLIN for duty as XI Corps Provost Marquee Corps	
	12th		Working parties as usual.	
			Capt. A.E.A. N.C. and Lt. ENTWOOD proceeded on Tour of the Bospital Front.	
	13th		Working parties & Guards as usual.	
			1st Essex Boxing Championships Held. Lt. APRAHART won the Feather and	
			Welterweight, 1st Lliong win 10.C. &c.	
			Lt. CRAYMER and 2/Lt. GIPP proceeded with 50 O.R.s to Grand Camp on BRUAY.	

Army Form C. 2118.

WAR DIARY
or
INTELLIGENCE SUMMARY.
(Erase heading not required.)

Instructions regarding War Diaries and Intelligence Summaries are contained in F. S. Regs., Part II. and the Staff Manual respectively. Title pages will be prepared in manuscript.

Place	Date	Hour	Summary of Events and Information	Remarks and references to Appendices
REIMS	March 9	11½	Working parties & guards as usual	
		15	Guards & working parties as usual	
			Lt. KEMP transferred	
			Lecture given on "Wire" the Hon. Major by Capt CRIMER M.C. 2nd Batt London Regt.	
		16"	Working party returned from trenches about 1600 hours	
			Brigade Divine Service	
		17"	All ranks were given an opportunity	
			The and pass of Lt. Dav. Foster Football Competition was played on the Reims ground. The 141 Rifle Meeting held H.Q. 1. C.	
		13"	2/Lt HAINES appointed to Brigade for demobilization	
		19"	In the course of his observation Lounge-Officer the sum Box came with 2.39 Ltt.	
			R.F.A. Return were adopted that no discussion reached	
			The Lieut Collins gave a concert to the Congt. Mingle at 20-30 hours	
		2"	Guards working parties as usual	
			Orders received today that a draft of 2 officers 140 O.Rs to stand by the Orders received for the Army of Occupation	
			Orders received later from 0.4.R. giving the numbers & the required numbers for the draft.	

Army Form C. 2118.

WAR DIARY
or
INTELLIGENCE SUMMARY.
(Erase heading not required.)

Instructions regarding War Diaries and Intelligence Summaries are contained in F. S. Regs., Part II. and the Staff Manual respectively. Title pages will be prepared in manuscript.

Place	Date	Hour	Summary of Events and Information	Remarks and references to Appendices
TERNAS.	March 22nd		In the relief for the period of the Divisional Train Inspection the 235 Mdl RFA took up I Sept Bde 1 Coy	
	23rd		The D.E.C. Divisional attended C.E. parade in the theatre at 11.00 hours.	
	24th		A party of 4 NCOs L.R.R.M.C. proceeded to England on special leave (Capt C.A. RFA MC was amongst yet) 2/Lt KING took over duties as O.C. Mall Major BRASS Station, vice 2/Lt CLARKE 19th Battalion	
	25th		Towards everything position as usual	
	26th		Men standing by for Busy of Inspection paraded in Inspecting order at ... hours for parade march	
	27th		Inspection parade in F.M.O for day	
	28th		At ... a.m the 2 Division (Capt? S.C. Cowan & 2Lt AR SMITH) ... a.m the left today to join the 12th 9th Royal Irish Rifles (lightly divisions) in the Army of Occupation	
			Major General Sir G.H. Gorringe K.C.M.G, etc. received his camps to his farewell or understanding command of the new 7. Division the 18th 19th 20th Lt. M.G Battalions 9th & Hull Infantries handed 9 officer engineering	

Army Form C. 2118.

WAR DIARY
or
INTELLIGENCE SUMMARY.
(Erase heading not required.)

Instructions regarding War Diaries and Intelligence Summaries are contained in F. S. Regs., Part II. and the Staff Manual respectively. Title pages will be prepared in manuscript.

Place	Date	Hour	Summary of Events and Information	Remarks and references to Appendices
	Mar 2/19		Major the L.C.C. thanked the Men & expressed for their work during the year. He then commanded them. B. Col. GREENE, L.C.M.C. C.C. 41st Bn. London called for three cheers for General GOODING, & on behalf of the second wished him God speed.	
		10:50	All available men were employed on fatigues.	
			Divine Service as usual.	
		3/19	Guards & Fatigues	

G. Neely.
LT. COL. COMDG.
LONDON IRISH RIFLES.

4th Brigade

12/3976

1st Bn Herts Regt.

Vol I.   1-11 — 31.12.14

1/17 Londons

1917

www.ingramcontent.com/pod-product-compliance
Lightning Source LLC
Chambersburg PA
CBHW081431300426
44108CB00016BA/2346